Advance Praise for Creating a Life Together

Before aspiring community builders hold their first meeting, confront their first realtor, or drive their first nail, they must buy this essential book: it will improve their chances for success immensely, and will certainly save them money, time, and heartbreak. In her friendly but firm (and occasionally funny) way, Diana Christian proffers an astonishing wealth of practical information and sensible, field-tested advice.

— ERNEST CALLENBACH, AUTHOR, *ECOTOPIA AND ECOTOPIA EMERGING*

Wow! The newest, most comprehensive bible for builders of intentional communities. Covers every aspect with vital information and dozens of examples of how successful communities faced the challenges and created their shared lives out of their visions. The cautionary tales of sadder experiences and how communities fail, will help in avoiding the pitfalls. Not since I wrote the Foreword to Ingrid Komar's *Living the Dream* (1983), which documented the Twin Oaks community, have I seen a more useful and inspiring book on this topic.

— HAZEL HENDERSON, AUTHOR *CREATING ALTERNATIVE FUTURES AND POLITICS OF THE SOLAR AGE.*

A really valuable resource for anyone thinking about intentional community. I wish I had it years ago.

— STARHAWK, AUTHOR OF *WEBS OF POWER*, *THE SPIRAL DANCE*, AND *THE FIFTH SACRED THING*, AND LONG-TIME COMMUNITY MEMBER.

Every potential ecovillager should read it. This book will be an essential guide and manual for the many Permaculture graduates who live in communities or design for them.

— BILL MOLLISON, COFOUNDER OF THE PERMACULTURE MOVEMENT, AND AUTHOR, *PERMACULTURE: A DESIGNER'S MANUAL*

Creating a new culture of living peacefully with each other and the planet is our number one need—and this is the right book at the right time. *Creating a Life Together* will help community founders avoid fatal mistakes. I can't wait to tell people about it.

— HILDUR JACKSON, COFOUNDER, GLOBAL ECOVILLAGE NETWORK (GEN); CO-EDITOR, *ECOVILLAGE LIVING: RESTORING THE EARTH AND HER PEOPLE*

Creating a Life Together

Practical Tools to Grow

Ecovillages and Intentional Communities

Diana Leafe Christian

Foreword by Patch Adams

NEW SOCIETY PUBLISHERS

Cataloguing in Publication Data:

A catalog record for this publication is available from the National Library of Canada.

Cover design by Diane McIntosh. Cover art by Sally A. Sellers, detail from "Family in B-flat" (1998) hand-dyed, hand painted and commercial cottons 45" x 81." Illustrations by Jacob Stevens.

Printed in Canada by Friesens, Tenth Printing, May 2018.

Paperback ISBN: 978-0-86571-471-7

Inquiries regarding requests to reprint all or part of *Creating a Life Together* should be addressed to New Society Publishers at the address below.

To order directly from the publishers, please add $5.00 shipping to the price of the first copy, and $1.00 for each additional copy (plus GST in Canada). Send check or money order to:

New Society Publishers

P.O. Box 189, Gabriola Island, BC V0R 1X0, Canada

1-800-567-6772

New Society Publishers' mission is to publish books that contribute in fundamental ways to building an ecologically sustainable and just society, and to do so with the least possible impact on the environment, in a manner that models this vision. We are committed to doing this not just through education, but through action. We are acting on our commitment to the world's remaining ancient forests by phasing out our paper supply from ancient forests worldwide. This book is one step towards ending global deforestation and climate change. It is printed on acid-free paper that is **100% old growth forest-free** (100% post-consumer recycled), processed chlorine free, and printed with vegetable based, low VOC inks. For further information, or to browse our full list of books and purchase securely, visit our website at: www.newsociety.com

NEW SOCIETY PUBLISHERS   www.newsociety.com

Dedication

For my friend Al Rasche for helping make this book possible,

and for my mother Rosetta Neff, for abiding loyalty, good humor,

and every kind of support.

Table of Contents

Acknowledgments

As someone who knew little of intentional communities in 1992, I'm grateful to those devoted activists in the Fellowship for Intentional Community who patiently educated me – Laird Schaub, Geoph Kozeny, Caroline Estes, Jenny Upton, Dan Questonberry, Tony Sirna, Harvey Baker, Elph Morgan, Jillian Downey, Tree Bressen, Betty Didcoct and Paul DeLapa.

I couldn't have written this book without being editor of *Communities* magazine for the last decade, and have learned much from its staff, columnists, contributors, and guest editors: Lance Scott, Billie Miracle, Ellie Sommer, Velma Kahn, Cecil Scheib, McCune Renwick-Porter, Jacob Stevens, Tristan Masat, Bill Metcalf, Albert Bates, Jan Bulman, Irwin Zucker, Douglas Stevenson, Carolyn Shaffer, Steve Niezgoda, Joyce Foote, Robert Foote, Deborah Altus, Tim Miller, Joe Peterson, Lois Arkin, Hank Obermeyer, Jeff Grossberg, Blair Voyvodic, Michael McIntyre, Daniel Greenberg, Jeff Clearwater, Rob Sandelin, Luc Reid, Larry Kaplowitz, Elana Kann, Bill Flemming, and Patricia Greene.

I am deeply grateful to the Fellowship for Intentional Community for generous permission to excerpt information from ten years of articles in *Communities* magazine, which helps illustrate community principles in every single chapter of this book. I appreciate the shared stories and insights of community veterans Judie Anders, Dave Jacke, John Charamella, Patch Adams, Brad Jarvis, Corinne McLaughlin, Gordon Davidson, Stephen Gaskin, Michael Traugot, Diamond Jamison, River Jamison, Susanna McDougal, Stephan Brown, Barbara Conroy, Don Lindemann, Katie McCamant, Chuck Durrett — and especially Colorado compadres Buzz Burrell, Denise Coté, Zev Paiss, Panther Wilde, the late Mike Mariner, Allen Butcher, Ben Lipman, David Lynch, John Cruickshank, John and Betsey McKinney, Judith Yarrow, Rob Jones, Jan Laser, Nancy Wood, and Jim Wetzel.

I am grateful to the people who helped set me on the path towards learning, teaching, and writing about communities: Dan Drasin, Dorothy Ives, Gordon-Michael Scallion, Ernest "Chick" Callenbach, Jerome Ostentowki, Bill Becker, Don Markle, and Hildur Jackson.

I'm especially obliged to the community founders who generously shared their stories — Velma Kahn, Tony Sirna, Arjuna daSilva, Valerie Naiman, Chuck Marsh, Peter Bane, Dianne Brause, Kenneth Mahaffey, Hank Obermeyer, Luc Reid, Dave Henson, and Adam Wolpert — heroes all.

Enormous thanks to the people who offered expert advice: Frances Forster, James Hamilton, Bob Watzke, Zev Paiss, Chris ScottHanson, Jim Leach, Dave Henson, Gregory Clark, Cindy Maddox, Carolyn Goldschmidt, Steve Goldstein, and Bill Goodman; and those who critiqued chapters: Tree Bressen, Geoph Kozeny, Velma Kahn, Patricia Allison, Harvey Baker, and Paul DeLapa.

Very special thanks to Rick Tobin, Brecharr Hemmaplardh, and Don Rose.

Foreword

BY PATCH ADAMS

I'M A COMMUNITY FOUNDER. I knew when I entered medical school in 1967 that I would create an intentional community to offer low-cost medical care. I knew health care delivery was in big trouble, and as a nerd activist interested in cybernetics, I wanted to create a model that addressed all the problems of care delivery. In order for health care delivery to be inexpensive, I thought the staff should live in the community and it would include farming and host of support facilities. I know the medicine I wanted to practice would include helping stimulate patients' living vital, independent lives. Concerned for the health of communities and society as much as of individuals and their families, I had read copious utopian and dystopian literature.

I was sure I wanted to do this in an intentional community. I visited Twin Oaks in 1969 and other communities as well, all of which all fed my hunger to live this lifestyle, which I knew would be good for both staff and patient. I knew I would start a community when I graduated in 1971, and wrote up an eight-page paper with our first mission statement.

The innocence of that document makes me smile today. Like any good nerd, I tried to find any literature to help guide me on how to make my community vision happen. Nothing. So I spoke with fellow communards and dove right in. I wonder what we would have done different-ly if we had run into this thorough, intelligent book back then. Maybe looking at all we had to do would have scared us away. We probably had fewer meetings than any founded community in history. We also made every known mistake. Yet for me, community living was a magical nine years. At a certain point in our process we realized that in order to continue with our hospital dream we would have to take most of the steps this book lays out so well.

Only a few community members wanted to continue in our medical service mission. The rest have all have all stayed together these 33 years as family, though no longer as an intentional community. In 1993, the incredible people who chose to continue to create our medical community realized we needed to do things differently, and made a commitment to the kinds of organizational structures this book suggests.

Very few communities would survive long without the depth of structure you'll find here. Whether you use this wisdom or not — it still is worth all the efforts to create and live in community. I've had no burnout or regrets. Community has made everything in my life easier and has allowed me to have huge dreams, inconceivable without community. The skills I've learned, practical and human, seem infinite. My love for humanity has thrived and expanded. Nothing about community has been easy, but it all has been fun. This is the work for political activists who want to live their solutions. If we are to survive as a species we will do so learning the ecstasy of community. We do have to get together.

Creating a Life Together shows what to pay attention to in forming new communities and ecovillages, and offers exercises to develop community intelligence. Do these exercises even if you don't agree with them; consider them training wheels. Of course no book can be complete; you still might make a million mistakes. I suggest reading this book and then visiting ten communities to see how they did it.

I thought it would take four years to build our free 40-bed hospital in community. Now, in our 33rd year, we may finally break ground this year. We're ready. We've learned that the journey to community is nurturing, and so will you. Good luck!

There is hardly anything more appealing, yet apparently more elusive, for humankind at the end of the 20th century than the prospect of living in harmony with nature and with each other.

— Robert and Diane Gilman, *Ecovillages and Sustainable Communities*

Do not be afraid to build castles in the sky.
That is where they belong.
But once the dreams are in place,
Your job is to build the foundation under them.

— Henry David Thoreau

～Introduction～

Creating A Life Together

"**I** FOUND THE LAND!" Jack exclaimed over the phone. As the originator of EarthDance Farm, a small forming community in northern Colorado, he had been searching for just the right community land for years, since long before he and a circle of acquaintances had begun meeting weekly to create community. He was so sure it was the right land, he said, that he'd plunked down $10,000 of his own savings as an option fee to take it off the market for two months so that we could decide.

I had joined the group several weeks earlier, and I knew nothing about intentional communities then. However, it had seemed in their meetings that something was missing.

"What's the purpose of your community?" I had finally asked. "What's your vision for it?" No one could really answer.

That Saturday we all drove out to the land to check it out.

And promptly fell apart. Confronted by the reality of buying land, no one wanted to commit. Frankly, there was nothing to commit *to*. No common purpose or vision, no organizational structure, no budget, no agreements. In fact we hadn't made decisions in the group at all, but had simply talked about how wonderful life in community would be. Although

Jack tried mightily to persuade us to go in with him on the land, there were no takers, and he barely got his money out before the option deadline.

The Successful Ten Percent

I've since learned that EarthDance Farm's experience is fairly common. Most aspiring ecovillages and community groups — probably 90 percent — never get off the ground; their envisioned communities never get built. They can't find the right land, don't have enough money, or get mired in conflict. Often they simply don't understand how much time, money, and organizational skill they'll need to pull off a project of this scope.

I wanted to know about the successful ten percent, those groups that actually created their communities. What did they do right?

I've sought the answer to this question ever since, in my years as editor of *Communities* magazine, and by visiting dozens of communities and interviewing scores of community founders. And I've seen a definite pattern. Generally, founders used the same kinds of skills, knowledge, and step-by-step processes to create widely different kinds of communities, from urban group households or rural ecovillages.

Creating a Life Together is an overview of that process, gleaned from some of the most innovative and successful community founders in North America. This is what they did, and what you can do, to create your community dream.

What Are Intentional Communities and Ecovillages?

A residential or land-based intentional community is a group of people who have chosen to live with or near enough to each other to carry out their shared lifestyle or common purpose together. Families living in a cohousing communities in the city, students living in student housing cooperatives near universities, and sustainability advocates living in rural back-to-the-land homesteads are all members of intentional communities.

Community is not just about living together, but about the reasons for doing so. "A group of people who have chosen to live together with a common purpose, working cooperatively to create a lifestyle that reflects their shared core values," is one way the non-profit Fellowship for Intentional Community describes it.

What most communities have in common is idealism: they're founded on a vision of living a better way, whether community members literally live together in shared group houses, or live near each other as neighbors. A community's ideals usually arise from something its members see as lacking or missing in the wider culture.

Ecovillages are intentional communities that aspire to create a more humane and sustainable way of life. One widely quoted definition (by Robert and Diane Gilman) defines ecovillages as "human-scale, full-featured settlements in which human activities are harmlessly integrated into the natural world in a way that is supportive of healthy human development, and which can be successfully continued into the indefinite future."

An intentional community aspiring to become an ecovillage attempts to have a population small enough that everyone knows each other and can influence the outcome of community decisions. It hopes to provide housing, work opportunities, and social and spiritual opportunities on-site, creating as self-sufficient a community as possible. Typically, an ecovillage builds ecologically sustainable housing, grows much of its own organic food, recycles its waste products harmlessly, and, as much as possible, generates its own off-grid power.

Sirius Ecovillage near Amherst, Massachusetts, grows a large percentage of its organic food, generates a portion of its own off-grid power, and offers tours and classes on sustainable living. EcoVillage at Ithaca has built the first two of its three planned ecologically oriented cohousing communities on 176 acres near Ithaca, New York, and operates its own organic Community Supported Agriculture farm for members and neighbors. We'll explore two aspiring ecovillages in the following chapters: Dancing Rabbit Ecovillage in Missouri, and Earthaven Ecovillage in North Carolina. I use the term "communities" in this to mean ecovillages as well as other forms of intentional community.

More and more people are yearning for more "community" in their lives; you may be one of them. These are people who feel increasingly isolated and alienated, and want something more satisfying. This can mean seeking to create community where they are, or it can mean seeking residential, land-based intentional community. It includes cohousing, shared group households, ecovillages, housing co-ops, environmental activist communities, Christian fellowship communities, rural homesteading communities, and so on.

Many peruse the hefty *Communities Directory*, which lists over 600 communities and where they are and how to join them. Others browse the web for individual community websites, beginning with such starting places as the Fellowship for Intentional Community (www.ic.org); The Cohousing Network, (www.cohousing.org); Ecovillage Network of the Americas (www.ena.ecovillage.org); or the Northwest Intentional Communities Association (www.ic.org/NICA).

Cohousing Communities

Cohousing is another increasingly popular form of contemporary intentional community. Cohousing communities are small neighborhoods of usually 10 to 40 households which are managed by the residents themselves, and which have usually been developed and designed by them as well (although increasingly cohousers partner with outside developers). Cohousers own their own relatively small housing units and share ownership of the whole property and their large community building (with kitchen, dining room/meeting space, and usually a children's play area, laundry facilities, and guest rooms). Cohousing residents conduct their community business through consensus-based meetings, and enjoy optional shared meals together three or four nights a week.

"Cohousers believe that it's more readily possible to live lighter on the planet if they cooperate with their neighbors, and their lives are easier, more economical, more interesting, and more fun," observes Chuck Durrett, one of two architects who introduced cohousing to North America from Denmark in 1986. By 2002, 68 completed cohousing communities were up and running in North America, and approximately 200 more were in various stages of development.

The growing interest in intentional communities, whether ecovillages, cohousing, or other kinds of communities, isn't just wishful thinking. By 2002 the yearning for community, and individual communities, has been favorably — and sometimes repeatedly — covered by the *New York Times, USA Today, The Boston Globe*, NBC's "Dateline," ABC's "Good Morning America," CNN, and National Public Radio.

Why Now?

I believe we're experiencing a culture-wide, yet deeply personal, phenomenon — as if some kind of "switch" has simultaneously flipped in the psyches of thousands of people. Aware that we're living in an increasingly fragmented, shallow, venal, costly, and downright dangerous society, and reeling from the presence of guns in the school yard and rogues in high office, we're longing for a way of life that's warmer, kinder, more wholesome, more affordable, more cooperative, and more connected.

This is partly because we're so unnaturally *disconnected*. Post-World War II trends toward nuclear families, single-family dwellings, urban and suburban sprawl, and job-related mobility have disconnected us from the web of human connections that nourished people in our grandparents' day, as well as numbing us with simulations of human interaction on TV sitcoms rather than living in a culture small-scale and stable enough that we'd have such interactions ourselves.

The people interested in intentional communities aren't extremists. They're the people next door. Many are in their 40s and 50s; they've raised families, built careers, and picked up and moved more times than they can count. They're tired of Madison Avenue's idea of the American Dream. They want to settle down, sink roots, and live in the good company of friends. Others are young people; fresh out of college, hyper-aware of our precarious environmental situation, and disgusted with the consumerist mall ethic, they say "No thanks."

We're also recognizing that living in community is literally good for us. Scientific research shows that our health improves when we live in a web of connection with others. "Of all the many influences on our health, interpersonal relationships are not only a factor, but increasingly are being recognized as the most *crucial* factor," physician Blair Vovoydic writes in *Communities* magazine. "Being connected to other people probably makes you physically healthier than if you lived alone." This appears to be especially true for older people, who tend to stay healthier longer, recover from illness more quickly, and live longer than the elderly not living in community.

It's also healthier for the planet. At a time when — every day — we're losing 200,000 acres of rainforest "lungs," we're spewing a million tons of toxic waste into the atmosphere, and 45,000 people die of starvation *every day*, living simply, cooperating, and sharing resources with others may be the only way of life that makes any sense.

"Small, independent, self-sufficient communities have the greatest ability to survive the normal cycles of boom-and-bust which our economy and culture go through, and an even better chance of surviving the major catastrophes which may loom ahead as our oil supply dwindles," writes Thom Hartmann in his book *The Last Hours of Ancient Sunlight*.

What better place than intentional communities to downsize possessions, share ownership of land and tools, grow healthy food, share meals, make decisions collaboratively, and together create the kind of culture that nourish-es our children as they grow up, and ourselves as we grow older? And what better place than intentional communities to show the rest of the world that even hyper-mobile North Americans can choose to live this way?

What You'll Learn Here

It's becoming increasingly obvious to many of us that intentional community living is one key to surviving, even thriving, in these disintegrating times. But, like members of the EarthDance Farm, few of us know where to start.

Creating a Life Together is an attempt to help your ecovillage or intentional community get off to a good start. It attempts to distill the hard experience of the founders of dozens of successful communities formed since the early '90s into solid advice on getting started as a group, creating vision documents, decision-making and governance, agreements and policies, buying and financing land, communication and process, and selecting people to join you. It's the information I was looking for when I began this journey. It's simply what works, what doesn't work, and how not to reinvent the wheel.

And this information is not only for people forming new communities — whether or not you already own your land. It can also be valuable for those of you thinking about joining community one day — since you, too, will need to know what works. And it's also for those of you already living in community, since you can only benefit from knowing what others have done in similar circumstances.

Because forming a rural community involves more variables than other kinds of communities (for example, how members might make a living), I focus more on rural communities. However, most of the steps and skills described in these chapters apply to urban and suburban communities as well. This book also focuses on communities in which decisions are made by all community members, and doesn't examine issues specific to ashrams, meditation centers, or other spiritual or therapeutic communities in which decisions are made by one leader or a small group. Why you need a legal entity (Chapter 8), and what you should consider before choosing a legal entity (in Chapter 15), apply to forming communities and ecovillages anywhere; however, information on specific legal entities (in Chapters 15 and 16) apply only to the United States.

Is This Information Really Necessary?

Many communities that formed in the 1970s and 1980s, including large, well-established ones, weren't familiar with most of this information when they started, and apparently didn't need it. Nonetheless, I urge you to learn these steps and skills. Why? First, because establishing an ecovillage or new community is not easy, then or now. Getting a group of people to agree on a common vision, make decisions collaboratively and fairly, and combine their money with others to own property together can bring up deep-seated emotional issues — often survival-level issues — that can knock a community off its foundations. I want you to have all the help you can get.

Second, since the mid-1980s, the cost of land and housing has skyrocketed relative to most people's assets and earning power. Zoning regulations and building codes are considerably more restrictive than they were in earlier decades. And because of media coverage that highlights any violent or extreme practices in a group, the "cult" stereotype has become part of the public consciousness, and may affect how potential neighbors feel about *your* group moving in next door.

Newly forming communities can flounder and sink for other reasons, too. Not being able to agree on location. Not having enough time to devote to research or group process. Not having enough access to capital. Not finding the right land. Based on the hard lessons of the "successful 10 percent" (and the "unsuccessful 90 percent"), today's community founders must be considerably more organized, purposeful, and better capitalized than their counterparts of earlier years.

Is This Advice "Corporate"?

As you skim these pages you'll see many figures and percentages — "business and finance" information — and you'll no find advice on the spiritual principles involved in forming a community. Is this book just some representation of "the system" you may be trying to leave behind? Why is there no mention of the spiritual aspects?

I'm presuming that your own spiritual impulses and visions about community are already well developed; that you know very well why you want to live in an ecovillage or intentional community or create your own. As for all the business and finance advice, consider it a set of tools designed to get you from your unique personal impulses of spirit to the manifestation of that vision in physical form. And while I'm not part of "the system," I study the system in order to learn how to use some of its more useful tools to create alternatives to it. As an old adage from India says, "It takes a thorn to remove a thorn." At the present time, anyway, it takes budgets and business plans, and a rudimentary understanding of real estate and financing, to create alternatives to a society in which these tools are necessary. Consider the skills and steps in this book to be the shovels and soil amendments you'll need to grow your own community, from the seeds of your vision into a flourishing organism.

How to Use this Book

Most of the skills to learn and steps to take in forming an ecovillage or intentional community are not linear, but simultaneous. So although the information is presented in a step-by-step way, some tasks must be undertaken together. For example, although you'll need to create a legal entity for owning land before you buy property together, what kind of land you want as well how you intend to organize ownership and decision making, makes all the difference in which legal structure(s) you choose in the first place.

I suggest first reading this book quickly, to get an overview, and then a second time, slowly and thoroughly, then collect and read other resources for more detailed information. I also suggest that everyone in your group read this book, not just those who are getting started and assuming leadership roles. The more of you who are informed — and hopefully disabused of common misconceptions about starting new ecovillages and communities — the more empowered and effective you'll be as a group.

So let's get started.

Part One: Planting the Seeds of Healthy Community

⮑ Chapter 1 ⮐

The Successful Ten Percent — and Why Ninety Percent Fail

ONE GRAY NORTHERN CALIFORNIA night in November 1988, six would-be community founders piled into a small pickup truck and headed for Oregon. Their vision at the time was to create a Community Land Trust with houses in the Bay Area and rural land within commuting distance. They'd just learned of an 87-acre property with a stream and 25 buildings in rural Oregon that had fallen to the IRS in the 1970s for $1.7 million in unpaid taxes. The former site of a Christian intentional community, the property had a large dining lodge and kitchen, 12 small rustic cabins, two dorms that could sleep 125, laundry and garden outbuildings, a large woodshop, an office/classroom complex, and a partially finished residential fourplex. Back taxes notwithstanding, it was what many community founders dream of — a rural property with many buildings — so off they went.

Ten hours later they clambered out of the cramped truck into the cold rain and surveyed the scene. "It was extraordinarily depressing," recalls Dianne Brause. What had once been groomed, beautiful lawn was now shoulder-high grass. The once-beautiful vegetable garden grew thistles eight feet high. Forty-five acres of for-

merly magnificent forest was an open field of stumps and brambles, clear-cut seven years earlier by the Christian group to raise money to pay their tax lawyers. Pushing through the wet walls of grass, the visitors examined the first few buildings. Most, empty and neglected for almost seven years, had broken windows, rotting roofs, and sagging steps. The group creaked open doors to find cold, dirty, foul-smelling rooms full of debris and mold. When the former owners realized the IRS would foreclose on their property, they stripped the buildings of everything moveable: furniture, carpets, sinks, stoves, vent fans, and fixtures. They had ripped the sprinklers out of the lawns and removed every light bulb. Now, as the group picked their way through litter, broken glass, and dead birds, they found no running water — the pipes had frozen and broken the previous year. Not only this, they said, but the property would probably now cost at least half a million dollars; its zoning had reverted from multiple occupancy to the county-wide regulation of "no more than five unrelated adults," and the place was probably still saddled with enormous IRS debt. Cold, soaked, and miserable, the group left. Obviously, the place was a bust.

But not for two members on that fateful day. Dianne Brause, a former conference center teacher, saw beautiful land with gentle meadows and some great trees left standing, excellent gardening potential, and all the right buildings — an ideal community and retreat/conference center. Kenneth Mahaffey, a businessman who bought, renovated, and rented out old houses, saw an excellent piece of real estate, an exciting land-purchase challenge, and the ideal site for a community. Dianne had experience and interest in community and good people skills; Kenneth had expertise in real estate and finance. Both were movers and shakers who made things happen.

Within six months they had closed on the property. Today it is Lost Valley Educational Center, a thriving community of 22 adults and seven children, with clean, renovated buildings, restored vegetable gardens, a reforestation project with sapling Douglas firs and hardwoods, and a vibrant conference center business.

Lost Valley — How One Group Did It

Kenneth and Dianne's first challenge was finding out who controlled the property and to whom they should submit a bid. Was the IRS still in charge? Since it had been seven years since the IRS takeover, was the huge tax lien about to expire? After much confusion and delay, they were finally able to send a bid via a local legal firm representing the unknown owners, though they were told they must not, under any circumstances, contact the IRS.

The property had been appraised at $557,000 a few years earlier, and before that, when it was still forested, at $750,000. The back property-tax bill turned out to be $50,000, but they believed it could be reduced. Many other parties had been interested in the property, and one had bid $250,000 a few months earlier, but

were no longer sure they could pay it. By guessing at their chances of success, the possible back-taxes outcome, the probable challenge to rezoning, and the property's state of ruin, Kenneth took a leap of faith and bid $80,000.

Over the next three months they heard nothing. Their inquiries led nowhere and they got conflicting stories about who really controlled the property. Finally Kenneth and Dianne contacted the IRS directly, and eventually learned that the legal owners were now the Seattle law firm that had fought the IRS on behalf of the previous owners. They called the Seattle lawyers, who said they knew nothing of the bid. The next day, however, they called back, saying, "If you can raise $90,000 we can close in three weeks."

With closing costs and lawyers' fees, the property would cost about $100,000. Kenneth raised the money from friends, creating three-month bridge loans at 8-10 percent interest. He stipulated in his sales offer that the IRS rescind their $1.7 million lien on the property. The seven-year period was up and the IRS had to decide whether to sue for the money or drop the claim. Fortunately, they chose to drop it.

Kenneth and Diane incorporated Lost Valley Center, Inc., a 501(c)3 non-profit educational organization. The property closed in April, 1989. Technically, Kenneth held the title, but the new non-profit considered itself the proud owner of 87 acres of grass, thistles, and run-down buildings. Although it still had a $50,000 back property-tax burden and uncertain future zoning, they'd scored a half-million dollar property. In a few months Kenneth remortgaged one of his real estate holdings and paid off the bridge loans. Then he loaned the organization another $100,000 to create a fund to repair and renovate the property.

Like many other community founders, they faced a serious zoning challenge. The previous owners had been allowed "multiple occupancy," but the county planning department decided that the property's grandfather clause was invalid because of the length of time between the previous use and current use of the property. So the property reverted to the county's normal zoning rules, meaning no more than five unrelated adults could live on the land, despite the fact it was 87 acres with 25 buildings. While they eventually did manage to get the multiple-occupancy zoning reinstated, buying the property without knowing this was quite a gamble. Usually, to be among "the ten percent," community founders need to resolve zoning issues before buying the land.

Two months later, in June, Dianne, Kenneth, and five others interested in becoming community pioneers moved to the land and set to work with a will.

The first month they cleared all the buildings of piles of junk, rebuilt the water system, restored the basic landscaping, and planted a quarter-acre vegetable garden. By August, they'd set up the woodshop and the Lost Valley Center's business offices, and repaired the dorm buildings, one of the fourplex residences, the dining hall, and five classrooms. They created a brochure for their conference and retreat center, and plastered local stores and bulletin boards with flyers — following advice to be as active and public as possible about their intended conference center activities. They went out of their way to meet their neighbors and join in neighborhood picnics and volleyball games, and invited the neighbors to their open houses. In September, joined by a few more pioneering residents, they renovated some of the cabins, set up their commercial kitchen, supplied their dorms with mattresses, blankets, and linens, and bought used furniture for all facilities. In October they hosted their first conference.

Another challenge was to show the county why the back property taxes of $50,000, should be reduced. Lost Valley pointed out that according to county law, since they and the previous owners were both 501(c) non-profits, they shouldn't be penalized for the length of time lapsed between the dissolution of the previous community and their own purchase of the land. The county agreed, and in January 1990 reduced the back taxes to about $10,000. The county also generously decided that the work of Lost Valley fell within their own tax-exempt guidelines, and wouldn't be liable for further property taxes as long as all activities on the property supported Lost Valley's own tax-exempt purposes.

Over the first four months of 1990, Lost Valley residents and volunteers also planted more gardens and began a reforestation project, starting 1,000 trees in their seed orchard and 800 baby Douglas fir and other trees in the clearcut. They developed a watershed restoration program with federal agencies, designed Ancient Forest Tour programs, and began agricultural research and educational projects. They held their first residential permaculture design course and began a bimonthly environmental education program. They continued renovating — cleaning or replacing all their carpets, installing fire safety systems, and renovating another cabin. They remodeled a small building as a staff kitchen and youth hostel and began hosting overnight guests.

Lost Valley was on its way.

What Works, What Doesn't Work?

Since the early 1990s, I've been intensely curious about what it takes for a newly forming community or ecovillage to succeed. So, first as publisher of a newsletter about forming communities and then as editor of *Communities* magazine, I interviewed dozens of people involved in the process of forming new communities and ecovillage projects as well as founders of established communities. I wanted to know what worked, what didn't work, and how not to reinvent the wheel.

I learned that no matter how inspired and visionary the founders, only about one out of ten new communities actually get built.* The other 90 percent seemed to go nowhere, occasionally because of lack of money or not finding the right land, but mostly because of conflict. And usually, conflict accompanied by heartbreak. And sometimes, conflict, heartbreak — and lawsuits.

What was going on here?! These people started out trying to create a way of life based on ideals of friendship, good will, cooperation, and fair decision-making. What had these founders not known?

The Successful Ten Percent

Lost Valley's story illustrates the major steps of forming a new community or ecovillage — establishing a core group with a particular vision and purpose, choosing a legal structure, finding and financing property, and moving in and renovating (or developing land). It also involves creating an internal community economy and refinancing any initial loans if necessary. (Since ecovillages are a form of intentional community, I'll use the term "community" to mean ecovillages as well as other forms of community).

Each of the communities we'll look at has undertaken a similar journey, and roughly in the same order. Most of the seven founders of Sowing Circle/Occidental Arts and Ecology Center in northern California were an already established group of friends and housemates who in 1995 formed a partnership (later replaced by a Limited Liability Company) to purchase property, and a 501(c)3 non-profit to manage their planned conference center business. They conducted a thorough property search, finding an 80-acre, million-dollar property with existing community buildings and cabins. They bought it for $850,000, paid for by a combination of owner financing and loans from their families, and second and third mortgages from friends and colleagues. They moved in and renovated for eight months, started up their conference center business, and refinanced with a single private loan five years later.

In 1998, dozens of web surfers from around the country coalesced around an Internet call for people to cofound an income-sharing community in rural New England. After planning the Meadowdance community via e-mail and in person for a year, the forming community group located 165 acres of nearly ideal land in rural Vermont for $250,000. Six group members willing to move ahead formed a Limited Liability Partnership and through members' loans raised most of the funds to buy and develop the property. They spent a year seeking a conditional use permit from the county for their large multipurpose community building, but, after spending $20,000 on tests, permits and fees, they didn't get it. So, they bought a house in town and started up their software testing and typing/editing businesses there. In 2002, after the businesses had started to take off, they began looking for rural land again.

Each of these communities are among "the ten percent" — the forming communities that actually get up and running. We'll learn more about each of them in later chapters.

But what about the other 90 percent of forming communities — the ones that fail?

---

*The figure is somewhat higher for forming cohousing communities. Approximately 25 percent seem to actually get built, according to *Cohousing* magazine editor Stella Tarnay.

Why Ninety Percent Fail

In the early 1990s, a founder I'll call Sharon bought land for a spiritual community I'll call Gracelight. At first it looked promising. Sharon had received unprecedented and unusually rapid zoning approval for a clustered-housing site plan. She met regularly with a group of friends and supporters who wanted to be part of the community. But over the next 18 months, first the original group and then a second group fell apart, disappointed and bitter. Sharon struggled with money issues, land-development issues, interpersonal issues. After two years she said she was no longer attempting community, and in fact loathed the idea of community and didn't even want to *hear* the "C"-word.

What had this founder not known?

- **How much money it would take to complete the land development process before she could legally transfer title to each incoming community member.** Sharon had no budget in advance, and no idea what it would cost to complete county requirements for a site plan and roads, utilities, etc.
- **How much each lot would eventually cost, and that she shouldn't have fostered hope in those who could never afford to buy in.** Sharon knew that some people in the group wouldn't be able to buy in, but counted on her sense that "it will all work out somehow."
- **That she'd need adequate legal documents and financial data to secure private financing.** Sharon believed that telling potential financial contributors her spiritual vision for Gracelight was sufficient. It didn't occur to her to provide a business plan, budget, or financial disclosure sheet, or to demonstrate to potential investors how and when they might get their money back.
- **That she should make it clear to everyone at the outset that as well as having a vision she was also serving as land developer.** Sharon didn't think of herself as a "developer," and never used the term, in spite of the fact that she financed and was responsible for the purchase and development of the land.
- **That she needed to tell people that she fully intended to be reimbursed for her land-purchase and development costs and make a profit to compensate her time and entrepreneurial risk.** Sharon didn't think in terms like "entrepreneurial risk," even though she was taking one. When group members in the first and second forming community groups finally brought up financial issues and asked pointed questions, she was offended. And group members were offended too, when they learned Sharon was going to make a profit. One can argue for or against making a profit on community land; the point is, Sharon didn't make her intentions clear at the outset.
- **That she needed to tell people from the beginning that, as the developer, she would make all land-development decisions.** Again, one can argue either way about one person making decisions about his or her own financial risks in forming a community — but Sharon should have made these clear.
- **That a process was needed for who was in the group and who wasn't, and for what kinds of decisions the group would make**

and which Sharon alone would make.

- That consensus was the wrong decision-making option for a group with no common vision or purpose, with one landowner and others with no financial risk, and with no clear distinction between those who were decision-making members of the group and those who were not. In fact, the group wasn't practicing consensus at all, but rather some vaguely conceived idea of it.

"Structural Conflict" — And Six Ways to Reduce It

After years of interviewing founders like Sharon and hearing their stories of community break-up, heartbreak, and even lawsuits, I began to see a pattern. Most new-community failures seemed to result from what I call "structural" conflict — problems that arise when founders don't explicitly put certain processes in place or make certain important decisions at the outset, creating one or more omissions in their organizational structure. These built-in structural problems seem to function like time bombs. Several weeks, months, or even years into the community-forming process the group erupts in major conflict that could have been largely prevented if they had handled these issues early on. Naturally, this triggers a great deal of interpersonal conflict at the same time, making the initial structural conflict much worse.

While interpersonal conflict is normal and expected, I believe that much of the structural conflict in failed communities could have been prevented, or at least greatly reduced, if the founders had paid attention to at least six crucial elements in the beginning. Each of these issues, if not addressed in the early stages of a forming community, can generate structural conflict "time bombs" later on.

1. **Identify your community vision and create vision documents** There's probably no more devastating source of structural conflict in community than various members having different visions for why you're there in the first place. This will erupt into all kinds of arguments about what seem like ordinary topics — how much money you spend on a particular project, or how much or how often you work on a task. It's really a matter of underlying differences (perhaps not always conscious) about what the community is *for*. All your community members need to be on the same page from the beginning, and must know what your shared community vision is, and know you all support it. Your shared vision should be thoroughly discussed, agreed upon, and written down at the get-go. (See Chapter 4.)

2. **Choose a fair, participatory decision-making process appropriate for your group. And if you choose consensus, get trained in it.** Unless you're forming a spiritual, religious or therapeutic community with a spiritual leader who'll make all decisions — and you all agree to this in advance — your members will resent any power imbalances. Resentment over power issues can become an enormous source of conflict in community. Decision-making is the most obvious point of power, and the more it is shared and participatory, the less this particular kind of conflict will come up. This means everyone in the group has a voice in decisions that will affect their lives in community, with a decision-making method that is fair and even-handed. How it works — the procedure for your decision-making method — has to be well-understood by everyone in the group.

A more specific source of community conflict is using the consensus decision-making process without thoroughly understanding it. What often passes for consensus in many groups is merely "pseudo-consensus" — which exhausts people, drains their energy and good will, generates a great deal of resentment all by itself, and causes people to despise the process they call "consensus." So if your group plans to use consensus, you'll prevent a great deal of structural conflict by getting trained in it first. (See Chapter 6.)

3. **Make clear agreements — in writing. (This includes choosing an appropriate legal entity for owning land together).** People remember things differently. Your agreements — from the most mundane to the most legally and financially significant — should absolutely be written down. Then if later you all remember things differently you can always look it up. The alternative — "we're right but you folks are wrong (and maybe you're even trying to cheat us)" — can break up a community faster than you can say, "You'll be hearing from our lawyer." (See Chapter 7.)

4. **Learn good communication and group process skills. Make clear communication and resolving conflicts a priority.** Being able to talk with one other about sensitive subjects and still feel connected is my definition of good communication skills. This includes methods for holding each other accountable for agreements. I consider it a set-up for structural conflict down the road if you *don't* address communication and group process skills and conflict resolution methods early on. Addressing these issues at the start will allow you to have procedures in place later on when things get tense — like practicing fire drill procedures now, when there's no fire. (See Chapter 17 and Chapter 18.)

5. **In choosing cofounders and new members, select for emotional maturity.** An often-overwhelming source of conflict is allowing someone to enter your forming community group, or later, to enter your community, who is not aligned to your vision and values. Or someone whose emotional pain — surfacing weeks or months later as disruptive attitudes or behaviors — can end up costing you untold hours of meeting time and draining your group of energy and well-being. A well-designed process for selecting and integrating new people into your group, and screening out those who don't resonate with your values, vision, or behavioral norms, can save repeated rounds of stress and conflict in the weeks and years ahead. (See Chapter 18.)

6. **Learn the head skills and heart skills you need to know.** Forming a new community is like simultaneously trying to start a new business and begin a marriage — and is every bit as serious as doing either. It requires many of the same planning and financial skills as launching a successful business enterprise, and the same capacities for trust, good will, and honest, kind interpersonal communication as marrying your sweetheart. Founders of successful new communities seem to know this. Yet those who get mired in severe problems have usually leapt in without a clue. Like Sharon, these well-meaning folks didn't know what they didn't know. So the sixth major way to reduce structural conflict is to take the time to learn what you'll need to know.

Community founders must cultivate both heart skills and head skills.. This means learning how to make fair, participatory group decisions;

how to speak from the heart; how to face conflict when it arises and deal with it constructively; and how to make cooperative decisions and craft fair agreements. It means learning how to create budgets, timelines, and strategic plans; and how to evaluate legal entities for land ownership or business or educational activities. It means learning the real estate market in your desired area, local zoning regulations, and, if needed, how to secure loans with reasonable terms. It means learning how to structure healthy and affordable internal community finances. It means learning about site planning and land development. It means doing all this with a sense of connection and shared adventure. Plunging into the land-search process or trying to raise money without first understanding these interrelated areas is a sure invitation to trouble.

Community founders tend to be specialists, but in fact they must be generalists. I've seen founders with spiritual ideals and compelling visions flounder and sink because they have no idea how to conduct a land search or negotiate a bank loan. I've seen founders with plenty of technical or business savvy — folks able to build a nifty composting toilet or craft a solid strategic plan — who didn't know the first thing about how to speak honestly and from the heart to another human being. And I've seen sensitive spiritual folks as well as type-A "get-the-job-done" folks crash and burn the first time they encountered any real conflict.

Not everyone in your forming group needs to have all these skills or all this information — that's one reason you're a group! Nor must your group possess all these skills and areas of expertise among yourselves when you begin. You can always hire training for your group or expertise in whatever you need, whether it be a consensus trainer, communication skills trainer, meeting facilitator, lawyer, accountant, project manager/developer, land-use planner, permaculture designer, and so on.

Many well-established North American communities never included most or all of these six structural ingredients at their origin, and don't see why they should have. "Hey, we're here now, aren't we?" In the 1960s, '70s, or early '80s, people usually just bought land and got started. Some of these communities are still with us today, and proud of it.

Nonetheless, for communities forming today, I recommend addressing all six of these issues early on, for all the reasons already noted.

What Will it Cost?

How much it will cost in total (and how much it will cost each founder) is a question that can only be estimated by creating a financial model and plugging in the numbers. To do that, you'll need to start with certain assumptions. Will you be rural, semi-rural, suburban, or urban? What are land values in your desired area? Will you renovate or develop your property? How many members will you have? Will you have community businesses? How will you structure your internal community finances to meet monthly land payments and other expenses? If your numbers show that your plan is too expensive or otherwise unworkable, revise some of your assumptions and try again.

How much it costs communities that have formed since the early 1990s (when it became harder to do than in previous decades) varies widely, depending on all the above factors, but mostly on land values. For example, in 1996 seven founders of Abundant Dawn community bought a beautiful 90-acre owner-financed parcel on a river with a farmhouse, cabin, and barn in rural southwestern Virginia for $130,000.

They paid $13,000 down, contributing slightly more than $1,800 each.

At the other end of the spectrum, in 1994 seven founders of Sowing Circle/Occidental Arts & Ecology Center bought an 80-acre, owner-financed fully-developed "turn-key" property in Sonoma County, California with rolling hills, panoramic views, stands of oak and redwood, two 20-year-old organic gardens, and 16 community buildings and cabins. They paid $850,000, with each member contributing about $20,000 to the $150,000 down payment.

Figure on several hundred thousand dollars or more to buy and develop your land, depending on your desired area and the magnitude of your plans. The cost per person will depend on how many founders and/or members split the costs. If you use owner financing, private financing, or bank financing, multiply that amount several times over for the true land-purchase cost, including all the principal and interest payments you'll be making over the years. (See Chapters 9, 10, 11, 12, and 14.)

How Long Does it Take?

It also takes enormous amounts of *time* to pull off a project of this magnitude. Even if you meet weekly, you'll still need people to work on various committees that work and/or meet between scheduled meetings — gathering information, calling officials, crunching the numbers, drafting proposals, and so on — for at least a year, or even two years or longer.

The founders of Dancing Rabbit Ecovillage in Missouri first explored their ideas and organized their initial group in 1993, began their land search in 1995, and bought land in 1996. They worked steadily to develop it and raise their population for the next six years, and they continue to do so. The founders of Earthaven Ecovillage

in North Carolina began with an original group in 1990, searched for land for four years, reorganized their group and bought land in 1994, and refinanced and began developing in 1995. They have spent the past seven years developing it and increasing their membership, and they also continue to do so.

Generally, the larger your group and/or the smaller your assets, the longer it'll take. And the fewer your numbers and the greater your assets, the faster it will happen. For example, the founder of Mariposa Grove, an urban community in Oakland, California, began looking for property in 1998, bought it in cash in 1999, and spent the next three years renovating it and attracting members. The two founders of Lost Valley Educational Center found their property in 1988, bought it (also paying cash) in 1989, and renovated it and got it ready to host workshop participants by 1990. They've spent the past 12 years continuing to develop the physical infrastructure and build the community.

So this is really a trick question. While it can take from a year to several years to find and buy property, develop it, and establish your membership and financial base, there's really no end point. Like a marriage or a business, growing a community is never really "done."

How Many People do You Need?

Forming community groups usually start out with one or two or a few people with an idea, grow larger (fluctuating in size as people attend a few meetings for awhile and get more involved or lose interest and leave), and shrink to a much smaller number when it's time to commit money to buy a particular piece of property.

See Figure 1 (on page 11) for some examples of how many people are involved in the communities we'll examine in this book.

TABLE 1: HOW MANY PEOPLE DO YOU NEED?

Community	Total Envisioned # of Members	Members at Early Meetings	Members at Property Purchase	Members in 2002
Lost Valley Rural (OR) 87 acres Founded 1988-89	20+	7 - 12	2	23
Earthaven Rural (NC) 320 acres Founded 1990-94	150	15 - 20	12 - 21	57
Sowing Circle/ Occidental Arts & Ecology Center Semi-rural (CA) 80 acres Founded 1991-94	10	5 - 12	7	11
Dancing Rabbit Rural (MO) 280 acres Founded 1993-96	500 - 1000	20 - 30	6	16
Abundant Dawn Rural (VA) 90 acres Founded 1994-96	40 - 60	12	7	9
Mariposa Grove Urban (CA) Founded 1998-99	12 - 13	0	1	9
Meadowdance Rural (VT) Founded 1998-00	50 - 75	30 - 40 online 20 in-person	6	9

SPIRITUAL COMMUNITIES: TROUBLE IN PARADISE

Newly forming spiritual communities seem to experience more structural conflict than most groups; probably because spiritual community founders sometimes tend towards a soft-focus, whole-picture orientation — what's popularly called "right-brained" thinking. This often frustrates and even repels other potential cofounders who may use more logical or systematic "left-brained" thinking. Like Sharon, founders of spiritual communities are sometimes accused of deceiving others about money and power issues, when in fact they simply hadn't focused on clear, explicit communication about finances and decision-making, and didn't realize such clarity was necessary. These founders often dismiss the primarily "left-brained" potential cofounders who could help them, considering them merely "bean counters," when the latter simply want to understand the financial, legal, and decision-making arrangements before they leap in wholeheartedly.

If you operate more in right-brained mode, I urge you to ally yourself with more left-brained compadres who can help ground your community ideals in workable business and legal strategies. And if you're a hardcore left-brainer, I urge you to hook up with more holistically oriented colleagues who will help you keep your heart open and help you remember why you want to bring forth this wonderful vision in the first place.

It doesn't just take information and skills, money, time, and people to form a community, but also a sense of connection, sometimes called "community glue" — born of group experiences like preparing and eating meals together, work parties, weekend trips, and long, intimate conversations. Gathering and weaving the thread of skills, information, money, time, people, and experiences is complex, and often overwhelming — what cohousing activist Zev Paiss calls "the longest, most expensive personal-growth workshop you'll ever take."

Next we'll take a look at the kind of person who pulls it off — that unsung hero, the community founder.

WE SET OUT TO CHANGE OUR WORLD...
by Roberta Wilson

As fate would have it, Winslow Cohousing on Bainbridge Island near Seattle, formed in 1988, ended up being the first owner-developed cohousing community in the U.S. We certainly didn't have much experience to go on. Only one of us had lived in an intentional community, and only a few had even visited any intentional communities. None of us had seen cohousing in Denmark, and of course there were no models of it close to home. What we had was McCamant and Durrett's *Cohousing* book and an incredible amount of energy.

As with all communities, we made some wise choices and some poor ones. We met every weekend for over two years, with many of us meeting in committees during the week. This vigorous schedule allowed us to buy land, get through the construction process, and move into our 30 duplexes and flats by Spring 1992, but it cost us potential members who couldn't devote such time to development. Finding loans for what looked to financial institutions like some kind of middle-income commune was difficult and may have cost one credit union representative his job. The stress resulting from engaging some of our own members to work for us hurt the group and hurt some of these members as well. Our original group was deeply bonded by the sheer effort of the project. Yet, after move-in we retreated to our individual homes to recuperate. While our idealism had carried us through the forming stages, we weren't quite prepared for the reality of living cooperatively — so many of us were used to having our own way in the world.

We also had the inevitable turnover. We had problems with new residents who either had their own heroic notions, or who soared and then dove as the honeymoon phase ended. We had kids who couldn't get along, a dog that bit, divorces and deaths, births and celebrations. For the most part, our surrounding neighbors were friendly. We figured out a work system, each serving on clusters — Administration, Process and Communication, Grounds, and Common Facilities. We figured out a meal system, with dinners five nights a week. We figured out how to work with consensus. We learned to keep good track of our finances, and we continued to work towards emotional literacy. We still struggle with issues such as member participation and how to make capital improvements, yet our meetings are now civil, efficient, and more emotionally honest. Folks have found their own level after the first years of feeling overwhelmed. Some of them have been disappointed with the lack of emotional intimacy, while others, especially teens, have felt uncomfortable living in a fishbowl.

At times, most of us have probably asked ourselves, "What am I *doing* here?" — a question, I believe, that arises from a complex calculation of time and energy spent and one's tolerance for conflict. Sometimes I've asked myself, after a difficult confrontation, why I should put so much of my life energy into something that seems, at the time, to give back little. Yet I'm sure that at other times each of us has surely declared: "I can't *imagine* living anywhere else!" — a response to the very personal exchanges that make living in community so rewarding. I can call my neighbor and ask her to turn off the coffee pot that I forgot. Children come to visit and play with my dog. A neighbor pauses from her chores a moment and tells me about her life. In the forest, we scatter the ashes of a member who died; in our orchard, we bury the family dog. A neighbor's sister comes to stay and offers massages. The children are delivered to school by adults who share the duty. Our community feels safe.

The idealism, dreams, and devotion, while still here, have given ground to the practical and the real experience of living in community — the good, the bad, and the ugly. Community is seeping into our cells, I believe, so that even the challenges become just part of who we each are. Cooperative culture is gaining ground over our individual upbringing in competition; slowly, we are giving up the need for absolute control. We set out to change our world, and now community is changing us.

Excerpted with permission from Communities Magazine, *Spring 2000.*

⤬ Chapter 2 ⤬

Your Role as Founder

VALERIE NAIMAN WAS A WOMAN with a mission.

In 1991, as she and a group of people interested in forming community in the mountains of western North Carolina began their land search, she sold her local business so she could devote full time to the project. To better understand the local real estate market and real estate financing, she studied for and got real estate sales and brokers' licenses, and took a job with a local realty company, which allowed the group to learn about any new properties as soon as they came on the market.

She also contacted communitarians nationwide, asking which legal entities they'd chosen for group land ownership, and why, and she learned as much as she could about the various legal entities communities could use to own property together. She studied Community Land Trusts by making calls to the School of Living in Pennsylvania, and by visiting the Institute for Community Economics in Ohio, organizations that help groups set up Community Land Trusts. She eventually didn't recommend this specific form of land ownership to the group, and they later created a Homeowner's Association to own property and a 501(c)3 non-profit to carry out its educational mission.

In 1993, the group found 320 acres of owner-financed land that fit most of their criteria. After the group spent over a year in confusion and conflict about the community's ultimate vision, and whether or not to buy this particular property, Valerie drew up and submitted a contract on the land herself, with a loophole in case she needed to get out of it. She hosted a "founders meeting" of tea and fundraising, inviting group members who shared the same community vision, and an interest in this particular property, as well as other local people interested in forming an intentional community. By the end of the afternoon they had raised the $100,000 down payment.

Over the next few months the group continued adding members and raising funds to begin developing the property, and bought it in December 1994.

The following year, Valerie visited the E. F. Schumacher Society in Massachusetts to learn how the group could create a small, private "shoe box bank" to raise funds. The group adopted this idea, created the EarthShares fund, and over the next few years raised enough money to pay off the owner-financers.

Other founders of "successful ten percent" communities have traveled a similar path. Recent college graduates Tony Sirna and Cecil Scheib were environmental activists with degrees in computer science and civil engineering respectively, before founding Dancing Rabbit in Missouri. They educated themselves well in real estate, zoning regulations, financing possibilities, and non-profit legal structures to buy their land and create the financial and legal structures that support their ecovillage dream.

In order to establish the Sowing Circle community and its non-profit educational organization, Occidental Arts and Ecology Center, cofounder Dave Henson left his environmental activist job and spent eight months as the group's full-time point person. He researched possible property sites and sources of financing and donations, negotiated with the owner of their chosen site, and drafted and instituted various financial and legal plans through which to carry out their purpose.

And Luc Reid, a software engineer and cofounder of Meadowdance community in Vermont, was an almost full-time on-line and off-line student of every aspect of community development he could find, learning as much as he could about what had and had not worked well in other recently formed communities.

Contrast these folks with Sharon and Gracelight community. Well-meaning and motivated, Sharon nevertheless hadn't a clue that she needed to educate herself in new fields and develop new skills to pull off a task of this magnitude. Community founders must anticipate challenges not faced by community founders of earlier times. These include the fact that "ideal" property isn't ideal if zoning regulations and building codes prevent you from developing it the way you want to. If your group wants rural land, a lack of decent-paying local jobs will affect your community's attractiveness to future members. Difficulty attracting members will affect your ability to pay back any land purchase and development loans, so your group must consider your site relative to available jobs before buying land. And the initial impression your group makes on potential neighbors will affect whether they will support your getting any needed conditional use permits or zoning variances.

What Kind of Person Founds a Community?

Certain recognizable characteristics stand out in successful community founders, or at least among "burning souls" — a cohousing term for vision-driven founders who work zealously to manifest their dreams.

Dianne Brause and Kenneth Mahaffey of Lost Valley are clearly burning souls. So are Valerie Naiman of Earthaven, Tony Sirna and Cecil Scheib of Dancing Rabbit, Dave Henson of Sowing Circle/OAEC, Luc Reid of Meadowdance, and other founders you'll meet in these pages.

Founders need to be visionaries — people who can imagine, visualize, or feel something that doesn't exist yet. Most of the group seeing the Lost Valley property for the first time saw a dreary wreck; Kenneth and Dianne saw a thriving community and well-appointed, successful conference center.

Founders must be leaders — people who can inspire others to believe a particular vision is possible and who motivate them to take action and make that vision come true. The people who joined Dianne and Kenneth at Lost Valley wouldn't have jumped into that uncertain venture, or worked so fiercely over the first year, without Dianne's and Kenneth's burning belief that Lost Valley would soon host successful workshops and conferences.

Founders of "the ten percent" are often successful entrepreneurs, or have at least one experienced entrepreneur in their group. Technically an entrepreneur is someone with the ability to organize and manage a business, assuming the risk for the sake of the profit, but I'm referring mainly to the aspect of instinctive business savvy — someone with an inner "radar" about what will work financially. Entrepreneurs take risks, based as much on intuition as on experience. They take the initiative. They're focused, task-oriented, on-point. They know how to create budgets and strategic plans. Kenneth Mahaffey was a successful real estate investor before cofounding Lost Valley; he took an enormous risk buying property that might require paying $50,000 of back taxes and might not have the necessary use permit restored. Valerie Naiman had been a successful movie costume designer and owner of a retail costume shop; she took a huge risk by selling her business and investing time and money to pursue legal structures and real estate for an untested, non-mainstream project, then investing substantial sums in Earthaven's down payment and EarthShares fund. Not all people with this ability use it to make money. Dave Henson, who has entrepreneurial savvy in spades, was a fairly well-known and effective environmental activist before cofounding the Sowing Circle/OAEC project.

And lastly, founders must be physical builders — people who know how to alter their property to help create their vision, from renovating a building to digging ponds, building cabins, or erecting solar panels. Kenneth Mahaffey and Dianne Brause and the first members threw themselves into cleaning and renovating the Lost Valley property, as did Dave Henson and his fellow cofounders at Sowing Circle/OAEC. As soon as they'd purchased their properties, Valerie Naiman and the cofounders of Earthaven, and Tony Sirna and Cecil Schaub and the cofounders of Dancing Rabbit, immediately began building roads, setting up camping areas, and creating the first rudimentary shelters on their undeveloped parcels of land.

Vision, leadership, entrepreneurial skill, and willingness to physically build must be present in your group, but not necessarily all in the same person. As founders you must certainly have vision — without which nothing will happen. You'll need leadership to inspire yourselves and those who'll join you to support that vision. You'll need one or more entrepreneurs who know what will work financially, and who are willing to take a risk — and thus inspire the rest of you to take a risk. And you'll need to get physical on the land to turn your vision into reality.

Given these "ingredients," here's my recipe for growing an intentional community:

1. Imagine, visualize, or feel something that doesn't exist yet.
2. Inspire yourselves and those that join you to believe your particular vision is possible and you can make it happen.
3. Use entrepreneurial skills to do all this within your estimated budget and time frame (revising either as necessary).
4. Use labor, tools, and energy to create the physical expression of your vision on your property.

What Else You'll Need

Your group will also need patience, faith, good communication skills, tenacity, and the willingness to acknowledge each other.

- **Have patience.** Forming an effective working group, learning good decision-making and group process skills, researching your options, acquiring and if necessary developing property simply takes time — from one to several years, depending on the scale of your plans, how many are in your group, how well capitalized you are, and other factors. Regardless of how everyone in your group would like things to progress more quickly, they probably won't. You'll also need to consider the timetables of others involved, including lawyers, zoning officials, and lenders. Elana Kann and Bill Fleming, project managers for Westwood Cohousing in Asheville, North Carolina, warn that founders must understand and accept the difference between what is and what is not in their control. Elana and Bill observe that probably 95 percent of the major variables involved in a forming community are not in the founders' control — land value and availability, banks' lending policies, and city or county zoning regulations. To make expectations more realistic and reduce anxiety, some experienced community founders recommend taking your most optimistic timing estimate at the beginning of your project and doubling it.

- **Faith.** Trust that it's meant to be, that you're being guided by a higher power. Dianne Brause would have been overwhelmed by fear and a sense of responsibility in what she and Kenneth and the others were attempting to pull off, but was repeatedly saved by her willingness to trust that it was meant to be. "After so many synchronistic events that didn't fit the scientific odds, I chose to act as if some higher force was really in charge, that the project was really a kind of sacred trust that we were privileged to take on," she recalls. "This belief allowed me to trust that things were actually being taken care of." Other founders have relayed similar stories of trust and courage in the face of what seemed like overwhelming odds against their project.

- **Good communication skills.** Your group will no doubt find strength in your members' diversity, yet that can also be a challenge. You'll need to learn how to hear and accept perspectives quite different from your own. Besides obvious differences of gender, age, economic circumstances, or spiritual or religious orientation, you may differ widely in your communication styles and in your needs for safety, self expression, recognition, and connection. Some will express themselves intensely, and often. Some will share how they feel; others will consider bringing up feelings irrelevant or annoying. Some will want to gather data, consider options, and plan extensively, while others will want to dispense with talking and "get on with it." In fact, the kinds of people attracted to forming community are typically explorers, doers, risk-takers, and entrepreneurs — and as such, likely to be impatient with the nuances of skilled group process or consensus decision making.

- **Tenacity.** You'll need determination and stamina. The ability to hold to a vision and persevere has made all the difference between groups that built their communities and those that felt too discouraged to continue. Sometimes it will seem like the process is going well and moving forward; other times it'll feel like you're stopped at every turn. Keep your eyes on the goal, lean into the wind, and keep traveling.

- **Willingness to acknowledge others.** You'll need to thank and acknowledge each other many times for ideas, proposals, legwork, research, patience, living room meeting space, snacks, tea, and childcare. There's no faster way to slow down progress than burnout, which usually results from too many long hours of contributing to a common cause without recognition or acknowledgment. You're all essentially volunteers — gifting the group with your time and life energy to fulfill your vision. You're going to need to feed each other with the basic nourishment that keeps volunteers going — the simple courtesy of heartfelt thanks.

"If Only I Had Known!"

"Why would anyone want to go *through* all this?" exclaimed Patricia Greene, after she'd given her heart and soul to forming a new community that disbanded after the first year.

Why don't they just *join* one?" ask some long-time activists in the communities movement. "So many communities have already done all the start-up work, why do that all over again?" Most community activists have met scores of shiny-eyed idealists sharing grandiose-sounding plans for community who clearly have no idea how much hard, humbling work is involved.

And it's true — growing a new community is at least as difficult as it is rewarding. I've heard more than one founder say: "If I'd had any *idea* how hard this would be I never would have done it!" After a pause, however, they usually add with a smile, "Thank God I *didn't* know, though, because here we are."

"Be careful what you tell your readers about forming community," warns a friend who lived for years at a permaculture-based community in New England. "Don't be so realistic about the process that you scare them off." He told me if I really wanted to help potential community founders achieve their goals, maybe I should say relatively little, so I don't discourage anyone who'd otherwise just plunge in and figure it out as they went along, as most community founders do. Whatever your level of interest in forming a new community, it's my hope that after reading this book you'll either say, "Great, I'm inspired. Let's get started," or, "Whew, I'm glad I found *that* out. I'll join one instead!"

I know a fine couple whom any community would covet as members. He's a carpenter, she's a writer. Both are lively, intelligent, spiritually inspired individuals who have decades of previous community experience between them. But no community they've visited has seemed quite right, in its location, its financial arrangements, or in its qualities of spiritual and intellectual "juice." I don't think this couple is too picky. They know just what they want and they haven't found it yet. I think they're simply community founders at heart. And you may be too.

So let's move on. Next chapter — getting your group off to a good start.

SUNDAYS AT DUMAWISH

*"We're Creating Something More Than
Mere Housing Here"*
by Virginia Lore

It is Sunday, which means that we will spend three to four hours today with our cohousing partners, talking about pavers and concrete mosaics, our new waiting list policy and how to save the birch trees on the west end of the property. About 40 of us will crowd into Kurt and Kara's living room, and, using colored cards, will make decisions in nine minutes that would have taken Kevin and me two days to debate. Small children will wander up from the childcare area downstairs for whispered consultations with their parents. They will be sent back down when the conversation gets too intense. Sometimes I'll go down with them. The intensity almost always gives me a headache.

There is plenty to be intense about. We're six months away from move-in, and the walls are being framed. We're one household away from full membership. Since Kevin and I joined this summer, we've seen five households join and one household withdraw. Our affiliate membership process is rigorous, and unit selection is based on the date of affiliate membership. These decisions have not been made without introspection, earnest discussion (mediation in two cases), and tears.

There are times when I would rather be anywhere than in another cohousing meeting. Today, for example. If I were less committed, I'd be home on the couch, eating popcorn and watching *The Big Chill*. So why will I go to the meeting instead?

I will go partly because I've skipped the last two weeks. Most of us have to take an occasional break from the fervor of the construction process. I have no qualms about trusting the community to make decisions, which will ultimately be best for the sum of us.

I will go partly because I want to see people. I miss the folks I don't see on the development committee. I want to see how much Eleanor has grown in the last two weeks, to hug Mem, and to find out how Bruce and Karen are enjoying the group. I look forward to Ethel's earthy laugh, Kurt's jokes, and to watching from across the room as Meg puts a quilt together.

Mostly, however, I will go out of faith. Cohousing is now both my religion and my politics. I continue to ask myself "Is this best for the group?" before putting up my green "Yes" card in response to a proposal, because I sense we are creating something larger than mere housing here.

If there is a cathedral for this new church of ours, it is the land. We have watched as the land was cleared and the grading completed. We have seen the retaining wall built — the earth pinned into place by grouting and rebar, held by shotcrete. We have watched from the street above the site the installation of the footings, the pouring of foundations. We have watched the units at the far end go up first — we've witnessed the snaky white neoprene tubing laid for the radiant floor heating, and come back to the meetings to tell each other, "They've started framing!"

This is what keeps me going to the meetings: in six months we will be neighbors, part of something we've all built together. If our process makes us more loving, unselfish and useful to each other, that is only to be expected. In this community, we will not only have potlucks and hold babies, but we will practice gentleness, honesty, love and compassion in a tribal setting. We'll have a place to eat, work, and make music among folks we have learned to trust, and it is this we will offer to the world around us.

It is as if we are both watching a miracle happen and creating it at the same time. Could there be any better way to spend a Sunday?

Excerpted with permission from
Communities *magazine, Spring 2000.*

⚎ Chapter 3 ⚎

Getting Off to a Good Start

Y OUR GROUP HAS GATHERED FOR your first meeting to talk about forming a new community. Where do you start?

I suggest starting with a general overview of the basic steps involved in growing an intentional community. You could begin by asking everyone in your in your group to skim through this book, then read it more thoroughly later on, and then read some of the recommended resources for more in-depth information.

There is also a wealth of information to be found on community websites. You'll find photos

of communities, vision statements, lists of values and goals, outlines of community processes, and community histories. By browsing community websites you'll get a wonderful sense of the rich and varied possibilities for community organization.

Visiting communities is another excellent way to empower your community dreams with real-life reality checks. I also suggest talking with as many founders as you can, of both communities that are thriving, as well as those that are struggling or didn't work out. My hope is that you'll begin your community journey with a great deal of information and increasingly realistic expectations.

While the following chapters describe steps community founders can take, don't assume these steps are linear. The process of growing a community is more organic — simultaneously ongoing *and* step by step. See Table 2 for an idea of what this can mean.

Cohousing communities have a slightly different process from other communities. Some additional key steps can include partnering with a developer, raising development financing, getting a construction loan, and securing individual mortgages. (See Chapter 12.) This is an increasingly popular model of intentional community in which people develop, build, and manage their

---

VISITING ESTABLISHED COMMUNITIES

Visiting communities can bring a sense of reality to the project — and hone your sense of what you want, and don't want, in your community. I suggest contacting any communities you'd like to visit ahead of time and asking whether they welcome visitors. Ask if you can offer several hours' labor when you visit them, as communities always need extra labor for work projects, and your being willing to work will make them more likely to invite you. Bring old clothes, work gloves. and food to share. You'll learn much and will probably have a great time. Be sure to send a thank-you note afterwards.

TABLE 2: THE COMMUNITY-GROWING PROCESS

Develop good communication skills ———-> ongoing —————————————————————————————-> **Learn to deal well with conflict** ——————> ongoing —————————————————————————————-> (Chapters 17-18)					

Organize your group ————-> (Chapter 3)	**Create your vision documents** ————-> (Chapter 4-5)	**Research the real estate market in your desired area** ————-> (Chapters 9-10)	**Research zoning issues in your desired area:** possible costs to get exceptions if needed ——-> (Chapter 11)	**Learn your financing options:** figure out your group's borrowing power ———-> (Chapter 12)	**Develop or renovate your property as needed** ————-> (Chapter 13)

Research communities: Learn as much as you can about how founders formed them ——-> (All chapters)	**Decision-making method:** choose (and learn how to use them) ————-> (chapter 6)	**Choose a location:** create site criteria———-> (Chapter 9-10) **Choose & set up your legal entity.** ———-> (Chap's 8, 15-16)	**Conduct your property search: choose your property** ——-> (Chapters 9-10)	**Finance and buy your property** ————-> (Chapter 12)	**Organize your internal community finances** (and reorganize as needed) ————-> (Chapter 14) <——————

Create community agreements & documents —————-> ongoing ———————————————————————-> (Chapter 7)					

Choose new people to join you —————-> ongoing ——————————————————————————-> (Chapter 19)					

Remember, most of the above steps are not linear, but can overlap.

own neighborhoods. They live in smaller-than-normal housing units and share ownership of community areas, usually including a common green, a garden space, and a large common building with a kitchen and dining room, children's play area, laundry facilities, and guest rooms. Members optionally share dinners together several evenings a week, and usually make decisions by consensus.

Don't Run Out and Buy Land — Yet

Many people interested in starting a community assume the first thing you should do is buy land. Even though a beautiful piece of property can be tempting, buying your property first is generally *not* a good idea — and can be a huge risk for conflict later because all the necessary structures haven't been put in place. I advise against it unless you've taken the following steps:

1. One person or a small group already has the necessary funds to buy it, and can cover its mortgage payments for a year or so.

2. The person or small group has set up an appropriate legal entity for property ownership, or sets it up soon after.

3. The documents of the legal entity (or other community documents) spell out the relationship of each future member's financial contribution toward ownership and decision-making rights, whether people will have equity in the property, and other financial issues.

4. The individual or small group buying the property have agreed on the vision for the community and have created its vision

---

MANY WAYS TO FORM COMMUNITY

Property and Housing

• Buy or rent several houses on the same block and share backyards; turn one into a community building.

• Buy or rent a large house and turn some of its rooms into common areas.

• Rent apartments in an apartment building; turn one apartment into shared common community space.

• Buy an apartment building (or buy several housing units in a planned community, condominium, or housing co-op) and do the same.

• Buy land with an existing house or houses (or an office building, retail store, factory building, warehouse, theater, church, or motel) and turn it into housing and common areas.

• Buy a former conference center or camp and do the same.

• Buy raw land and start from scratch.

Ownership

• The community can own the whole property and lease housing facilities or homesites to members.

• Members can hold title to their individual housing units or lots and houses, and share ownership of common land and community buildings.

Degree of Closeness

• Community members can be closely involved in each other's lives — sharing living space or kitchens, living in close proximity, sharing equipment and tools, or having a car co-op.

• Members can be less involved — living in separate housing units or in separate houses (in clustered housing, in more widely spaced but still clustered housing, or on separate lots), or sharing fewer resources in common.

Degree of Financial Interdependence

• Community members can work for community businesses (and/or outside businesses), share incomes, and share a common treasury.

• They can have a hybrid economy — working for community businesses and sharing profits for food, housing, medical insurance and other necessities, but keeping any outside earnings or assets separate.

• They can have fully independent incomes, and share some or many community expenses.

documents, and anyone joining subsequently must necessarily agree to this vision. Or these will be created by the initial buyers and the people joining them soon after — but *none of the new people will put their money in* until the vision is fully agreed upon and written down, and everyone knows what it is they're agreeing to join.

Why all these safeguards should be in place will become clear as you read on.

When You Already Own the Property

Many aspiring community founders are people who'd like to turn their family-owned land into an intentional community, or groups of friends who have just purchased land together and ask, "Now what?"

If your group has already purchased land, every chapter in this book is still relevant to your situation, except perhaps Chapter 10 on finding the right property and Chapter 12 on financing it. Definitely read "Legal Barriers to Sustainable Development" and "Shopping for Counties — Zoning Regulations, Building Codes, Sustainable Homesteads, and Jobs" in Chapter 9, as well as Chapter 11 on zoning — you still may have these issues to deal with.

Frankly, property owners who want to turn their already-owned land into the site for an intentional community often have the greatest challenge, even though it may seem as if they have already overcome the largest hurdle. When one or more people are the owner-landlords and the rest are tenants, or when a land-based business is also involved and one or more people are the owner-employers and the rest employees, there's an imbalance of power. The owners have enormous power over everyone else, who can be evicted or fired at any time. And the owners have privileges the others probably do not, such as, for example, the right to all financial knowledge concerning the property or business, and the right to enter or lock others out of any building on the property.

The owners often have a genuine desire to experience a sense of community in the group, as well as a strong desire to retain control over all aspects of property use and any activities which could affect property value — since, after all they bear sole financial risk for it. But these two desires are essentially incompatible. You can't simultaneously have "community" and total control over the whole property. This situation often resembles a "feudal lord and serfs" situation. People move there believing the place is a community, yet have no financial/legal risk or responsibility and no real decision-making power, even when the landlord/employers may have set up some kind of "consensus" process (which they can of course override anytime). Not to mention that the tenants/employees may consciously or unconsciously resent the owners for having all the power. Or that the owners may truly believe they don't want power over anyone — but are unwilling to relinquish it until or unless others shoulder their load of the financial, legal, maintenance, and other responsibilities. Or that however benign the owners, the others may project all kinds of parental/authority-figure issues onto them, further clouding the issue. Such inadvertent "fiefdoms" tend to repel competent, solvent, and informed community seekers, yet attract people with few skills and limited funds who are, perhaps unconsciously, seeking a generous "parent" to take care of them. The owners end up functioning like a substitute mom or dad — whether or not they welcome the role — with a passel of community "children" to look after.

This isn't community — no matter how badly everyone wants it!

A situation like this *can* work, however, when there are agreements about how people can buy in to property ownership and how the size of their financial contribution (equal shares? unequal shares?) relates to decision-making rights. There must also be a legal entity for owning the property together, which ideally outlines these agreements in its bylaws or operating agreements. (See Chapter 9.) The group must also find a way to legally protect the owner from the ongoing financial and legal responsibilities such as mortgage payments, property taxes, insurance, and maintenance costs, and legally share these responsibilities, such as through a Triple Net Lease document. (See Chapter 12.)

What if some or all potential community members cannot afford the entire buy-in fee at once, but can make a down payment and mortgage payments over time? One solution would be for the owner to become the owner-financer — the "bank" — and set up promissory notes with each person. (See Chapter 12.)

What if the property is worth so much money, say, several million dollars, that the owner cannot find enough (or any) other potential community members who, even with owner-financing, can afford to buy in and equally share property ownership? One solution could be to subdivide a smaller portion of the property and make it available to shared group ownership. Another possibility is individual member ownership of separate lots (or a cohousing-type arrangement with individually owned housing units and shared common property). A clause in community membership documents could outline members' rights and responsibilities about using and enjoying the adjoining larger property. The owner would still own and control the expensive property, and could be one member among many in shared ownership of the subdivided property.

What if the owner wants to preserve the property in perpetuity as wilderness, or farmland, or community, for example, and doesn't mind taking a financial loss in terms of the right to sell it one day at full market value? The owner can place a conservation easement on the property or create a land trust or community land trust before seeking like-minded fellow members. (See Chapter 16.)

If you're a property owner seeking to create community on your land, please take these issues into account. Be willing to release total control and find ways for people to become fully participating, responsibility-sharing fellow community members. And if you cannot or don't want to release full control but still want live in close proximity with others, please do so and enjoy it — but don't advertise it as "community"!

Organizing Your Group

Following are some start-up suggestions and recommendations from other founders:

Decide how often you'll meet, and where. It helps to schedule meetings on the same day at regular intervals, for example, every Sunday from 1:30 to 5:00. You might begin by meeting monthly or every other week, but when you begin exploring financial and legal options and start your land search, you'll most likely need to meet weekly, with smaller committees working on various tasks between meetings.

At the same time, you'll need to be flexible in your expectations about meeting participation. Weekly meetings can become tiresome, especially for parents of small children. Some groups have found ways to make participation easier for people, by arranging for childcare during meetings, sending meeting agendas out ahead of time, or using e-mail or phone surveys to gather input and ideas. Since some people will have considerably more time to devote to the project than others, some groups have created an internal "time bank" system of credits for hours spent in meetings, committee work, and research tasks. The general idea is that each member "owes" the community a certain number of credits over a period of several years. This way people who can't offer much project time in the present have the opportunity to make up for it later.

Choose a decision-making method; decide how you'll run meetings. If you chose consensus as your decision-making method, get trained in it as a group, or you could end up operating from widely divergent assumptions about how it's done, or crippling your meetings with "pseudo-consensus." (See Chapter 6.)

You'll also need to decide how meetings will be run. Most groups learn, after time, to allow newcomers and visitors to offer ideas and opinions, but to limit decision-making rights to group members. Some suggestions and information about conducting meetings are offered below.

- *Facilitation.* Having a facilitator can make all the difference in how productively and smoothly your meetings run. You can arrange for one or more group members to be trained in facilitation, or you can have all members take a facilitation workshop, and rotate the role in your group. You could also exchange meeting facilitation with other communities or with forming-community groups in your area.

- *Agendas.* Having meeting agendas created ahead of time and sent out to everyone in your group before meetings makes a huge difference in how well your meetings function. Agenda planners schedule each item for discussion in a particular meeting, and note expected amounts of discussion time for each. People won't be able to attend every meeting, and knowing what topics will be decided or discussed ahead of time allows them to attend particular meetings, based on their own priorities.

- *Evaluation.* Allow time at the end of the meeting for evaluation, listing on a large piece of easel paper what you did well and what could have been better. Doing this regularly will help your group improve communication and meeting skills.

- *Minutes.* Decide who will take notes or minutes, what you'll include in them, how they'll be distributed, and by whom. Encourage people in your group who are good at taking minutes to do it regularly. Distribute the completed minutes to everyone by e-mail and/or postal mail.

Decide on some general principles for your community. As a preliminary step, and as preparation for your later visioning process, ask yourselves what are the general principles upon which you'll base your community. Define your bottom lines in terms of:

- **Potential location** and relationship to the land (urban or rural, small gardens or large farming operation, and so on).

- **Preferred distances from cities,** major airports, educational resource centers such as colleges or universities, wilderness or recreation areas, and other places important to your group.

- **Lifestyle issues** (whether you'll have diet preferences, or will be oriented to single

SOWING CIRCLE'S GENERAL PRINCIPLES

Here's what Sowing Circle founders agreed on and wrote down as their principles:

1. We'll support an educational center.
2. We'll be non-dogmatic and diverse.
3. We're not attached to any one lifestyle, diet, or spiritual purpose.
4. We'll consider each person in a couple relationship as a single, individual member.
5. We'll each make equal financial contributions and have equal shares of ownership.
6. We'll each have equal decision-making rights and each contribute equal amounts of labor.
7. We'll share expenses and reduce our level of consumption.

people, families with children, or multiple generations; pet issues; sexual orientation and gender issues; drug-use issues).

- **Preferred financial set up** (whether everyone will contribute the same or different amounts, or contributions will be tied to decision-making rights; or which expenses the community might share).

- **Spiritual issues** (whether you'll have a preferred spiritual orientation or practice, be spiritually eclectic, or secular).

- **Political issues** (whether you'll be activists, or will support politically active members).

- **Educational issues** (whether you'll offer classes, or will be a model and demonstrate site, and so on).

Create a preliminary financial model. As noted in Chapter 1, you'll need to create a rough financial model to get a general idea of the amount of money to raise. Read Chapters 9 through 16 to get a sense of the steps involved. Then consider your probable type of location (urban, suburban, semi-rural, or rural), your preferred area and current property values there, and whether you'll seek raw land, developed property, or a fully developed turn-key property, in order to estimate likely down payment and mortgage costs. Also estimate the costs of attracting more members (if applicable), creating your legal entity, searching for likely properties and investigating the best ones, and any property development or renovation. Divide these by your estimated final number of members for a rough estimate of how much the project may cost each member household. If you don't have information for some of these variables, take your best guess. Compare this information with your group's probable assets and borrowing power (see "Getting Real About Finances"). As noted earlier, if the numbers are too high, revise your assumptions (for example about your desired location or number of members), and try again.

Work out a preliminary timeline. Ask yourselves the length of time in which you'd ideally like to accomplish everything necessary to move to community and set up your physical infrastructure. Creating a preliminary timeline based on this estimate will provide a baseline for comparing your expectations to the reality as it unfolds. You will most likely need to revise it many times as you progress through the steps.

Timelines, like budgets and flow charts, are planning tools to help you anticipate what might be needed at various points, and to give yourselves a series of small goals to help you achieve larger milestones. Timelines can also be helpful by serving as a kind of visualization tool. It's the process of planning — not necessarily any given plan — that's important.

Create a decision log. A record of decisions is an invaluable reference. Update it frequently, post a copy on the wall before meetings, make copies available for members to take with them. Give a copy to each new member who joins the group.

When a group doesn't create a decision log, people tend to continually revisit the decisions that have already been made, which wastes time and drains the group's energy. Stand by your decisions and resist the temptation to revise previous decisions because new group members may want something else. It's fine to revisit a decision when there is a good reason to do so, but don't do it frivolously. (See Appendix 2 for Buffalo Creek's decision log.)

Agree on criteria for group membership. What qualifies someone to become a decision-making member of your group? Are there a minimum number of functions or meetings newcomers must attend before having decision-making rights? (See Chapter 18.) Many groups find that a small, non-refundable financial investment ($100 or so), and/or a smaller dues fee of perhaps $10 a month tends to generate group commitment and helps separate out the mildly curious.

Identify your vision and create your vision documents. The light that will guide all your efforts, this will be one of your first major tasks as a group. (See Chapters 4 and 5.)

Keep accurate financial records. In the beginning you'll probably have minor expenses such as refreshments, copying, and postage costs. As you become more committed, expenses might include consensus facilitation training, expenses associated with visiting communities or attending communities conferences, and so on. While more significant expenses will arise later, you'll need to decide at the outset how to keep financial records, taking into account how much dues or financial contributions will be, and whether any part of these are refundable, and so on.

Begin writing community policies and agreements. At some point you'll need to draft agreements and policies, with regard to financial expectations, communication processes, behavioral norms, and other issues. Some of these you'll need now as a forming-community group; others later, as shared owners of your property. (See Chapter 7.)

Help each other stay accountable. Before long you'll need to draft documents and budgets, visit properties, and research financing options, zoning regulations, and other matters. You'll probably assign yourselves tasks and completion dates, as many of these tasks will need to be completed by a particular date so the group can take the next step. Yet, because unexpected work or family commitments or the inability to manage time wisely, people often don't do what they say they will, with negative consequences for the group. You'll need relatively painless, guilt-free ways to help you stay accountable to each other, such as task reviews, task wall charts, buddy systems, and other means. Sowing Circle founders agreed that one person would call each person to ask if he or she had completed their tasks. It was set up as an official tracking system, not a criticism, so no one would feel singled out. (See Chapter 17.)

Establish guidelines for group process. This means making decisions cooperatively, communicating honestly, and holding each other accountable for responsibilities. It means giving feedback and asking for change without making each other wrong, and facing and resolving conflict.

While many groups don't deal with these issues until they're forced to, I believe learning these skills early in your group life is one of the most significant aspects of creating a healthy community. Some groups set aside a separate meeting once a month where members can openly express their frustrations or concerns and seek to resolve them. Some amount of conflict is normal and expected. It's important to create a conflict resolution plan and practice it before you have any significant conflict, like hav-ing a fire drill before you have a real fire. (See Chapters 17 and 18.)

Identify goals, record and celebrate your progress. Groups, like individuals, feel energized and successful when they see themselves progressing steadily toward their goals. To help focus your efforts, you can write down each of your goals on a timeline chart (for example, creating your visioning documents, getting consensus training, creating your site criteria). Post the

"MAGICAL THINKING" AND THE ANTI-BUSINESS ATTITUDE

Bill Fleming, a cohousing founder, cautions community groups against using "magical thinking," a term for a belief common to four-year olds in which simply imagining something means it will happen. "Mommy, I can fly to the moon!"

Community founders engage in magical thinking when they disdain facts and research gathered by other members on, say, legal options or environmental issues, and consider the research results to be mere opinions, no more valid than anyone else's. Magical thinking is in play when people distrust the process of counting or measuring anything to predict likely outcomes (acres, square feet, years, dollars, amounts of principal and interest) in favor of intuitive guesses and inner guidance, or by dismissing tools such as budgets and business plans as being "oppressive" or "restricting our creative flow."

This is related to the pervasive anti-business feeling which is common in communities — distrust or outright fear of financial planning, borrowing money, interest on loans, contracts and written agreements, corporations and other legal entities, and the like. I can understand it. In my younger years I was against anything remotely related to business, multinational corporations, or the government. Like many other countercultural folk, I was also intimidated by tools and processes used by the mainstream, didn't understand how they worked, and turned them into symbols of everything I rejected.

But over time I learned not to mistake the tool for the motivation. I learned "business" is not the same thing as deceitful business practices, money is not the same thing as domination and the lust for power, legal structures are not the same as corporate greed.

Every community formed since the early 1990s that I know of, has been motivated by a spiritual impulse and/or by environmental and social justice concerns. Their founders learned to understand and use tools also used by mainstream culture — creating legal entities, buying property, borrowing money, paying interest — in order to create viable alternatives *to* mainstream culture. They use these tools to help create the kind of world where people share resources, make decisions cooperatively, and are mindful of their relationships with the Earth, their plant and animal relations, and each other.

I urge you to do the same.

chart on the wall before meetings, estimating the date by which you'd like to accomplish each goal. Highlight or circle each goal as you achieve it. Revise the timeline often, since it probably won't be accurate for long, but always show your already-achieved goals. Celebrate when you reach certain milestones; honor and acknowledge what you've done. Creating community is a huge undertaking, yet here you are doing it, step by measurable step.

Getting Real about Finances

One of the most common pitfalls for forming-community groups is unrealistic expectations about how much it will cost. To become familiar with the kinds of expenses associated with buying and developing community property, read Chapters 9 through12 on locating, buying, and financing community land (and keep in mind that these prices will most likely be higher now). You can get an overview of property prices in the area you're considering by looking in the real estate sections of the papers or calling a few realty companies there.

How much can you contribute? At some point you'll then need to discuss your individual financial situations openly, including whatever income or assets you each could make available to the project. People are reluctant to share their personal financial information for many reasons — normally it's no one else's business, and it violates a cultural taboo. Wealthier people are often reluctant to discuss their finances for fear of making themselves vulnerable to reactions ranging from resentment to outright violence, while those with fewer assets wish to avoid pity or even dismissal by others.

Here's an exercise you can use to begin the discussion while preserving everyone's financial

privacy. Write the following on a sheet of easel paper and hang it where everyone can see it:

A: **Down Payment/Development.** Amount you could pay as an equal financial contribution for the down payment and property development.

B: **Monthly Member Assessments.** Amount you could pay on an ongoing basis as monthly member assessment fee for property payments (principal and interest on any loan(s) for property acquisition; property taxes, insurance, repair and maintenance fund).

C: **Potential Private Loans.** (If applicable) Amount you could make available to the group as a private loan for property purchase and development.

Hand out identical pieces of paper and ask each person to write down an amount for A, B, and if applicable to them, C, without identifying themselves. Collect the papers, add up each amount, and write these totals on the easel paper. Without anyone's feeling embarrassed, you can get a general sense of what your group can afford at this point.

If you're like most groups, you'll probably need to borrow money for property acquisition, thus your other financial baseline is your group's total borrowing power. Two exercises in "Assessing Your Potential Borrowing Power" (see Chapter 10) can help you figure this out easily.

At some point, members will need to stop being anonymous and let the group know how much each may be able to contribute to the down payment and other land-purchase expenses, and everyone's potential borrowing power. I suggest having general discussions first, then schedule a discussion at a subsequent meeting where you'll tell how much you could contribute, so everyone will have a chance to think about it ahead of time.

No doubt a few group members will have far greater assets than most others, and some will have far less. More affluent members will be able to contribute more money than others, either as the project's required contribution, or as a private loan (and sometimes, though it's rare, as an outright donation to the project). Keep in mind that your group will have several choices with regard to handling contributions to the property purchase and development. Some examples include:

- You can each pay equal contributions, and tie those contributions to equal property ownership rights and responsibilities and decision-making rights, as Sowing Circle/OAEC founders did.

- The community could pay for its property purchase and development with loaned funds, with *no* requirement for a buy-in fee, and all members could pay monthly fees that reimburse the loan(s), as Dancing Rabbit did.

- You could gather equal contributions from founders that guaranteed the right to build on a plot of land, as Earthaven founders did.

- One member could buy the property, and essentially loan this amount to the other group members, who would pay the member back over time.

- One member could buy the property and the community could refinance as a housing co-op, with the founder being reimbursed all funds except his or her co-op share, as Mariposa Grove plans to do.

When someone can't afford it. When a member can't afford the buy-in fee, some groups reluctantly decide that they won't be able to join the community. Other groups figure out ways to make it financially possible for everyone to join. For example:

- The community could loan the person part of the money for the required down payment from its development fund, as Sowing Circle/OAEC did. The person then reimburses the development fund over time. Alternatively, another group member, or several members, could loan the person part of the required contribution.

- The community could buy the property with equal contributions from most founders, but allow some founders to pay half down and the rest in monthly payments with interest, as Earthaven did.

- The community could buy the property with equal contributions from most founders, but allow some founders to pay with the equivalent of so many years' labor for the community at some agreed-upon hourly wage, through a labor contract, as Earthaven did with some early members.

- The person doesn't contribute to the land purchase, but pays the community a monthly rental fee to live in community-owned housing. The community would need clear agreements about whether the property-use and decision-making rights are different for founders who are tenants. Alternatively, the tenant-members could save money over time to pay the buy-in fee.

- The person could rent a room or a rental unit, or share housing with another community member. Again, doing this would require clear agreements about any distinctions in property use and decision-making rights.

- If the amount of financial contribution is tied to the size and cost of the housing unit, the community could create studio-sized housing units for founders with fewer assets, as some cohousing communities have done.

- In "lot model" cohousing communities, in which each member buys a lot and builds their own dwelling, the community could allow the member to use the kitchen and shower facilities of its common house, and build a small sleeping hut on his or her site, while saving enough money is to build a house, as Sharingwood Cohousing in Washington did.

There are most likely many other ways to help founders without enough funds for the buy-in fee. Sometimes the process of accommodating people in this situation can backfire, so it's critical to put any alternative arrangements in writing in advance, to protect both the community in general and the specific members involved. (See Chapter 18 for Pueblo Encantata's experience with one such arrangement.)

Collecting Funds

While your expenses will be minor at first, once you're about to create a legal entity and begin your land search, you'll need several thousand dollars from each committed member for costs associated with forming a legal entity and the land-search process. When you find a likely property, expenses can include an option fee to take the property off the market and, if needed, costs associated with researching its feasibility for your group and/or getting an exception to zoning regulations. Community groups create different methods for collecting funds; for example, collecting a small monthly amount and assessing yourselves larger lump sums at key points along the way.

If you hire a member of your group to devote full or part-time to the project for a time, that's another expense. (Or you could do as one group did, and give the person a deep discount on buy-in costs and/or the first choice of homesite or living space.)

Raising Money from Supporters

You might also raise funds from others. Earthaven cofounder Valerie Naiman suggests having a document showing your community's

YOUR COMMUNITY NAME

One of the most rewarding aspects of creating a new community is choosing a name. It will not only inspire your group and invoke your vision, but will reflect your values and aspirations to potential cofounders, lenders, zoning officials, and neighbors. Positive-affirmation and nature-affiliated names such as "Abundant Dawn," "Earthaven," and "Meadowdance" seem to work well. I *don't* recommend pretentious, flowery, or overly idealistic names, since (perhaps because their founders were never grounded in business, legal, and financial realities?) communities with such names often tend to end up as part of the "ninety percent." Even if a community with a pretentious name gets off the ground, being called "Harmony Bliss Spirit" can prove downright embarrassing during the inevitable periods when people feel disillusioned or find themselves embroiled in conflict.

mission and purpose, values, and goals to show to friends, family, and others who might want to support your community project. You could organize fundraising events such as benefit parties, with donated live music or catering, or benefit auctions with donated auction items, as well as offering supporters the opportunity to give low-interest loans. Along with membership dues, gifts and friendly loans from supporters can total several thousand dollars.

Attracting and Integrating New Members

At some point you may decide you'd like other people to join your group. You might want to simply tell friends and acquaintances what you're doing and invite them to a meeting, or you could cast a wider net and draw from the public.

If you decide to draw from the public, target your promotion to people with values and interests compatible with your future community. If you're planning an ecologically sustainable community with organic gardens, for example, mail press releases to local environmental organizations and post flyers at health food stores, farmers' markets, and organic-food restaurants.

Use aspects of your vision statement and your mission in your flyers or brochures. For example, "We're seeking to form a community of _____(kinds of people)___, to buy ___(number of acres)___ in ___(county/counties)___ in order to _____(purpose of community)_____. If it's a longer brochure, include a few paragraphs summarizing the key aspects of the values and goals of your community. Use this in any press releases you may send out as well.

One of the best ways to attract like-minded people is a community website. I suggest creating one as soon as your group feels committed enough. The purpose of your flyers, brochures,

press releases, and classified ads should be to whet people's appetites and send them straight to your website, where they'll learn much more about your interests, values, and plans. This is where you reveal as much of yourselves as possible. Use your vision statement and other vision documents ("This is what we're about"), your decision log ("This is what we've done so far, and what we ask new people to agree to"), and your "How to Join Us" document ("These are the steps and requirements for joining our group"). Make sure you clearly describe the financial requirements for participating, once you've decided on them. You can include photos of yourselves looking like a friendly and engaging bunch of folks, perhaps a "Frequently Asked Questions" document, relevant agreements or policies, and photos of your intended property once you've found it. Be sure to make it simple to request information through the website, and designate a member of your group to handle these inquiries.

You'll want the information on your website to draw only the people who resonate with your group's particular values and vision. If you don't use a website, you can use brochures and packets of printed materials to accomplish the same goals. "It's more important to reach the *right* people than simply a lot of people," notes Meadowdance cofounder Luc Reid.

You could follow up any inquiries by sending out a thank-you letter and a questionnaire for inquirers to fill out and return.

A next step could be for interested people to visit your group. Have a regular procedure of welcoming visitors at the beginning of meetings, and introduce everyone around the circle. If they show an interest in becoming members, give them a copy of your vision documents and your "How to Join Us" document (even though they may have already seen these on your website), a current version of your decision log, and other relevant materials. Explain your process for when and how new members can participate in meetings and when they'll have full decision-making rights. (Some communities require new members to take a consensus workshop before becoming full members.) Community consultant Rob Sandelin suggests assigning new members a "buddy" who will be available by phone to answer any questions about your process and your progress so far.

Creating "Community Glue"

Forming a community is not really about your property-purchase and development goals, but about generating a sense of community — a kind of group well-being in which you've connected with each other emotionally and know each other deeply.

Rudolf Steiner said that shared physical activities — when people move the body and vocal chords — bonds people at such deep levels that their connection tends to last. This certainly confirms most groups' experience of what makes people feel connected and committed to each other — working together in shared labor, eating together, telling each other their life's experiences, speaking from the heart about personal or interpersonal issues, singing, dancing, doing rituals, and celebrating birthdays and holidays.

Most groups have weekly or monthly potlucks, often associated with business meetings, which certainly contributes to community glue, as well as making decisions together and personal sharing, such as check-ins and wisdom circles. (These are explored more fully in Chapter 17.)

One of the best ways for a group to experience a sense of community is to rent a rustic lodge with kitchen facilities for the weekend, with activities that might include preparing food and eating meals together, hiking and swimming, playing volleyball or other sports, making music and singing, and telling stories around the campfire.

Storytelling is an excellent way to create intimacy on deeper levels, especially if the topics are self-revealing and personal. One way groups can do this is to tell their life stories, focusing especially on life-changing events or those that affected them deeply. Another is to ask each person to share for 20 minutes or so about the attitudes in their family of origin on such normally taboo subjects as religion, money, or social class. Such sessions can not only lead to a much closer sense of connection, but can also help people understand how each group member might approach such community issues as sharing common property or handling community finances.

If the group is small enough, or if there's enough time, each person can tell stories in turn.

BREAKING BREAD TOGETHER

In some communities individual households have kitchens and eat meals at home, with shared meals one or more times a week. Other communities have central kitchen and dining facilities where members share three meals a day. How many shared meals are necessary to make a difference in community glue?

"Count up the number of days in a week that a group shares meals, and you'll have a reasonably good barometer for measuring the closeness of that community," observes community activist Geoph Kozeny. "When the frequency gets up to four meals a week or so, somehow the social glue gets stronger."

Almost every community described in this book begins common meals by standing in a circle and holding hands and either taking a moment of silence, offering a prayer, or singing a song.

If time is more limited, people can put their names in a hat and draw out as many names as there is time for, with future meetings planned so everyone will get a chance. Shyer members can choose not to speak, but will still enjoy listening to other people's stories. The group can use a kitchen timer to help each other keep to their agreed times. Storytelling evenings are so enjoyable they can be repeated many times.

Pioneers, Settlers, and the Flow of Members

Two kinds of people are usually attracted to forming communities — pioneers and settlers. Pioneers take risks and leap into the unknown. They start the group, do the research, find the land. Settlers wait and see if the pioneer group can pull it off. They come in later, when more is known about the project, and when there's something more visible to join. Settlers need the pioneers to break trail for them. Pioneers need the settlers to join when it's time to raise money and make the project happen. Pioneers are like entrepreneurs. Settlers are like wait-and-see investors. Forming community groups need both.

In most groups, relatively few people meeting in the early months will actually end up moving into the community (although it's possible a tight group of friends will go the whole distance. "The group you start with won't be the group you'll end up with," says Sowing Circle cofounder Adam Wolpert. "Even some of your key founding group members may not be there when you buy your property."

People usually leave when you reach certain milestones:

- When you identify your community vision and write your vision documents, some people could realize it's not for them and leave. However, new people will join, attracted by your group and your community vision.

- When you agree on criteria for your property more members could exit — that's not really the kind of land they wanted. But new people will join — it's exactly the kind of land they wanted.

- When you agree on financial criteria for your community, you could have another exodus — some can't afford it. But more will come, and your financial criteria will let them know whether they can afford it.

- When you decide to purchase a particular property there may be a stampede for the door. Some back off because it's not the right property after all. Others flee because it's a supreme reality check. Now that they're staring community full in the face — gulp! They realize they're not ready for it; it's too huge a commitment, too great a lifestyle change.

However, after this point, many more people may join the group — because they like you, they like your vision, they can afford it — and they like your beautiful property! This is often the time when settlers, watching from the sidelines, get active again, and bring their checkbooks.

You're on your way. Next, your first significant step towards community — identifying your community vision.

≋ Chapter 4 ≋

Community Vision — What It Is,
Why You Need It

IT WAS CRISIS TIME at a community I'll call Willow Bend. This small community in the rural Midwest launched itself in the early nineties with no vision or vision statement. That means they had no shared expression of their desired future, no "why we're here" agreement that aligned community members and inspired them to work toward their shared aspirations.

Then the bottom fell out of the market for the wooden children's toys they manufactured as their primary community business. Overnight they lost almost half of their annual income base. Under severe financial strain, the members held long meetings to figure out what to do. Unfortunately different Willow Benders had widely different ideas about their purpose for being a community.

"We're here to show people a low-consumption lifestyle that works financially," says Tom. "We've got to recoup our losses somehow."

"No way!" exclaims Kathleen. "We're just here to enjoy ourselves and not have to work for the man. We'll just eat beans for awhile."

"How can you say that?," asks Andy, incredulous. "We're supposed to radicalize people! We're supposed to show that you don't have to compete so much and can share things equally and all get along!"

Except they weren't getting along, and were competing mightily themselves, for the underlying basis of Willow Bend's reality. With no common vision, they had nothing to return to — no common touchstone of values, purpose, or aspirations about why their community life mattered, how it fit into the larger world. Because they use consensus decision making, no majority of Willow Benders with the same vision could determine the vision for the whole group. On the surface it looks like they were arguing about money. But they were actually expressing the inherent structural conflict of not all standing on the same ground. And unlike folks in forming-community groups, people with different visions can't simply go their separate ways and start different communities. Willow Bend was their home, and no one could ask anyone else to leave because of their "wrong" vision. As the conflict grew intense several people saw no way out and left the community. Now Willow Bend had two crises — not enough money and not enough people to carry out the tasks of their other community businesses.

I hope this (true) story illustrates why it's so important to establish why we're here as a basis for creating community — and why everyone in the community needs to be on the same page.

Kat Kinkade, cofounder of Twin Oaks community in Virginia, describes a similar circumstance. Once some friends of hers were appalled by what they read in the vision documents of a particular community. But when they met someone from that community whom they liked very much, they decided to visit, and found everyone there to be friendly, warm, and charming. Figuring that actions speak louder than words they decided to ignore the community's declared vision and values and join anyway.

But as Kat's friends lived there over the months, they found themselves increasingly at odds with the community's founders. While everyone was warm and courteous at first, the newcomers' values and goals weren't compatible with the community's, and soon they were embroiled in serious conflict over the direction the community. Eventually the dissension and distrust grew so bitter that Kat's friends left the community — and so did several other members, disillusioned by the bad blood generated by power struggles over vision and values.

"This left the group weak, angry, and exhausted," says Kat. "It was a community tragedy, and not an uncommon one." I've heard this same story more than once about other communities.

So the first major task members of a forming community group is to clarify and write down their vision, and make sure they all agree on it.

Some well-known, long-lived, apparently successful communities don't have and never had a common vision, or at least, never wrote anything down. This can work — but in my opinion it doesn't work well for long. Not having a common vision can blow a community apart when a major challenge or crisis occurs. Or it can slowly erode everyone's vitality and well-being over the years as each conflict arising from different visions adds to the accumulation of resentment.

"A common vision is neither necessary nor sufficient for starting a new community, since many have gotten by without one, and some that had one failed," observes community activist Tree Bressen. "But a common vision greatly increases the probability of success. If your group is going to all the trouble to start a community, can you afford not to give yourselves the best possible chance?"

Sound a Clear Note

A vision doesn't start out as necessarily "visual," and although written down, it's much more than a collection of words. It begins as a quality of energy that grabs you and doesn't let go. It's like a beam of energy leading your group from where you are to where you want to go.

Your vision must be articulated in a way that others can understand easily. It must be simple, clear, and authentic. As Sirius cofounders Corrine McLaughlin and Gordon Davidson say, it must "sound a clear note on inner levels," so it will attract others who resonate with that note.

"It's like a tuning fork against which you measure your resonance," says Adam Wolpert, cofounder of Sowing Circle/Occidental Arts & Ecology Center. "It shows how well you're doing in the theory-practice gap. It helps you aim high."

Once it's written down, a well-crafted vision:

- Describes the shared future you want to create.

- Reveals and announces your group's core values.

- Expresses something each of you can identify with.
- Helps unify your effort.
- Gives you a reference point to return to during confusion or disagreement.
- Keeps your group inspired.
- Draws out the commitment of the people in your group.

"By describing what we want to have happen," says Adam Wolpert, "it's like an insurance policy for the future, for what we *don't* want to have happen."

Elements of a Community's Vision

The terms "mission," "purpose," "values," "goals," "objectives," "aspirations," "interests," and "strategy" are often associated with a community's vision. These words mean different things to different communities, as you'll see in the sample vision documents. Here's how I use these terms.

Vision. This is the shared future you want to create, your shared image of what's possible, the thing that motivates your actions to create community. It's often expressed as the "who," the "what" and the "why" of your endeavor. Ideally it's described in the present tense, as if it were happening now.

Mission, Purpose. Your group's mission or purpose expresses your vision in concrete, physical terms. It's what you'll be physically doing as well as experiencing as you manifest your shared image of what's possible. To understand the difference between "vision" and "mission," consider a community with the vision: "A world where everyone has adequate, healthy shelter." Its mission, to express this vision physically, could be: "To build a model demonstration village using low-cost natural building materials, and through outreach programs teach our building methods, particularly in Third-world countries."

Values. Your group's vision arises out of its shared values, the characteristics and processes you deem worthy. Values are expressed by how you behave now, and how you intend to behave, on a daily basis, as you live in community. In the above example, the community might hold values of sustainability, fairness, kindness, generosity, service, accessibility, thrift, and conservation of resources.

Interests. This includes experiences, states of being, or physical things people may be interested in relative to your future community. Interests usually arise from values and can be expressed as goals. Many of you may be interested in composting, perhaps because you value sustainability, and express that as a goal to build compost for your future community garden.

Goals, Objectives. Goals or objectives are milestones you commit yourselves to accomplish, but short-term, often in a few months or a year. Your community's goals are measurable: you know when you've accomplished them. In the above example, the group might want to finish building their model village in three years, and in the following year begin their outreach program to countries in Central America.

Aspirations. These are strong desires or ambitions for inspired, elevated goals, arising from values. Your community may have a goal to construct a meeting hall for 100 people in two years, and, because you value beauty and sacred space, your aspiration is to build a meeting hall that will be beautiful, calming, and uplifting.

Strategy. Your strategy affirms a series of goals in a particular time-frame. If your vision expresses the "who," "what," and "why" of your community, your strategy encompasses the "how," "where," and "when." It usually involves budgets and cash-flow projections and time lines. Altering your vision will completely change the future you're creating, but altering your strategy only changes how you end up getting there. In the above example, the group's strategy for achieving their goals might be to raise $500,000 and share low-cost building methods in the first two years by offering public workshops and seeking grants from private donors and public foundations.

As we'll see in the next chapter, a community's vision arises in part from the resonance of its individual members' combined values, interests, aspirations, and goals.

Nature's Spirit, an aspiring spiritual community in South Carolina, expressed the difference between their vision (their dream), mission (their physical activities), and goals (their specific, measurable actions) this way:

Vision: A world that values the diversity of all life and provides for its sustainability by living in harmony with nature and spirit.

Mission: To create a community in which we work to expand our consciousness by living in the question: How does one live sustainably in harmony with nature and spirit? This will enable us to be of service, share our experiences, and link with similar local and global efforts.

Goals:

- Procure and care for a commons — a land trust that will ecologically support a small village of 50+ people.

- Build a self-sustaining infrastructure to support our basic needs.

- Create homes, gathering places and guest facilities using sustainable building methods and energy sources.

- Maintain an organic stewardship of the land that will provide for our own and others' food needs while giving back to the Earth.

- Create and nurture a spiritual center as the core of our community.

- Create an interdependent social system.

- Initiate necessary enterprises to assure economic viability with minimal dependence on institutional structures and the market system.

- Establish educational, leadership, internship, and exchange programs that will enable us to be of service to others, communicate and share our experiences, and link with similar local and global efforts.

Your Vision Documents and Vision Statement

Some communities have formal vision documents that describe in inspirational terms the shared future they hope to create together. Other groups may have various documents that give a sense of their vision, often conveyed through a vision statement, possibly a brief description of their purpose or mission, inspirational or factual paragraphs about their community and what they hope for it, and sometimes lists of shared values and goals. These can appear in internal agreements and covenants or formal documents associated with the legal entity through which the community owns land (corporate bylaws, partnership agreements, or operating agreements), and in promotional literature such as website text, brochures, and information packets for prospective members.

Your community's vision is not the same thing as its *vision statement*, although a vision statement serves some of the same functions. The vision statement is your vision articulated — a condensed version in a few sentences. "It's like a notice posted at the gate to all who would like to enter," says Stephen Brown, cofounder of the former Shenoa Retreat and Conference Center in California. "It says, in effect, 'This is what we are about; *this* is what we hope to accomplish; *this* is what guides us'."

Shenoa Retreat and Learning Center: We have joined together to create a center for renewal, education, and service, dedicated to the positive transformation of our world.

Harmony Village Cohousing: We are creating a cooperative neighborhood of diverse individuals sharing human resources within an ecologically responsible community setting.

Meadowdance Community: We are an egalitarian, child-centered community that welcomes human diversity, ecological sensibility, mutual learning, and joy.

Earthaven Ecovillage (from "ReMembership Covenant"): (We are) an evolving village-scale community dedicated to caring for people and the Earth by learning, practicing and demonstrating the skills for creating holistic sustainable culture, in recognition and celebration of the Oneness of all life.

A well-crafted vision statement:
- Offers a clear, concise, compelling expression of your group's vision and mission

(and sometimes, its goals).
- Is short, ideally about 20-40 words.
- Embodies the same quality of energy as your vision.
- Helps focus your group's energy like a lens.
- Offers a shorthand reminder of why you're forming community.
- Helps awaken your vision as a energetic presence.
- Is easily memorized, and ideally each of you can recite it.
- Communicates your group's core purpose to others quickly: "This is what we're about."
- Allows your group to be specific about what it is — and is not.
- Is what potential new members want to see first.

And, like your community vision itself, the vision statement:
- Is something every member can identify with.
- Helps unify your effort.
- Keeps your group inspired.
- Reveals and announces your core values.
- Gives you a reference point to return to during confusion or disagreement.

Like the examples above, your vision statement should be fairly clear and unambiguous. There seems to be a high correlation between clear, specific, and grounded vision statements and communities that actually get built — and between flowery, vague, or downright pretentious vision statements and communities that never get off the ground.

(Note: Some of the communities from which I excerpted sample vision statements, pg. 39, use the terms "vision statement" and "mission statement" differently than I've just described. But you'll get the gist.)

Do It *First*

Identify and articulate your vision first, *before* buying property together. If not, you could end up like one eco-spiritual community in the Northeast. Six years after moving to their land, and after finishing a major building project, they began having differences about what their next steps should be. They couldn't understand why their conflict was so intense. Why were they so at odds with each other? What was wrong with those other people? Finally the group called in a group process consultant who asked each member to fill out a questionnaire about what they valued and aspired to in their community. The

EXCERPT FROM VISION DOCUMENTS, DANCING RABBIT ECOVILLAGE

Our Mission: To create a society, the size of a small town or village, made up of individuals and communities of various sizes and social structures, which allows and encourages its members to live sustainably. ("Sustainably" means in such a manner that, within the defined area, no resources are consumed faster than their natural replenishment, and the enclosed system can continue indefinitely without degradation of its internal resource base or the standard of living of the people and the rest of the ecosystem within it, and without contributing to the non-sustainability of ecosystems outside.)

We encourage this sustainable society to grow to have the size and recognition necessary to have an influence on the global community by example, education, and research.

While Dancing Rabbit is still a small community in the pioneering stage, we call ourselves an ecovillage because our vision is of something much more than what we currently are.

We intend to grow to be a small locally self-reliant town of 500 to 1000 residents, committed to radical environmental sustainability. We will be housed in a variety of living arrangements, eat a variety of foods, and work on varied projects. It will be a society flexible enough to include egalitarian communities, cohousing, and individual households. But while we may have different approaches to some issues, the common desire for environmental sustainability will underlie all key decisions at Dancing Rabbit.

Although Dancing Rabbit will strive for self-sufficiency and economic independence, we will not be sequestered from mainstream America. Rather, outreach and education are integral to our goals. We will vigorously promote ourselves as a viable example of sustainable living and spread our ideas and discoveries through visitor programs, academic and other publications, speaking engagements, and the like.

(See Appendix 1 for more sample vision documents.)

questionnaire revealed that community members lived in either one of two subtle but different paradigms of reality, expressed by the following two vision statements:

1. We are an educational organization and model demonstration site based on ecological principles. We live as a residential community in order to facilitate our work hosting classes and workshops.
2. We are a community of supportive friends valuing an ecologically sound, sustainable lifestyle, and to help others, we offer classes and workshops in these topics.

Some community members believed the first was the community's reason for being, others believed the second — and until that time *no one knew the other reality existed.* It was a stunning revelation. Different people had different visions, which they incorrectly assumed everyone shared. Although by this time people were arguing most of the time, their core problem wasn't interpersonal conflict. Their problem was structural — *built into* the system. Theirs was definitely a "time-bomb" kind of conflict, with members unable to see it's not that "John's being unreasonable" or "Sue's irresponsible again," but that John and Sue were each operating from a different assumption about why the community was there in the first place. And what should they do with such structural conflict? Which people should stay in the community and which had the "wrong" vision and should move out?

Having a clear, grounded, inspired vision and vision statement does not in itself ensure a com-

munity's success. I knew two forming communities with beautiful vision statements that broke up. One halted because its members were young parents with too many responsibilities to spend the time that creating a community requires. The other was geographically challenged — its members were aligned in vision, but members had strong loyalties to two different locations. Some forming community groups with well-aligned visions have broken up for other reasons, such as losing their chosen property to a competing buyer with more money. And some new communities with great visions that have already moved to their property and begun building, have sometimes been brought down by conflicts with neighbors, zoning regulations that restricted their expansion, or the departure of too many members. Although it doesn't solve everything, at least an inspired common vision gives a challenged community a central core to rally around during challenges like these, and encourages them to have the heart to persevere.

Other structural-conflict issues can break up communities as well — coming to grief over how decisions should be made, or what their agreements were, or through exhausting interpersonal conflict. Nevertheless, and I can't emphasize this strongly enough — for the best chance of success, make creating your vision and vision statement the *first* thing you do.

How do you do this? We'll explore that next.

Chapter 5

Creating Vision Documents

THE PROCESS OF COMMUNITY visioning can be exciting and challenging. It involves deeply held values, strong interests, and high aspirations. It brings up both known and hidden expectations and assumptions.

The members of your group may hold many shared values and some differing values, and similar as well as wildly different ideas and expectations. Some of these may be realistic, others not. Your task is to unearth, sift, and refine these ideas and expectations until you come up with a grounded yet inspiring description of your shared community future.

This generally involves two steps:

1. **Exploring the territory.** You explore your dreams, hopes, and expectations for community in a series of visioning sessions, writing down highlights of what you learn, ideally on large sheets of easel paper. The sessions can include wide-ranging discussions, deep personal sharing, and visioning exercises. It's best if these sessions are long — half-day, day-long, or weekend meetings.

2. **Writing it down.** A smaller task force or committee uses this material to draft a preliminary vision description and vision statement. The whole group critiques the work, makes suggestions for improvement, and sends it back to the small group for revision. The back-and-forth process between the task force and whole group can occur as many times as needed until it's done. The larger or the more diverse your group, the longer this process may take.

Some groups finish within a few weeks or months, but only if they're relatively small, their members know each other well, or they're fairly homogeneous in interests and values. But if your group is large, your members diverse, or your plans ambitious, it can take more than a year. The six cofounders of Shenoa Retreat and Conference Center spent a year and a half identifying and crafting their vision documents. The 15 to 20 members of Earthaven's original group spent two years.

Some community veterans say it's better if the group is relatively small, for example between three to five people, or at least no more than ten. Visioning with a smaller number of people helps reduce the likelihood that the group will try to contort itself this way and that in order to include the diverse visions often found in a larger group.

"It's far better to start with a very small group, even two or three people who have a strong agreement about the purpose of the community, and allow it to unfold organically from that strong and firm nucleus or seed, than it is to start with 20 people who have no clear agreement or purpose, and then try to discover one," advise Robert and Dianne Gilman in their book *Ecovillages and Sustainable Communities.*

However, regardless of the size of your group, everyone needs to contribute to the vision. It doesn't work if especially influential people articulate the vision and everyone else just goes along with it. When people don't "vote" for the vision at the outset by helping create it, they end up "voting" for it later, through their behavior. Those aligned with the vision will vote "Yes" by behaving consistently with it; those who were never really aligned may vote "No" on the vision by balking at or unconsciously sabotaging certain processes or tasks later. If everyone in the group participates in the visioning process and buys into it at the beginning, the community functions as a more harmonious, cohesive whole later on.

More Than One Vision?

You may not be able to resolve vision differences easily. Let's say you discover that most people in your group want a rural self-reliant homestead at least an hour's drive from the city, but others want a country place that's no more than 30 minutes from their city jobs. Among both the hour-away and job-commuter groups, some definitely want open, honest feedback but others want none of that "touchy-feely stuff." Some of the for-process as well as anti-process people want a homeschooling co-op; others don't. With diversity like this, you're probably not destined to end up in the same community. But your visioning process wouldn't be wasted. It could help bring clarity to what each of you does and does not want in a community — a helpful first step.

A scenario like this could have several outcomes:

1. The vision of the original group members remains constant and the people who resonate with it remain involved. Those who don't, leave the group.
2. Some people leave your group, disappointed that more people didn't share their vision. New people join your group, attracted by the vision articulated by the largest number of remaining group members, or by the most influential members.
3. Your group disbands. Too many people wanted too many different things.
4. Your group splits into two or more smaller groups.

What's typical? Smaller groups of long-time friends, especially those who have already worked together on visionary, spiritually oriented, or activist projects tend to align to a common vision. Larger groups, especially those whose participants don't know each other well (such as people responding to public announcements about forming a community), tend to experience high attrition and/or splinter into smaller groups. This is fine. One or more of the smaller groups may go on to form a community.

If a group is small and based primarily on deep connections or shared friendships, most members will tend to stay in the group and alter any expression of community vision to fit everyone's interests and desires. The founders of Sowing Circle/OAEC in northern California were long-time friends and environmental activists, some of whom had been housemates on and off for 15 years. They wanted a community that would operate an educational center and demonstration site based on ecological principles. One artist member supported this vision, yet wanted to continue painting and teaching painting. So the when the community established its non-profit center, they included arts and called it the Occidental Arts and Ecology Center, offering workshops on landscape painting along with those on organic gardening and permaculture design.

This kind of coalescing of interests usually works best if a founding group is fairly small. Most of the seven founders of Abundant Dawn community in rural Virginia had previously lived in large income-sharing communes. Some wanted an income-sharing community; others wanted independent finances. Since friendship and connection was their major draw, they formed smaller subcommunity "pods" within Abundant Dawn. Founders favoring income-sharing became the Tekiah pod, those favoring independent incomes became the Dayspring Circle pod, and they all still got to live in community together.

However, if a forming community is not based on existing friendships but on an idea that it would be nice to live in community, then the original founders will probably hold to their particular visions and others will drop out, especially if the initial forming group is large, or if its members were attracted through flyers or other public means. Such a group tends to have multiple values, aspirations, and expectations, making the visioning process more complex. Some communities, particularly cohousing communities, begin with this challenge.

When your group is diverse, do you adopt a vision that will cause some people to stay and others to leave, or do you try to mold the vision to meet everyone's different values and interests?

Don't try to create a one-size-fits-all vision. "All too often there's the temptation to accommodate or shape the vision to suit the needs of each person, either because the group needs to recruit new members or because they have a misguided sense of wanting to take care of everyone or be 'all things to all people,'" says Stephen Brown. "To be successful, a forming community, like a business, needs to hold a relatively narrow focus and sharply defined objectives. If the community tries to do too much, by attempting to meet the needs of all who come along, it will spread itself too thin and either not get off the ground or run out of steam fairly early on. The vision therefore also defines what the project does not intend to accomplish. If your vision is too broad or comprehensive, and tries to please all of the people all of the time, it will fall of its own awkward expansiveness, trying to be in too many places at once."

How do you handle it if, after weeks or months of visioning sessions, you discover you are really two potential communities? What if many people leave, or the group splits in two? This can feel chaotic and disorienting — and newly bonded group members or long-time friends can feel loss knowing their friends won't be joining them in the same community future. If this happens it's perfectly OK; it's part of the process.

"A key challenge for the group at this time is to help everyone discover his or her own vision, and, in so doing, allow everyone to see which visions are sufficiently aligned to serve as the basis for the group vision and which visions need to find expression elsewhere," observe Diane and Robert Gilman in *Eco-Villages and Sustainable Communities.* "It is important to avoid the expectation that every initial member of the group *should* continue with the group, since for some that could mean either suppressing their own vision or attempting to force a vision on others that the others do not truly share. Honor each person's contribution *and* don't be afraid to sort out who will and who won't continue with the group."

Finding out that you have multiple directions and diverse ideas, and that you may in fact be two different potential communities is not a sign of failure but a step along the way. Even with the best of intentions, if your group discovers that you're not all on the same page, you can still wish each other well and form two communities. (And you don't have to lose each other as friends.)

A Sacred Time

Your visioning process is one of the single most important tasks you'll undertake as a forming community. This is where you'll speak form the heart about what really matters to you. It's a sacred time. Your voices may become suddenly soft, or tight with emotion. You may get tears in your eyes. You'll be unearthing — birthing — something here. Listen for that deep sense of purpose, that group entity that wants to be born. And listen equally, for what seems "off," or unrealistic, or something only personal growth or therapy could provide. This is the time to ask yourselves: "Are these expectations realistic? Do they make sense?"

Visioning seems to involve both the process of exploring and that of revealing, much like Michelangelo finding the sculpture hidden within the marble. Something new emerges, sparked by the potent brew of individual values, ideals, aspirations, and expectations.

If you haven't done so already, it's important to decide now who is and is not a committed, decision-making member of your group. You may have some less committed members, people who attend meetings only occasionally or who have only recently joined, or people who feel more tentative about the idea of community or about your group specifically. You may want to consider asking these people not to participate in the visioning process. Or, you might want to include them in the processes but (with everyone's knowledge and consent ahead of time) give less weight to their interests and suggestions than you do those of the more committed members. This can be a difficult issue to bring up for discussion, as some people believe "it's not community" if you consider excluding or limiting anyone's participation. But consider it practically. If six of you meet regularly and have similar interests, and a seventh person comes occasionally, or is present for some but not all of your meetings, or has substantially different ideas about community than the rest of you, should that person's values and desires be part of your shared community future? Maybe they should, and maybe not, but I believe you'll be better off discussing and deciding this with everyone involved ahead of time.

"That's Not Community!" — Hidden Expectations and Structural Conflict

Most people drawn to community have expectations or assumptions about what "community" means. They believe they know why they want to live in community, and what they'll expect to find there. Some expectations or assumptions focus on activities — we'll share some resources, we'll share some meals, we'll cooperate on decisions. Others arise from painful experiences from the past and focus on emotional states the person hopes to feel in community — connection, inclusion, acceptance. Past emotional pain can motivate people toward community because at some level they believe community will provide what's missing from their lives. "Missing" factors that propel people toward community can include affection, acceptance, inclusion, and emotional safety. This can involve conscious loss and known expectations — "It's going to be like a warm and loving family" — as well as unfelt pain and unconscious expectations ("…and I will be totally loved and accepted, finally!").

Hidden expectations about community usually aren't realistic. They often take on a golden, nostalgic quality, like looking back on a paradise lost. Here's what one member of a forming community wrote about her personal vision of community:

Like a warm embrace, a gathering of friends, laughter on sunny days, caring and offering support in times of need, like coming home. Warm, homey, spiritually rooted, peaceful, joyous, celebratory, connected, close, respectful, emotionally honest, trusting. Home!

There is absolutely nothing wrong with this vision. It's probably what we all want. The question is — can we expect community to provide it?

"The fantasy of creating an 'ideal' community tends to transform a simple discussion into a magical blend of fact and fiction," writes Zev Paiss in *Cohousing* magazine. "Visions of community are fertile grounds for the expression and growth of long-suppressed dreams. And the opportunity to express these feelings can have an urgent quality in the early discussion stages."

Suppressed pain and hidden expectations or assumptions about community can be a prime source of structural conflict "time bombs" that erupt weeks, months, or years later. This happens for two reasons.

First, living in community cannot erase buried emotional pain. When people find that after living in community they're *still* yearning for something valuable and elusive (although they may not know what it is), they tend to feel angry and disappointed. Not knowing the source of their discomfort, they tend to blame the community, or other members, for it.

Second, hidden expectations about community differ widely from one group member to another. This comes up when we each think we're behaving in good community fashion but someone else is aghast at how our behavior "betrays" community ideals. Someone will express frustration, even outrage, when we've just breached an invisible rule in that person's own personal paradigm. "How can you *say* that? That's not community!" Or, "How could you *do* such a thing? That's not community!"

The community visioning process can offer your group an excellent opportunity to flush hidden expectations to the surface and examine them rationally.

"Don't go into all this psychology stuff," advised one experienced community friend. "It sounds like therapy talk. Community isn't about psychology. It's about neighbors learning a high level of functioning together so they can make decisions and get the work done."

I disagree. Community *does* involve psychology stuff — which, in my opinion, is why roughly 90 percent of new communities fail. Forming a community is deeply psychological. Emotional pain and hidden expectations exert a powerful pull on people, and community founders are no exception. Put a group of people in a community visioning session, and you have dozens of different needs and expectations, known and unknown, ricocheting invisibly around the room.

I bring this up so your group can use the visioning process to identify, if possible, any hidden expectations and bring them in to the light of day. Knowing what everyone wants (and *really* wants), will help your group see where you may be on the same page and where you may not be.

And the best time to examine this is now, in your visioning meetings, before you go out and buy land together. You don't want to find wildly differing pain-driven expectations later, when everyone's financial investment, homes, and community self-image are on the line. The more time you spend on this issue now, the less you'll spend later. The exercises below can help your group with the visioning process. See Exercise 7 for help with accessing hidden expectations.

Exploring the Territory

The following exercises are offered to help trigger insights and stimulate the process of sharing, discussing, unearthing, and revealing the components of your community vision. They're offered as a smorgasbord of options: you may be inspired to choose some or all of them, modify them, use exercises from other sources, or make up your own.

As mentioned earlier, this may take several half-day or day-long sessions over several weeks. I suggest meeting in a cozy room with enough tea, snacks, pillows, and childcare to be comfortable and relaxed for many hours. Choose a facilitator, or arrange for an outside facilitator. To remind you of your goal, make the following poster on a large sheet of easel paper and hang it where everyone can see it.

OUR COMMUNITY VISION

- Shared future we want to create
- Reveals & announces our core values
- Each of us can identify with it
- Helps unify our effort
- Reference point we can return to
- Keeps us all inspired

The group will need lined paper for each person (legal pads work well), pens or pencils, pads of extra-large (4" x 6") yellow sticky notes, both red and green paper stick-on dots, sheets of easel paper and blue masking tape (it doesn't pull paint off walls), and large sheets of easel paper covering roughly a 4' x 8' area of wall space, or a large whiteboard.

Exercise #1: Individual Values, Group Values

The first exercise is designed to help people become more aware of what they may want to experience in community living.

Depending on the size of the group, it can take from one long day and evening, to a weekend (or two different day-long sessions). The exercise works in a large home or facility where people can go off by themselves and concentrate.

The exercise begins by writing five different two- or three-page recollections of experiences in which you felt especially fulfilled in a community-like setting or a shared group activity. These settings can include:

- your family
- summer camp, as a child or as a camp counselor
- hiking or camping trips with friends
- a college dorm, fraternity or sorority, or student co-op
- a shared group household or intentional community
- an activist or service project, a shared work task
- a therapy group, 12-step group, ritual group, or men's or women's group
- a theatrical or musical presentation

- a team sports activity or shared athletic event
- your workplace
- the military

You're looking for times when you felt profoundly happy with other people, as if you were blessed to be there, as if you had "come home" — when you not only enjoyed the experience, but felt connected and bonded with the other people present.

If you can only think of positive times that weren't all that profound, that's fine. Just write about some experiences you enjoyed with others. If you can't think of five different times, that's OK too. Just write as many as you can.

While writing these stories focus mostly on what you felt and thought during these experiences, rather than going into detail about what happened.

This is focused work that requires concentration. Some people can do it anywhere; others will need privacy and quiet. Make sure people get the quiet they need. If some people finish before others, ask them to go elsewhere if they want to talk with others so they won't disturb those still working. Writing five little stories can take several hours. Take breaks as needed, and when everyone has finished, take a break.

Each person will end up with an overview of activities they especially like to do and states of being they especially like to feel in a community-like setting.

Next, form into groups of three. One person at a time reads their stories and the other two listen, taking notes if they like, and reflect back to the speaker what the stories tell them about that person's values, beliefs, and aspirations. The first person writes these insights down, adding any more that come up.

After everyone has had a turn, each person selects five or six of the values, beliefs, or aspirations that are most personally significant, and writes the essence of each in a phrase or short sentence (not in a single word) on large yellow sticky notes.

Each person reads out their phrases and hands them to the facilitator, who sticks them on the wall of easel paper or a large whiteboard. The group can ask clarifying questions but doesn't otherwise comment on the statements, or agree or disagree with them.

After everyone has finished, the whole group, or a few people from the group, clusters the sticky notes into whatever natural categories they seem to fall into. These may include "interpersonal relations," "shared meals," "governance and decision-making," "celebration," "shared work," "children," "ecological values," "spiritual values," and so on.

The facilitator gives each person half the number of stick-on red dots as there are people doing the exercise (e.g., three dots if you are six people; five if you are ten, etc.). Each person places a red dot next to the clusters that are most important to him or her personally in a future community.

Now the facilitator gives each person the same number of green stick-on dots as there are people in the room (in other words, twice the number of red dots). Within the clusters, each person places a green dot next to the individual phrases that are most important to him or her personally.

Sit back and look at where the dots are. This is an indication of what's most important to you as individuals and as a group, and how aligned or divergent your values and interests may be.

Talk about what you see. Do most of you share the same values and interests?

(To keep this work for the writing-it-down phase of your visioning process, ask someone to copy the clusters, phrases, and red and green dot indicators onto one or more sheets of easel paper you can hang in the room.)

Exercise #2: Individual Values, Group Values

Here is a shorter and simpler exercise designed to get at the same kind of information, although it's far less rich and revealing than the first exercise.

Pass out five or six extra-large yellow sticky notes to each person. Everyone answers the questions, "What values do you hold personally for community?" and "What values do you think we share in common?" on the sticky notes, with one answer per note. It works best if this is done silently. At the end of five minutes, everyone places their sticky notes on the wall of easel paper or a large whiteboard. As in the above exercise, the whole group or a few people cluster the sticky notes into categories of similar values.

Don't be concerned if people don't just write values, but also write interests or ideals. The exercise will still give you an idea of how aligned you may be, individually and as a group.

Hand out the same proportions of red and green sticky dots as in the above exercise, and ask each person to put red dots on the clusters and green dots on the individual sticky notes that express the values they hold most dearly.

As in the above exercise, sit back and look at where the dots are. (And to keep this work for the future, ask someone to copy it down on one or more sheets of easel paper you can hang up.)

Exercise #3: Brainstorming

This exercise is similar to the first two. Brainstorming offers a quick overview of your whole group's many interests, values, and ideals.

In this process you each call out words or phrases that embody what you're seeking in community. The facilitator and a second person write the words and phrases down on the large yellow sticky notes, which they stick onto the wall space covered with easel paper or a whiteboard. As you call out your words and phrases, don't hold back. Say anything and everything that comes to mind. Don't criticize or comment on anyone else's offerings — this is a time to let ideas pop up like popcorn, without censoring.

Cluster the post-its into categories, and place your red and green stick-on dots, as above.

Look at the clusters and dots, and talk about what this shows you about yourselves. (And have someone copy it onto one or more easel papers you can hang up, as above.)

Brainstorming is like a snapshot of your group at a given point in time. If you do this exercise in the early stages of the visioning process you'll get a quick overview of what the group generally wants at that time. If you do it again towards the end of the visioning sessions, you may get different results.

Exercise #4: Non-neogtiables

Each of you lists on a piece of paper those things, situations, and systems that *must* be or *must not* be present before you will seriously consider going forward with the community. Then everyone reads their lists and a scribe writes them on a large sheet of easel paper for everyone to see. This exercise will show you places where various individuals in the group may seem incompatible, but don't worry; this is just a beginning step. "The exercise is amazingly revealing, because it forces us to examine what is really important to us," says cohousing consultant Zev Paiss. I recommend doing this exercise at least twice, once in the middle of your visioning sessions and again at the end (which may be weeks later), because what people consider "non-negotiables" can change so much over the course of visioning work.

"Despite the apparent solidity of the term 'non-negotiable,'" notes Zev, "as we learn about our personal priorities and experience working with others to develop a collective vision, those items most important to us inevitably change."

Exercise #5: Where do we Draw the Line?

Process consultant Rob Sandelin uses this exercise to help groups disagreeing over different choices or strategies. It shows that a group can agree on a common value, but not agree on the lengths to which each person would go to express that value.

Let's say everyone in your group assumes you're all on the same page about what you mean by "ecological living." But some of you want the community to grow most of its own organic food and everyone eat vegetarian, and others want each household to make its own decisions about this, and offer a choice of omnivore or vegetarian food at common meals.

On a large sheet of easel paper that everyone can see, create a list, and, in increasing order of effort, time, or "strictness," outline the different actions people can take to express the value or principle you're discussing. Items at the top of a list on "ecological values," for example, might include: "Buy organic produce," "Recycle trash," and "Compost kitchen scraps." Farther down you'd find actions that take more effort or commitment, such as: "Eat vegetarian;" or "Flush the toilet rarely." The bottom, listing the most "radical" actions, might say "Use only off-grid power," "Build only with recycled lumber," and "Don't use a car unless you're car-pooling."

When your list is complete, give everyone as many red dots each as the number of items on the list, and ask each person to put dots by the actions they are personally willing to actually do in their daily lives (not actions that they simply support theoretically). Some will have dots left over, since probably everyone won't be willing to do everything on the list.

This exercise presumes that people aren't simply "for" or "against" various values but differ in the matter of degree, which show up in what they are willing to actually do. It can help your group see, immediately and visually, where you fall as individuals in terms of specific actions you will or will not take regarding seemingly shared values. Doing this process with a variety of these shared values — "honesty," "love of nature," "spirituality," and so on — can help you see whether most of you, in fact, are aligned in vision, and if any of you differ radically. (Better to find this out now.)

Exercise #6: The Public/Private Scale

This exercise is used by Rob Sandelin to help groups get a sense of how strongly their members feel about a sensitive issue that some members may not want to speak about openly. Let's say you're discussing an aspect of your future community life that seems to bring up discomfort and apprehension, but no one is coming out and saying what's bothering them. If you suspect that some people do or don't want something but don't want to say so publicly, you can use this exercise.

On a sheet of easel pad paper, write a horizontal line numbered from one to nine, with the numbers one, five, and nine larger than the others. Below is an example of what your paper will look like:

1	2	3	4	5	6	7	8	9
Opposed to it				So-so				Advocate it

Give everyone a blank slip of paper and ask them to write the number that corresponds to their level of support for the principle, activity, or situation you've been talking about. A nine means you wholeheartedly support it; a one means you're adamantly opposed to it; a five means you could go either way. The other numbers are graduations of support or lack of support for the subject. Collect the slips of paper and make check marks at every number the people have written. You may have one mark at 9, three marks at 3, and three at 2, for example. Now you'll have an immediate and visual way to see how the group as a whole really feels about the subject. It can be a real eye-opener. You may find that only one or two people strongly support something, and most others don't care or actively oppose it. Depending on what your scale tells you, there may be no need to discuss the subject further. Without having to embarrass anyone publicly, you now have a realistic indicator of the spread of opinion in your group about a particular value or ideal.

"This technique is a quick and powerful way for an individual to see where they fit in with the rest of the group," says Rob. "If the scale shows everybody is at the 7-9 range and I am the only person that is at a 2, that is very valuable to me to know. Conversely, it is very helpful for the group to know that one of its members is not aligned with everybody else."

Exercise #7: Hidden Expectations

This exercise, derived from art therapy, operates on the principal that you can bypass your thinking process and access your unconscious mind. It involves answering questions, but this time, answer them as fast as you can with your pen or pencil in your non-dominant hand. (If you're right-handed, use your left hand; if you're left-handed, use your right.)

Writing as fast as possible with the non-dominant hand is what makes the exercise work. Your writing (or printing, if that's what comes out) will tend to be large and scrawling, even primitive. It may reveal expectations about community that you know very well, as well as expectations that may be important to you but about which you may be barely aware. You may have strong feelings as you write.

Prepare the questions in advance, in questionnaire form, with a copy for each person. Leave at least half a page of blank space for each answer. It should take about eight double-sided pages.

The exercise takes about 20-30 minutes, and seems to work best when everyone in the room does it at the same time. The exercise doesn't necessarily trigger deep insights in everyone, and it doesn't do it every single time. But it can offer a powerful source of insight for some.

You don't have to share your answers with anyone, so be as candid and uninhibited as you like. Don't *think* when you're writing. Just write as fast as you can and let your non-dominant hand do the work.

1. What do you want more than anything? For yourself.
2. What do you want more than anything? For the world.
3. What do you want more than anything? For your children.
4. What do other people do that hurts you?
5. What do you fear?
6. What makes you mad?
7. What makes you cry?
8. If you could go back in your childhood and change your mother (or primary female caretaker), what would you change?
9. If you could go back in your childhood and

change your father (or primary male care-taker), what would you change?

10. What didn't you get as a child?

11. If you could make something in your child-hood better, what would it be?

12. If you could make something in your child-hood go away, what would it be?

13. What do you need to feel safe?

14. What do you need to feel loved?

15. What do you need to feel happy?

16. What kind of community do you want?

When everyone is finished, take a break. When you return, gather in groups of three and invite anyone who wishes to share what they learned to do so within the small groups. Speaking is optional. Some people will speak, some won't; hearing some people describe their insights can motivate others to share their own.

When each small group is finished, return to your whole group, and again invite people to share what they've learned. Don't write anything down at this point, but just listen, and then talk about any expectations — known or hidden — that anyone may want to talk about. This process can be very revealing, and it can also help you feel closer and more bonded as a group.

The point of this exercise, however, is not necessarily for you to *share* any conscious and hidden expectations with the group, but simply to *uncover* them. It's an opportunity to look them in the face, so to speak, and ask whether or not they are realistic, or if they serve you. If you discover that you expect companionship and play-fulness in community, for example, which might be a fairly conscious expectation arising from growing up in group of active brothers and sis-ters, that's fine. This seems like an expectation that serves you: being more aware of this expec-tation can motivate you to consciously create

congenial, playful aspects of your community's social life.

However, discovering that you might have hidden expectations that in community you'll always be included and never be left out, or that you'll always be fully accepted and never criti-cized, or that you'll always be totally emotionally safe and never experience conflict — watch out. Expectations like these can be time bombs. You can take the space now to defuse them by nam-ing them, sharing them (if you wish), examining them more closely, asking yourself if they seem realistic, and becoming willing to laugh about them and let go of them.

If everyone in your group is doing this, it can have a profound effect on your shared vision for community, which can be considerably more realistic and grounded than it might otherwise have been. Congratulations!

Sharing from the Heart

You can certainly combine elements from these various exercises and make up your own. You can repeat "Non-negotiables" and "Brainstorming" as many times as you like, to see how the group's ideas are shifting or coalescing. You can bring in "Public/Private Scale" and "Where Do We Draw the Line?" anytime to get a sense of how everyone in the group feels about something, not just the most outspoken ones. The whole idea is to stim-ulate awareness of what you each really want, and get a sense of your group's shared or differing components of vision. Ideally, the ideas from pre-vious discussions and exercises will be captured on large sheets of easel paper on the walls.

Really get into this with each other, as you share what you aspire to, deeply yearn for, expect, hope, and fear about living in communi-ty. These conversations can be tense, they can be deep. And they're often funny. It's a good time for a sense of humor, as you might find out that the two most inspired "burning souls" in your group have opposite hidden expectations. Consider these revelations to be part of the process.

At this stage you're not creating strategy — how you'll get there — but simply working at identifying and visualizing the various aspects of your shared future. Have a note-taker write down the main points of your discussions, type them up, and save them for the more comprehensive writing process to come.

You may discover aspects of your future community that some of you want and some of you are indifferent about or don't want. You can negotiate, trying to meet everyone's interests while not limiting anyone's opportunities. If that isn't possible, you can see if some people are willing to let go of some part of their personal desires so the group may gain alignment on a wider part of the vision. You may want our community to raise horses because you love them; for example, and I may want us to raise fields of wheat because I secretly fear famine. Can either of us let go of these personal desires so we can all live in our rural, self-reliant homestead? You may want us to operate a coffeehouse in our storefront space because you love the arts and intellectual pursuits; I may want us to run a soup kitchen because I yearn to serve the homeless. Can either of us let go of this so we can all create our vibrant urban community?

With differences like these, it's a time for deep and heartfelt sharing, of asking ourselves "Is this realistic?" "Will this work for me?" "Will this work for all of us?" "What's really important to each of us?" "What can I live without; what's not negotiable?" There is no real rule — you will need to navigate this unfolding territory as you think best.

Writing it Down

To help with the writing process, I suggest making the following posters on large sheets of easel paper (see below), and hanging them up as reminders of you what you're aiming for.

OUR VISION DOCUMENTS

- Can include Vision, Mission, sometimes Goals
- Vision: Shared future we want to create
- Mission: What we'll be doing to create it
- Goals: Shorter-term milestones we commit to
- Vision Statement: Vision articulated briefly

DECISION-MAKING AND THE VISIONING PROCESS

Many experienced communitarians believe that consensus is the appropriate process for deciding an issue as critical as the visioning process. "The consensus process itself fosters an attitude that can help forge a bond and build trust in your group," observes consensus facilitator Betty Didcoct. "When the input of everyone is honored, who knows what might surface — a strong single vision that draws everyone, or multiple visions that suggest the presence of more than one potential forming community."

Other community activists, such as Rob Sandelin, suggest not using consensus for your visioning process. For consensus to work well your group must have a common purpose, and when you're still in the visioning process, it doesn't have it yet. A group needs a method, he says, such as, say, 75 percent voting, in which some people can diverge radically from others about what they want in the community without bringing the whole process to a crashing halt. I personally agree with this view, although there are groups out there who employed consensus for their visioning process and it worked just fine.

ASSESSING YOUR VISION DOCUMENTS

You may want to test your vision documents and vision statement against the following criteria:

For you as an individual:

1. Do you feel good when you read the written expression of your vision?
2. Is it meaningful for you? If not, how would it need to be changed to make it meaningful?
3. Does it resonate with your personal sense of identity? Do you feel as if you can "own" it?
4. Does it inspire you?

For your group:

1. Is your vision document simple, clean, and authentic?
2. Does it reveal and announce your group's core values?
3. Does it focus on the "who," "what," and "why" of your project?
4. Is it fairly concrete and grounded (not vague or flowery)?
5. After you read it, can you remember it? Do you "see" it?
6. Does it express your purpose?
7. Does it inspire your group?
8. Does it generate excitement?
9. Does it show what your community will be like when your vision is achieved?
10. Does it express passion, conviction, and commitment?
11. Is it possible in the current zoning, building-code, and lending environment?

Your Vision Statement:

1. Is it clear, concise, and compelling?
2. Does it express your vision and purpose?
3. Does it also reveal and announce your core values?
4. Is it fairly short? Can you memorize it?
5. Can you identify with it?
6. Does it inspire you?
7. Do others "get it" right away?
8. Does it seem reasonable? Is it unrealistic? Is it too ambitious?

OUR VISION STATEMENT

- Expresses vision and mission/purpose
- Clear, concise, compelling
- Ideally short, 20-40 words
- Ideally memorized
- Helps awaken vision
- It's what others see first

One way to do this is for everyone to go home and write their own idea of what the community's vision statement would be. At the next meeting read each person's version, then get into groups of three and merge them. Then select a committee of three or four people to write a rough draft of vision documents and/or a vision statement based on the groups' merged statements. Include in this writing group, if possible, a visionary thinker, a systems thinker, and someone skilled with words. It works best having a small group write something to present to the group because it's much easier to respond to something already written than it is for everyone to sit around and try to write the whole thing as a group. At the next meeting, the group reviews the first draft, decides what it likes and doesn't, makes suggestions and refinements, and sends the amended draft back to the small group for more work. This round robin word-crafting process can occur as many times as needed until the full group pronounces the vision documents complete.

Next — power imbalances in communities, and how your decision making and other self-governance methods can spread power equally among members.

≈ Chapter 6 ≈

Power, Decision-making, and Governance

MOST INTENTIONAL COMMUNITIES, other than those led by a single spiritual teacher or leader, intend that power be shared equally among members. But certain members may still have considerably more power than others. Much of the conflict in a core group or community occurs over issues of unequal distribution of power.

Sometimes the power imbalance is caused by one or more people dominating meetings and committees. These folks might have a dominating communication style — interrupting, talking loudly, "talking over" others, or speaking with such intensity and certainty that no one can oppose them. This means they end up having a lot of the power in the group.

Or maybe they have fine communication skills but unintentionally dominate meetings and committees because they have more information about issues than others do. These people arrive with a briefcase, clipboard, pocket calculator, and a sheaf of documents about how it's done. Who could disagree?

Still others are fine communicators and don't know any more than anyone else, but they've got such energy and force in their personality that people instinctively look to them for leadership. Without meaning to, they've got a lot of power in the group. Some appreciate them; others resent them.

Sometimes the power imbalance involves someone being more influential than others because of his or her role in the community. In some communities one person, often a founder, seems to have considerably more influence over decisions than others, even if the community uses democratic decision-making. The power-person might have established the original vision for the community, put up all or most of the money, and/or lived there the longest. Other community members habitually defer to his or her opinion, even if the group officially believes everyone has equal say.

Power — The Ability to Influence

People who have power and privilege in a group usually aren't aware of it. They usually exercise it innocently and don't notice that it's not reciprocal.

Joel Kramer and Diana Alstad in *The Guru Papers* define "power" as the ability of a person or system to influence other persons or systems — and it's neither good nor bad. They distinguish between plain and simple "power" and "the *authoritarian* use of power." (Italics mine.) When people have authoritarian power, they enforce or perpetuate their power by punishing or ignoring those who disagree with them. This distinction helped me see that the authoritarian use of power is something most of us want to avoid, yet "power" — our ability to influence each other — is not only *not* negative, but something which, if we encourage it equally in our group, can benefit all of us.

I see decision making as the main power-point in a community — who makes decisions and how they make them. Power imbalances can be greatly reduced by using a fair, participatory decision-making method that spreads power equally and offers checks and balances against power abuses. (Everyone's having good communication skills certainly helps too.) *Not* having a fair, participatory decision-making method early in your group will almost certainly generate conflict over power imbalances at some point. I consider this another kind of structural conflict, because putting this kind of decision-making method in place at the beginning is a "structure" which can help protect against it.

(Of course, simply having a fair decision making method doesn't address power imbalances triggered by dominating, intimidating, or manipulative behaviors outside of meetings, taking unilateral actions that affect the community without first checking with others, or breaking community agreements. These issues will be addressed in Chapters 17 and 18.)

Focused Power, Widespread Power

If a community chooses a single person or a committee to make certain decisions, they've got focused power — which is good for decisions which must be made quickly or which require special expertise.

With majority-rule voting, power is theoretically spread widely, and everyone has it. However, in controversial issues, where the vote may be split 51-49 percent, half the group has all the power, the other half has none.

Consensus decision-making is a group decision-making process in which all present must agree before action is taken. It's based on the belief that everyone has a piece of the truth. The intention is that each person in a meeting is given the time and space to speak their truth, and is listened to with respect. If done correctly, this method can help to spread power throughout the whole group, and is the method chosen most often by contemporary community founders.

How Consensus Works

While there are many styles of consensus, in general it works like this: Members don't vote Yes

---

SOWING CIRCLE'S REASONS FOR CHOOSING CONSENSUS

Sowing Circle/OAEC founders chose consensus for five reasons, which they describe in one of their community documents:

Consensus creates and strengthens a spirit of trust, cooperation, and respect among the Partners (members):

- By incorporating the clearest thinking of all Partners, consensus increases the likelihood of new, better, and more creative decisions.

- Because all have participated in its formation, everyone has a stake in implementing decisions.

- Consensus significantly lessens the possibility that a minority will feel that an unacceptable decision has been imposed on them.

- Consensus safeguards against ego/adversary attitudes, uninformed decision-making, "rubber stamping" of decisions, coercion, self-interested positions, mistrust, and half-hearted agreements.

or No on motions. Rather, proposals are introduced, discussed, and eventually decided upon. Proposals don't necessarily remain as they were introduced, but are improved or modified to meet people's concerns as necessary. When it's time to decide, people either give consent to the proposal, stand aside from it, or block it.

Giving consent doesn't necessarily mean loving every aspect of the final version of the proposal, but being able to live with it and being willing to support it.

Standing aside is an act of what's sometimes called "principled non-participation," in which someone can't personally support the proposal, but doesn't want to stop the rest of the group from adopting it. People who stand aside are noted in the minutes, and, depending on the group's agreements, may not have to help implement it (but they are still subject to it).

Blocking the proposal stops it from being adopted, at least for the time being. It is not used for personal reasons, or because someone doesn't like how the decision may affect them personally. "Blocking is a serious matter," writes consensus teacher Bea Briggs, "to be done only when one truly believes that the pending proposal, if adopted, would violate the morals, ethics, or safety of the whole group." Caroline Estes, another well-known consensus teacher, often says that people who understand consensus well will only block a proposal three or four times in their lifetime — and in 50 years of consensus practice, she's never blocked once. (Caroline further notes that people who often want to block a group's proposals are probably operating on a different set of values than other members and may be in the wrong group.)

A proposal is passed when everyone in the meeting gives consent, even if one or more people stand aside. It is not passed if at least one person blocks it. (Some groups don't proceed if more than one person stands aside, believing that the group doesn't have enough unity to go forward with the proposal.)

When a group uses consensus to make a decision, they can only change that decision by reaching another consensus. It may take longer to make decisions using consensus than it does when using majority-rule voting, especially at first. However, implementing a proposal once it's agreed upon usually takes far less time. Majority-rule voting, in which up to half the people can be unhappy with a decision, often generates foot-dragging and other forms of unconscious sabotage when it comes to implementing the proposal. With consensus, a decision often takes longer to decide, but far less time to implement since everyone's behind it.

A consensus meeting is not "run" by a chairperson, but served by agenda planners and a facilitator. For each meeting, the agenda planners create an agenda which will help the group address relevant topics in a certain order and within certain time frames for a well-paced, effective meeting. The facilitator's job is to consider the needs of the group as a whole, create an atmosphere of trust and safety, help those who want to do so to participate in the discussion (and not let anyone dominate), help the group stick to its agenda contract, keep the group focused and on task, and assess how well the group is agreeing, before testing for consensus.

Consensus is essentially a conservative approach to decision making — if everyone in your group cannot support the proposal, you don't adopt the proposal, or you change the proposal. While in the consensus process theoretically one person can stop a group from moving forward on a proposal, this is a rare event in a well-trained group. People objecting to a proposal voice their concerns openly from the beginning, and the group attempts to modify and refine the proposal to meet these concerns. If, after much discussion, there isn't much support for the modified proposal, the facilitator doesn't call for a decision, but lays aside the proposal for a future meeting, or calls for a committee to suggest new solutions at a later meeting.

Consensus generates an entirely different dynamic among meeting participants than majority-rule voting. With the latter, competing factions usually try to win converts to their position by criticizing the other position and creating an "us versus them" atmosphere. But consensus creates an incentive for supporters of a proposal to seek out those who disagree with them and really try to understand their objections — and to reform the proposal to incorporate the other members' concerns. Conflicts and differences can arise using consensus as often as they do when using other forms of decision making, but in consensus conflicts are seen as a catalyst to creating more innovative solutions and crafting an agreement out of all the different concerns that people raise. So consensus is not compromise, which weakens everyone's interests, but a creative meta-solution, which, ideally, strengthens everyone's interests.

Because the consensus facilitator draws out the ideas and concerns of each member and doesn't let the more articulate or energetic members dominate, consensus empowers a group *as a group*. Majority-rule voting usually rewards the most aggressive members but disempowers the group as a whole.

Done well, consensus can transform meetings from overlong, frustrating, draining sessions that go nowhere and elicit people's worst behaviors, to spirited, stimulating events where everyone's ideas are valued and the group comes up with surprisingly creative and workable solutions.

In a well-trained group with good facilitation, using consensus can elevate the consciousness of a group. It's not just a decision-making technique, but a philosophy of inclusion, drawing out the ideas, insights, and wisdom of everyone's "piece of the truth."

But it's not a panacea and it won't work in every situation. To get the full power and impact of this process, certain elements must be present.

What You Need to Make Consensus Work

Willingness to learn the process. Consensus needs to be taught thoroughly, and its basic principles periodically reviewed. I can't emphasize strongly enough the need for training: the more people in your group who understand consensus, the better it will work. Training often takes place in one or more weekends or multi-day workshops, with plenty of opportunity to practice. Fortunately there's a wealth of consensus trainers who can help, and articles and books to get you started. (See resources for more information on consensus trainers, see www.CreatingALifeTogether.org).

Common purpose. Without a shared vision and common purpose to focus and unify your efforts, your group can bounce around endlessly between confusion, frustration, and grim battles for control. In the times when you find yourselves yelling at each other or your momentum halted by apathy or despair, you need a common touchstone to return to. You need to remember where you're going and why you're going there — one of the reasons you spend so much time and energy creating your community vision.

Willingness to share power. For many, consensus requires a kind of paradigm shift — from an impatient "I know best" attitude to a simple acceptance of and respect for other human beings. Folks who are used to being in charge — alpha males and females, articulate dynamos, and people who usually think they know better than others — can have an especially hard time with consensus at first. If your group is top-heavy with such folks you might want to think twice about using this method, and ask if they are willing to give up such roles and innate assumptions. And related to this:

Willingness to let go of personal attachments in the best interests of the group. If your main concern is what the decision will be and whether it'll be the one you want, it's unlikely you're practicing deep listening, holistic thinking, and letting go of your preconceived ideas, say consensus trainers Betty Didcoct and Paul DeLapa.

Trusting in the process, and trusting each other. This means believing that by continuing to share ideas and concerns about a proposal with each other, you will come up with a much better solution than any one of you could have thought of alone. It's believing that there is a solution, and that together you'll reach it. It's assuming that everyone is doing his or her best to listen to one another's point of view. It takes willingness just to sit patiently through the ongoing discussion, even though you don't yet know how it will turn out or how the issue will get solved.

Humility. "I have come to believe that one of the foundations of successful consensus process is personal humility," says consensus facilitator Rob Sandelin. "When you can consider that your beliefs about a community issue may be wrong,

then you are ready to fully engage in consensus. For example, I may not like the boy my daughter is dating and think he isn't a good companion for her, but I realize I might be wrong, that I might have misjudged him, and that the situation is safe enough that I can give my permission for her to date him knowing she will learn from the experience. Consensus is often about giving permission to go ahead, even if you are concerned about the outcome. You give permission in order to have experiences to learn from."

Equal access to power. Consensus requires a level playing field. It doesn't work well when one person in a group is the employer, who could theoretically fire or demote the others; or when one member is the land owner, who could theoretically sell the land or evict the others.

Physical participation, and the right people present. In consensus no one decides by proxy. (although in well-trained groups, the interests of absent members are taken into account). Participation requires that people be there because agreements are built on what comes out of the discussion. And good decisions require good information to start with. Group members who might implement a decision, or have information or perspectives relative to a topic, need to attend the meeting.

The right topics. Not all topics require that the whole group be present to decide. Some things can be decided by area managers or committees, based on the whole group's input.

Well-crafted agendas. When a few designated people plan an agenda ahead of time, and when the whole group reviews, revises, and approves it at the beginning of a meeting, the group has just made a contract with itself for how they'll spend time in that meeting. Making such a contract and sticking to it goes a long way towards having effective, satisfying, upbeat meetings. Having no agenda, or an agenda controlled only by certain people, or a poorly crafted agenda, can diminish the group's trust and subject them to confused, dragging, time-wasting meetings.

Skilled facilitation. The facilitator is not the group's leader or chairperson, but its servant, charged with the job of helping the group make the best decisions possible. The facilitator is empowered to help the group keep its process and agenda contract with itself, move forward in its discussion and decision-making tasks, and intervene when necessary. The facilitator doesn't participate in the discussion. (In many communities several members learn facilitation so they can rotate the role. Some communities trade facilitation with other nearby communities, so everyone can take part in the discussion.) The facilitator is neutral about the topics being discussed, and treats everyone equally, showing no favorites. He or she helps spread the power throughout the group by asking, "Have we heard from everyone?" "Does anyone have anything to add?" The facilitator seeks solutions, asking, "Are there any other ideas?" The facilitator helps the group focus on where it is in the discussion by summarizing what's been said so far, by drawing out and clarifying decisions, and by asking, "Are we ready to move on?" With a skilled facilitator, community meetings which used to be irritating or unproductive can move more swiftly, which means its members tend to remain alert and energized, enjoy themselves, and get more done.

I used to think consensus wouldn't work in a group with an aggressive member who'd steamroller over others; or an angry, suspicious person who might block a decision out of sheer contrariness. But I've learned that a good facilitator, like a kind of aikido master, can redirect the overly verbal, draw out shy folks, diffuse aggressive behavior, stop cross-talk, and repeatedly bring a group back to its task of making good decisions. "A good facilitator can save you up to 50 percent of the group's time," notes Bea Briggs. "A poor one can easily cost the group as much."

Enough time. Making good decisions takes time, especially when people are first learning new procedures. Arrange enough time in your meetings so that you won't feel rushed; as your group builds trust and experience together, you'll get more efficient at making decisions with this method.

"Pseudoconsensus" and Structural Conflict

"Many groups aren't trained in how to use consensus," says Caroline Estes. "When I get called in to help, it's usually because the group doesn't understand the process."

When a group thinks it knows how to use consensus, but doesn't, it's a set-up for structural conflict. They proceed in ignorance, sowing seeds of frustration and resentment that can fester for years to come. Many political activists in the 1960s and '70s assumed they were using consensus, but were often just guessing at it. This is what I call "pseudoconsensus," and it's widespread in communities. Here are some of its forms:

- *Big League Complex.* The main problem in many forming community groups, says Caroline Estes, is when people are used to having their own way, or they believe they know better than others. I call this the "Big League Complex." It seems particularly prevalent when the group has a high percentage of business executives or people in the helping professions, as is the case with many cohousing communities. "Participants in a consensus group must be willing to give up hierarchical roles and privileges and to function as equals," writes Bea Briggs. "The contributions of experts, professionals, and elders are, of course, welcome, but they must not be allowed to silence the voices of the other members."

- *Decision by endurance.* Another pseudo-consensus notion is the belief that people need to stay in the room until they make a decision, no matter how long it takes (even if that means until four in the morning, as many '60s-era political activists well recall.) If people believe they must keep talking about something for hours and hours until they all agree, their meeting is not well-facilitated and/or their agenda wasn't well planned. A good facilitator keeps to the agenda's planned schedule and suggests unconcluded items be tabled for future meetings and/or sends items to committee.

- *Everyone decides everything.* Some groups flounder in frustration and burnout because they believe everyone in the group must be involved in every decision, no matter how small. Not true. The whole group is usually needed for deciding major policy issues; smaller issues can often be decided by committees, operating with general guidelines from or oversight by the whole group.

- *"I block, I block!"* Pseudoconsensus seems especially prevalent in cohousing com-

munities, whose members often seem to misunderstand blocking. I've heard of cohousing core groups in which people sometimes blocked proposals because, for example, someone wanted *this* kind of front door and no other, saying, "I'm sorry but that just doesn't work for me." This is not consensus; it's self-indulgence. Then there was the forming cohousing group where a member living in another state, reading about a particular proposal on the agenda of the next meeting, sent word that he disagreed with the proposal and was blocking in advance, so there'd be no need to discuss it. This poor fellow didn't have a clue that you don't do this with consensus — but the group hadn't a clue either, since they let him do it! A trained group knows blocking is used only when someone's "piece of the truth" shows them something important the rest of the group hasn't seen. One uses this privilege after a time of earnest, objective, soul-searching. Not understanding the blocking privilege is what can make pseudo-consensus dangerous. A whole group can be held hostage to such tyranny. (C.T. Butler's Formal Consensus process has a further safeguard, which some consensus facilitators call the "principled objection" — a block can only stand if it is consistent with the group's stated purpose. If the group believes it's not consistent with their purpose, the block is not valid.)

Consensus is like a chain saw. It can chop a lot of wood, but it can also chop your leg! The point — you have to be trained to use consensus, or its improper use can hurt you. *Not* getting trained in consensus is another form of structural conflict.

Rob Sandelin says, "If even one person in your group doesn't fully understand consensus — don't use it."

Agreement-Seeking — When You Don't Want to use Full Consensus

Agreement-seeking methods fall in between majority-rule voting and consensus and can include elements of both.

Super-majority voting. As in consensus, people try to build agreement for a proposal and modify the proposal as needed, but they vote for or against it. The proposal must receive many more "Yes" votes than a simple majority to pass. Depending on what the group has decided in advance, the required majority can be anywhere from 55 to, say, 95 percent.

Voting fallback. The group attempts to come to consensus once, or twice, and if they don't reach consensus, they fall back to a percentage of voting the group has previously decided on, anywhere from majority-rule (51 percent) to, say, a 95 percent vote.

Consensus-minus-one or consensus-minus-two. In consensus-minus-one, a proposal still passes even if someone blocks it (it takes two to block the proposal for it not to pass). In consensus-minus-two, a proposal still passes even if two people block (it takes three people to block the proposal for it not to pass). Consensus trainer Lysbeth Borie believes these terms are misnomers, since neither is actually "consensus," and suggests these methods might be more accurately termed agreement-minus-one or unity-minus-one.

The sunset clause. In consensus, once a decision is made, it requires a consensus of the whole to change it. With a sunset clause, the group agrees on a proposal for a certain period of time; say a month, six months, a year, etc., at which time the decision is automatically discontinued and the situation reverts to what it was before. The decision can be continued (or continued and modified) only by a consensus of the whole.

A sunset clause is a way for people who aren't fully supportive of a proposal to allow the whole group to try it for a while without requiring the agreement of the whole group to rescind or modify it later if it doesn't work out.

Consensus teacher Tree Bressen points out that in order for sunset clauses to work well, the group must have a well-functioning agenda list and tracking mechanism for decisions so that the item will be brought up again later. Otherwise those group members who went along with the decision reluctantly may not be so willing the next time someone proposes a sunset clause.

Multi-winner Voting

Another decision-making method that spreads power equally in a group involves finding a way for the greatest number of members to get the most of what they want. Multi-winner voting is a system adopted from European parliamentary elections in which each person gets a certain number of votes to spread across a range of choices.

Sharingwood Cohousing in Washington State uses multi-winner voting as a proportional spending method for its annual discretionary funding allocation. Once a year Sharingwood members hold a "budget party" to decide what projects they'll fund the following year. They dress up in fancy clothes for wine and cheese in their Common House. Each member receives an envelope of play money as they enter, which represents his or her real power in the decision making. This is the amount of money in the discretionary budget fund for the following year, divided by the number of community members — "voters" — who attend the budget party.

Various members or committees sponsor projects they'd like to see funded the following year, and set up displays in the room, which the guests visit during the evening. A "New Retaining Wall" display, for example, might have a short sample rock wall and a member-advocate of the project who explains the benefits of the project.

Party guests spend various amounts of their play money on one or more of the proposed projects they like best. As soon as a project gets wholly funded its sponsors ring a bell and announce it — "The retaining wall is funded!" — to everyone's cheers. Since more projects are proposed for the next year than Sharingwood has money for, not all projects get enough play-money funding. At the end of the budget party sponsors of the least-funded projects donate their contributions to the almost-funded projects. This way the greatest number of people fund the greatest number of their favorite projects.

Community Governance — Spreading Power Widely

In communities, as well as in core groups, everyone needn't decide everything — it's too unwieldy. So how does a group manage decisions so that power is balanced and everyone has input into decisions, yet meetings don't take too long, and people aren't driven crazy with details? The "ten percent" communities profiled in this book all govern themselves with whole-group-meetings and a series of smaller committees.

Let's consider the method used by Earthaven Ecovillage in North Carolina. Full group meetings, called Council, are held over two days, one weekend a month. In Council, significant and wide-ranging community and policy issues are decided upon. Day-to-day work is accomplished by smaller committees overseeing finance, physical infrastructure, membership issues, and so on. Committees are set up by the Council, and report to it. The committees decide on issues and distribute a record of their minutes and all decisions to members by email and by posting them in the kitchen and Council Hall. After posting, the community has three weeks in which to offer concerns regarding a decision. In that event, the proposal goes back to the discussion stage for further refinement and revision, which is also posted for three weeks for everyone's OK. If a committee decision is not challenged in the three-week period, it stands. This way, every community member who reads the committee minutes can keep track of each committee's activity, and oversee all community decisions. Additionally, committees may bring proposals about more significant issues to Council for discussion and decision by the group.

More than One Form of Decision Making?

As we've seen, although consensus often takes longer than other methods, its decisions are usually implemented faster. However, because forming-community groups must sometimes decide things quickly, particularly when a land-purchase may be involved, some community veterans recommend having an alternate, faster process in place.

And some groups might have more than one decision-making method, using different methods for different kinds of decisions. If some community members own the property and others are tenants, for example, the group might use consensus for most decisions, and a supermajority method solely for decisions affecting property value; or have a decision-making body (that uses consensus) comprised only of property owners who make decisions affecting property value. (However, doing so will probably bring up power issues, unless all members understand who makes which decisions, and agree to this when they enter the community.) It's important to be flexible, and know when it's appropriate to be inclusive and when to be more directive in decision-making. You must agree in advance on which method you're using before starting a meeting.

STYLES OF CONSENSUS

Quaker style. Consensus was developed by Quakers in seventeenth century England as an extension of their beliefs in equality, nonviolence, and everyday accessibility to divine guidance. In Quaker meetings people sit silently, seek a place of inner tranquility and guidance, and don't offer their opinions unless they believe they're divinely inspired to do so.

Native American style. Certain Native American tribes have traditionally made decisions in the context of being moved by Spirit before speaking, respectfully listening to one another, and giving particular weight to the voice of community elders.

"Community" style. Derived from these traditions and by the contemporary communities movement, what I call "community" style considers emotions that come up in meetings as potentially relevant input for decisions. If someone is angry or tearful in a meeting, for example, a community-style facilitator would use the person's upset as an opportunity to find out what "pieces of truth" about a proposal or a group dynamic those feelings may contain.

Consensus by individual guidance. Developed by various community activists in the early '80s (including Betty Didcott, and members of Sirius community), this method involves meditating and seeking spiritual guidance before beginning the meeting, so that any decisions may be informed by intuition and spiritual guidance. It's very similar to the practices of Quakers and Native Americans, but without a specifically religious or cultural context.

Formal Consensus. Facilitator C.T. Butler developed this as a step-by-step (hence "formal") process to address the typical problems of consensus as used by members of political activist groups. The first step, once a proposal is made, is to ask only clarifying questions. In the next step, people state only objections and concerns, which are written on a large easel pad and grouped according to topic. In the third step these groups of concerns are addressed, one at a time, with discussion and suggestions for refining or modifying the proposal. The last step is calling for consensus. The steps can occur sequentially in one meeting, but for more complex or controversial topics are usually spread across several different meetings. Proposals can be blocked only when the group agrees that the person's reasons for the block are based in the group's vision and values, called the "principled objection." If not, the block is considered invalid and the proposal passes anyway. This step prevents a group from being covertly disrupted by someone not aligned with the group's vision and values, as is often found in non-profit organizations and cohousing communities He finds that this way of treating blocking allows non-profits and cohousers to include these people without being held hostage to their ability to block the group from moving towards its intended purpose.

Other community activists caution against using a so-called "fallback" decision-making method in addition to consensus, for two reasons. First, if someone blocks a proposal, the people who want the proposal to pass can just sit back and say, "No matter, we'll just switch to 75 percent voting now and pass it anyway." The group won't try to keep re-crafting and honing the proposal to meet that one person's concerns. In consensus, the idea is that when concerns about a proposal are met, *it makes a better decision*. A "fallback" method is likely to result in lower-quality decisions. (And as consensus trainer Patricia Allison points out, willingness to stop the consensus process and simply vote because someone has blocking concerns means they group's not really using consensus.) Second, many facilitators point out that consensus is not just a method but a philosophy of inclusion. When individuals are less able to influence the group's decisions because it has switched to a faster method, they see it as breaking down the trust and cohesion of the group. If there's pressure on the group to decide something quickly, people won't feel the time or space to get in touch with and express their concerns. They could feel pressured into deciding something they don't really want, and end up leaving the group as a result.

I believe this issue hinges on whether you want to start a new community primarily to build its physical infrastructure and see who'll join you over time, or to create a place where you can enjoy connection and friendship with your existing group. If your reason is mostly to create a community and live with whomever resonates with its vision, you may want to use a faster decision-making method than consensus (such as super-majority voting), in these circumstances, regardless of the current members you may lose.

If your reason is to create a community with your current group of friends, you may want a more inclusive method like consensus that builds support and connection, regardless of the great land deals you might have to pass up.

What Decision-making Method Should You Use?

If you want to spread power widely, help bond the group more deeply, and evoke the shared wisdom of the group for decisions, consider using consensus or an agreement-seeking method (or both). For spreading resources across a range of choices, try multi-winner voting.

And for accomplishing many tasks without taking the whole group's time, consider setting up systems like Earthaven's Council and committee structure.

If you've chosen consensus, here are some ways to get trained in it:

- Read Bea Briggs' *Introduction to Consensus* for an excellent overview of the process itself, and especially how to facilitate a consensus meeting. I suggest studying it, section by section, as a group.

- Study the Formal Consensus process in C.T. Butler's book, *On Consensus and Conflict*. I recommend Formal Consensus for inexperienced groups, as I think its step-by-step process is easier to learn and easier for beginners to facilitate.

- Visit other community groups or political activist groups, and as a guest, observe their consensus process.

- Hire a consensus trainer to come out and train your group.

- Offer support to any group members who want to learn facilitation (including financial help for additional training), so you'll end up with a team of people who can rotate the job of facilitating your meetings.

Some core groups and communities go all out to understand and practice consensus well, and their meetings show it. Sharingwood cohousing gives whatever approval and financial support necessary for the ongoing training of its process team. Members of Earthaven's core group arranged trainings by both Caroline Estes and C.T. Butler.

In Part Two we'll look at some of the technical tips and tools for growing a community — from making agreements and setting up legal entities to finding, financing, and developing your community property — and how you'll raise enough money internally to pay property loans and operating expenses.

Part Two:
Sprouting New Community:

Techniques & Tools

Chapter 7

Agreements & Policies: "Good Documents Make Good Friends"

"You'll be hearing from our lawyers!" said Steve and Sandy, faces grim, as they left the porch and strode to their car. Stunned, Darren and Maria stood in their doorway and watched the couple disappear down the long gravel road. Steve and Sandy had left a community I'll call Cottonwood Springs a few days earlier, saying they no longer wanted to be part of it. They'd just returned to demand their $22,000 membership and site-lease fees back.

"But, but ... you know we've spent all the money," Darren replied, not believing his ears. "On the balloon payment, the new roof, the pump repair."

The lawyers showed up the next day with the papers for a lawsuit. Steve and Sandy wanted not only the return of their $22,000 for membership and site-lease fees, but $15,000 more for legal fees and damages, and $4,200 for "back wages" — a retroactive $10 for every hour they had worked in the new community since they'd joined two months before.

This was a nightmare for Darren and Maria. After meeting for three years with other community-interested folks, they had found their ideal land, an owner-financed 83-acre ranch in rural

Montana, but no one else in the group was quite ready to make the jump yet. Gambling on the power of their vision, the couple put most of their life's savings into the down payment and moved to the ranch, bringing their home-based pottery business with them.

For two years they hosted a series of visitors, but no one became a member.

"That's why we didn't finish our bylaws," says Maria, "since we didn't want to make unilateral decisions about the community without knowing the wishes of any future members. We wanted everyone to create it together."

Steve and Sandy were the first visitors who really seemed "right." They loved the land and the vision of a self-reliant homesteading community, and had great skills — he was a builder, she was a gardener. They had enough money for membership and site-lease fees, and were even able to move to the property and live in their RV. Best of all, they'd arrived in time to avert a looming financial crisis, since the first $13,000 balloon payment for the property was due in a few weeks. The newcomers seemed like the answer to Darren and Maria's prayers.

The first month everyone was elated. Enjoying each other's company, they put in long hours of hard, rewarding work reroofing the barn that would become their kitchen/dining room, replacing the well-pump, and upgrading the irrigation system.

"It was fine with us that we hadn't worked on the bylaws any further," recalls Maria, "because we were working so hard to finish the roof and irrigation system while the weather was still good. We knew we'd get to it later."

The second month Sandy began to point out aspects of Cottonwood Spring's site plan that she didn't like. Could she and Steve put their house over there, rather than where the plan indicated houses should be? Could they build their house with standard construction materials rather than the more labor-intensive alternative materials Darren and Maria wanted for community homes?

Sandy and Maria began to get on each other's nerves. Maria wanted Sandy to stop trying to change Cottonwood Springs into something it wasn't. She hadn't counted on new people wanting *this* much change. Sandy was frustrated, feeling unable to co-create the kind of community she and Steve had envisioned. Maria assumed that initial power struggles were normal, given that community living brings up people's issues. Also, as a long-time veteran of group process issues, Maria saw conflict not as a problem but as an opportunity to ultimately get more connected, once the conflict was resolved through deep personal sharing and coming to common agreement. But such ideas were foreign to Sandy, who took the increasing tension as a sign that things weren't working out. Relations between the founders and newcomers deteriorated until Darren and Maria proposed they have a serious process meeting. But this was too weird for Steve

and Sandy, who thought, "*That's* not community!" They felt that they had no choice but to leave.

And that's when the newcomers found out that there was no provision for departing members to get their money back.

All Darren and Maria had shown them were written descriptions of their ideas and visions, and a half-finished set of bylaws, "which," Maria recalls, "they *said* they agreed with." But with no signed contracts or legal documents, there were no agreements about what either party could or could not do. The newcomers were under no obligation to stick with the founder's visions and plans; the founders were under no obligation to pay anyone anything. Everyone was unhappy; but for a scrap of signed paper, there hangs the tale.

They settled out of court. By refinancing the property (made possible by the balloon payment and recent property improvements), Darren and Maria returned Steve and Sandy's $22,000 membership and site fees, but no additional claims. Although the founders didn't lose their property, they lost a great deal — a new friendship, the excitement of creating a real community at last, and a good deal of their own energy and heart for community. Steve and Sandy got their money back, but not their injured pride or dignity, and certainly not their community dreams. Disgusted and embittered, they never wanted to see another intentional community again.

Remembering Things Differently

True stories just like this one happen all too often.

Some forming communities have made verbal agreements — but ... what was it we said again? I may remember that, according to our work-equity agreement, if we were to disband our community and sell the property. I'd be compensated in actual earned wages, in real dollar amounts. But *you* may remember agreeing that I'd be compensated only as a percentage of the sale price. This would never become a problem — unless we decide to disband and sell our property. Why wouldn't normally savvy folks like us write it all down?

Heartbreaking though it is — because it's so simple to prevent — many forming communities flounder or sink because its founders don't write down their agreements at the outset. Months or years later, when they try to conjure up what they thought they agreed on, they remember things differently. Unfortunately, even people with the greatest goodwill can recall a conversation or an agreement in such divergent ways that each may wonder if the other is trying to cheat or abuse or manipulate them. This is one of the most common and most devastating structural-conflict time bombs.

Why do so many would-be communitarians not put agreements in writing? Why does this kind of structural conflict happen so often?

I believe many idealistic, visionary people think the only reason to sign an agreement or contract would be to prevent someone else from cheating them. And who wants to suggest that their community colleagues might do that?! It's too embarrassing to bring up; it's not polite; it's in poor taste. "If I suggested we write this down and sign it, what kind of rude person might they think I am?"

Then there's the anguish of people who'd like the world to be a better place — want to help it *become* a better place — and can't bring themselves to agree to such documents because on some level, wouldn't that just be *inducing* distrust and suspicion? Couldn't we keep distrust and potential cheating away from us by simply not ever thinking about it?

Well-meaning folks such as these can keep their scruples if they keep in mind these three tendencies of the recollection process:

1. Jack remembers vividly what he *meant* — what he believed and mentally pictured vividly — but not what he actually *said*. (People often don't say what they mean: not in an attempt to deceive, but because of poor communication skills.) Not knowing what Jack meant, Jill recalls only his actual words. But that's not what he remembers at all.

2. Jill is sure she remembers what Jack said — but she didn't actually pay close attention to his words at the time. Rather, she was unconsciously so focused on what she herself believed about the subject, that she thought Jack had said what she believed. But it's not what he said at all. He remembers what he said — but not what Jill was *thinking* while he said it!

3. Jack says something and, seeing Jill nodding in agreement, he assumes that the communication that he *intended* in his mind was the communication that was *received* in her mind. But it wasn't. Jill interpreted what she heard him say as something else entirely. Once again, they're not remembering the same thing.

Giving Yourselves Every Chance of Success

Communication can get so fouled up, and so fast — it makes no sense *not* to just check it out by having a group member write down what everyone thinks they're agreeing to and then read it back, or have everyone read it. *Now* is the time to say, "Wait a minute; this isn't what we just said," rather than dredging up remembered differences months or years later, when people's life savings or their major life decisions may be at stake.

Obviously, you'll improve how well everyone remembers an agreement if you not only write it down, but also ask everyone to sign it. While not appropriate for every kind of agreement or written document, pretending you're the Ben Franklins and John Hancocks of your own Declarations can be rewarding, especially if documents are signed ceremonially. Of course, it's also a good idea to keep your agreements in a safe place (or in two different safe places), and refer to them as needed.

"But just having written documents, or having them with our signatures, doesn't guarantee anything," you might say. "Anyone can break those agreements anytime. What's a piece of paper?"

Formal written contracts between people, and documents for legal structures such as bylaws are only binding when someone not abiding by them is taken to court and forced to comply on pain of fines or jail. And while this is certainly not something you'll want to see happen, this potential consequence does serve as a kind of deterrent.

A more powerful deterrent is social pressure. Legal documents and formal contracts as well as other kinds of written agreements, such as meeting minutes, decision logs, behavioral norms, and so on, can easily be breached, but not without everyone in the community knowing they were breached and by whom. Social pressure and the possibility of group displeasure can be a strong motivator for keeping agreements, even among people who believe that they wouldn't need such pressure to keep agreements. Social pressure works most of the time, and it's certainly better than what happened to the folks at Cottonwood Springs.

"Good documents make good friends," notes Vinnie McKenny, founder of Elixir Farm, a successful herb farm and small intentional community in Missouri. Vinnie knows whereof she speaks. She not only has created a successful business and several non-profit projects with various friends, but also has a strong background in the administration side of philanthropic giving and has worked with significant donors. Vinnie knows how the world works, in my opinion, and knows the value of making everything agreed upon between even the best of friends crystal clear and unambiguous — and written down.

Your Community's Agreements and Policies

You'll have agreements, often called "policies" or "guidelines," both in the forming-community stage and later, when you're living on your property. The forming-stage documents could include vision documents and policies about your group's membership and decision-making processes, communication norms, finances, and the land-search process. These are often recorded in meeting minutes, decision logs, covenants, and informal contracts.

As you establish a legal entity, purchase property, and move to the community, you'll probably make additional agreements for the following kinds of community issues:

- Community labor and one-time or periodic fees owed.
- Land-use and ecological guidelines.
- How ongoing or periodic community expenses will be paid; what happens in the event of cost overruns.
- Policies for dogs and other pets, children, noise, tool use, conserving water or electric power, or the use of drugs , alcohol, tobacco, or firearms.
- The processes by which new members join the community.

- New members' expected financial contributions and labor requirements.

- The processes by which members may leave the community, including how, or if, they will be reimbursed any of their membership fees or other expenses.

- Behavioral norms, including how the community will handle people violating those norms, and the consequences for doing so.

- Grounds for, and the process of, asking someone to leave the community.

Some of these agreements will be recorded in the formal documents associated with the legal entity you'll form to purchase land together, or to conduct any non-profit activities or operate a community-owned business. These can include Articles of Incorporation and Bylaws (corporations), Partnership Agreements (partnerships), or operating agreements (Limited Liability Companies), for example, depending on which legal structure(s) you choose. (These will be examined more closely in Chapters 15 and 16.) Other agreements may be recorded in documents such as leases, promissory notes, real estate deeds, and contracts, and still others may be in simple policies your group drafts, approves, and implements.

Many forming communities are so overwhelmed with organizational or construction tasks in their early years — or simply don't anticipate what they might need — that they create certain policies and agreements only when a crisis reveals the need for them.

That's what happened to the Community Alternatives Society in Vancouver. While they had agreements about financial and labor requirements, and guidelines about how they'd use and maintain their common facilities, they

had no policy about people's behavior, since they all seemed to behave reasonably well. The normal conflicts were handled by their communication processes, and their differences of opinion were addressed in consensus meetings. But after living together in relative harmony for 11 years, they discovered that a member had done something so unacceptable it forced the issue. They realized they needed rules about behavior, and more importantly, an agreement about what to do if anyone breached them. The group came up with one of the wisest and most humane community behavioral policies I've seen, with not only a clear description of members' rights and responsibilities, but also a graduated series of consequences when someone violated them.

Other communities anticipate the kinds of agreements they'll need over time and begin creating them early on, as did the founders of Abundant Dawn community in Virginia (most of whom had previously lived in other communities). They began working on their policies and agreements in 1994, three years before they found and moved to their land. Some of these were a collection of different agreements they made over time, that they later compiled as a policy on a given subject. In other cases they just sat down and created a policy step by step. As of this writing, eight years later, some agreements are completed; others are approved by the whole group but need more work; still others are in draft form and not yet approved. They've saved the actual writing of some formal contracts and leases until they've agreed on the policies which those contracts will contain.

Their agreements, some of which are listed below, illustrate the kinds of issues most forming communities address sooner or later, depending on their living arrangements and the degree of shared resources. These are the kinds of issues your group will need to consider. I suggest you use Abundant Dawn's list to stimulate your own thinking on which agreements your group wants to make, and when.

Creating agreements like these is serious business and requires a lot of time and care. (Abundant Dawn's founders estimate that the number of person-hours they've spent creating their agreements, both in committees and community meetings, to be in the thousands.) Some people might consider the number and complexity of Abundant Dawn's agreements excessive, but I think it's smart. This is a community founded by experienced communitarians — and it's one of the ten percent.

Abundant Dawn's Agreements

Vision Statement. The who, what, and why of Abundant Dawn community.

Articles of Incorporation and Bylaws. Part of Abundant Dawn's documents as a non-exempt non-profit.

Membership Policy. Rights and responsibilities for different kinds of membership, commitments, sabbaticals, part-time members, how membership ends.

Community Structure Overview. Sections on community legal structure, community culture, decision-making and governance, pod structure, forming pods, pod joining fee. (A "pod" is a smaller subcommunity within Abundant Dawn.) This document addresses balancing members' desire for freedom with their desire not to be negatively impacted by the choices made by their neighbors (with regard to noise, nudity, etc.).

Food Policy. Description of bulk food purchase and distribution, use of the community garden, and how food resources are shared.

Conflict Resolution Document. More of an evolving plan than a policy, this document describes methods for resolving conflicts, including but not limited to full-group process meetings.

Financial Policy. The Financial Overview encompasses all agreements about money, including all community income sources and expenses, members' financial obligations, what the community does and doesn't pay for, and what happens in a financial emergency. The Formula Agreement describes their formula for determining the monthly fees owed by each pod or subcommunity within Abundant Dawn, based on the pod's current number of people and cars, and each pod member's annual income.

Visitor Policy. Guidelines for how to host visitors seeking a community to join.

On-Land Business Policy. How members own and operate businesses in the community, including financial relationships, community control, non-members as co-owners or employees, permission, and contracts.

Land Planning. Overall site plan for community land.

Environmental Guidelines for Building. Description of the various sustainability factors to consider in building a home.

Forestry Policy. Guidelines for use and care of forest, including when and how trees can be cut, how firewood can be gathered, etc.

Pet Policy. How many dogs and cats each pod may have, and how to minimize the animals' impact (especially the impact of outdoor cats and dogs) on both the wildlife that was already there, as well as on other community members.

Expulsion Policy. What may be an expellable offense, and how a member would be asked to leave, financial resolution, etc.

End of Abundant Dawn Community as We Know It. If the group could not continue as a community, this agreement shows how they would dissolve the legal entity, sell their property to a land trust or become a land trust, continue to live in the homes they've built, and disburse any assets. This was an extremely difficult agreement to create, and few communities ever think about this in advance. (But it's good planning.)

One of your group's most significant set of agreements will be those embedded in the documents of the legal entity through which you'll own property together. We'll look at those next.

YOUR PET POLICY

Once you move to your property your community will definitely need a pet policy, since pets, especially dogs, create some of the thorniest conflicts faced by communities. In the early 1980s, for example, a group of city dwellers moved to the rural Midwest to begin their new spiritual community. While they had no agreements at all, (believing that spiritual folks like themselves didn't need any), they forgot that dogs no longer contained in yards naturally become that bane of communities—a hunting pack. Their now-liberated dogs exuberantly followed their instincts and killed a number of small mammals, including kittens and cats belonging to other members. The community erupted in gut-wrenching conflict. Some members were furious over the loss of their pets and feared the dogs might kill other cats or even attack their children. The dog owners were furious and defensive, since their own beloved family dog couldn't be guilty — it was *other* members' dogs. It got so ugly that some fathers threatened to shoot the dogs on sight. Stunned by the uproar, the community finally decided they might need rules after all, and agreed that all community dogs would be fenced.

Dog packs, dogs barking, dog droppings, dogs with fleas, dogs digging up gardens, and dogs scaring off wildlife are some of the issues that arise over man's best friend in community. Cats too, can be an issue in communities, as some experts estimate that one cat kills roughly 100 small animals and birds over the course of a year. And yet, sometimes communities want dogs to deter deer who eat gardens, or cats to eliminate the rodents that get into food supplies. So while Fido and Fluffy may indeed be welcome, they need to be managed. Some communities have agreements that dogs and cats must wear small neck bells to warn wildlife of their approach, or that dogs be fenced and leashed.

Recognizing that pets could be important members of the family, Earthaven's founders allowed people to keep their dogs when they moved to the land (although no more than five or six total on the property), but not get new pets when their pets died. Abundant Dawn crafted a unique plan that regulates the number of dogs and cats per neighborhood, based on neighborhood population. (See "Pet Policy, Abundant Dawn." Appendix 2, pg. 235.)

⊰ Chapter 8 ⊱

Making It Real: Establishing Your Legal Entity

"**N**o — I DON'T WANT US TO have any legal entities or form a corporation! Corporations and lawyers are what's wrong with this country!" So declared a cofounder of a start-up community I was once involved with. She was willing to create community agreements and policies, but not a legal corporation. While I knew our group needed a legal entity to own property together, I certainly saw her point. Corporations are entities which under the law are treated as if they had the rights of actual people, but allow the real people who run them to incur debts, violate the environment, or harm others with no consequence to them personally. And when most people think "corporation," they think big, multinational corporations. Armed with millions of dollars and fleets of lawyers, large corporations can deny, evade, and delay prosecution for environmental and other crimes for which an individual person would be swiftly thrown in jail. No wonder many of the people most interested in creating a more cooperative, alternative culture are averse to "corporations" and "legal entities."

Yet form them we must, if we are to protect ourselves from potentially ruinous lawsuits, exorbitant taxes, or sudden responsibility for paying debts we didn't agree to. Legal entities are themselves neutral. (And only some legal entities are literally corporations.) It's when people use these structures to harm others and avoid responsibility that they become objectionable. We can use these structures to create a more sustainable, cooperative way of life and, by demonstration, influence our culture for the better.

Why You Need a Legal Entity — Before Buying Your Property

Why does your community need to form a legal entity? First, you'll need one to purchase your property, and to own it together over the years. (Technically you can purchase property as a group with no legal entity, but your default choices — Tenancy in Common and Joint Tenancy — are not recommended. See Chapter 15.) Second, you'll need a legal entity (which could be a separate one) to own and manage any community-owned businesses or to manage any non-profit activities — especially if you want to receive tax-deductible donations for those activities.

Consider the consequences if you don't have a legal entity. Serious, potentially community-killing conflicts can arise regarding:

- property rights and responsibilities of members
- vulnerability to creditors and lawsuits

with regard to members' personal assets

- financial compensation for departing members
- issues about who-all holds title to property and what happens if the group disbands and sells its assets

Not to mention that without choosing a particular entity you might end up paying exorbitant, unnecessary taxes. Not having a legal entity for your community is definitely a structural-conflict time bomb that could someday blow your group apart.

WHY FORM A LEGAL ENTITY?

1. Having a legal entity will make the process of buying land easier. A seller or lending institution will take a legal entity with tens of thousands in the bank and a brief credit history more seriously than a collection of individuals trying to buy property together.
2. Any agreements the group makes as part of the documents of its legal entity (such as operating agreements or bylaws), will be compatible with state law, and thus legally enforceable. If a member violates one of these agreements, the other members will have the force of law behind them to induce the errant member to comply.
3. Some legal entities are more compatible than others for the various ways you can own property together, such as: (a) everyone owns the property in common; (b) each household own its own individual plot; or (c) each household owns its own individual plot and everyone together owns the rest of the property in common.
4. Since the IRS and the state will tax your community according to whichever legal entity you have chosen, you might as well pick one that saves the most taxes relative to your community's particular circumstances.

Thus the criteria for choosing your community's legal entity for property ownership usually depends on how well it can (1) protect your members from potential lawsuits or other financial liability, (2) prevent unnecessary taxation, (3) allow your community to hold title to land and structure land use and decision-making rights the way you like, (4) allow your community to accomplish its purpose, and (5) reflect your values. (See Chapter 15.)

Some communities have different legal entities for each kind of activity; others conduct various activities under one legal structure. And since no legal entities are designed specifically for intentional communities (except 501(d) nonprofits created for the Shakers) we must borrow from the various legal structures designed for operating businesses, pooling money for investments, or holding land in common, and shape these structures to fit our community's particular needs.

"Wait a minute, *our* community won't be like that," you might say. "We're going to create something beautiful and noble — not some *business*." Ah, but your financial dealings need to be conducted in a businesslike way. After all, you'll probably be dealing with hundreds of thousands of dollars and you'll need clear, fair agreements. And, when you get right down to it, your community *is* a business, since it involves your putting this money together and agreeing how you'll spend it, how you'll raise more of it when needed, and how you'll deal fairly with any surplus or deficit.

Using a Lawyer

Yes, you should definitely have a real estate lawyer when you buy your property, and a lawyer with tax-law experience to help you set up the legal entity with which you'll own your property. Wait until you've learned as much as possible about your community's most likely legal options before you hire one, though. For one thing, you will be empowered, because information is power. You will also avoid paying a lawyer to spend several expensive sessions demystifying the realm of business legalities before even beginning to draw up a document. You will not feel like supplicants or amateurs. You won't be overwhelmed or intimidated.

I also recommend hiring an experienced tax accountant or CPA. The point, after all, is to choose a legal entity which not only reflects your values, but also saves you the most tax money. Tax accountants and CPAs often know more about the nuances of these financial issues than lawyers.

Few lawyers or accountants know anything about intentional communities — another reason for learning as much as you can about possible legal entities and picking several likely ones before you see the lawyer. At an hourly fee that could be several hundred dollars, you don't want to have to *pay* the lawyer or accountant to educate him or her as to what an intentional community is before naively asking for a suggested legal structure. You'll want to have written a clear, concise definition of your planned intentional community, along with several possible legal options for accomplishing, it before you walk in the door.

Most lawyers don't know an extensive amount about the entire range of business and investment entities, but tend to specialize, and will likely steer you towards the entities they know most about. This can work to your disadvantage, as your community can end up wearing the wrong legal structure like an ill-fitting shoe. Know which structures seem the best match before you seek legal help, then pick specialists in the structures *you* want.

But before any of this, your whole community needs to be absolutely aligned and clear on what it is you're trying to do.

"Remember," says Dave Henson, of Sowing Circle/OAEC, "your lawyer (or your CPA) works for *you*. Their advice on organizational questions is only as good as your community's clarity about your economic and organizational goals."

Once you and the lawyer (or you and your tax accountant) have picked a legal entity, you can save far more in lawyer's fees if you draft your start-up and operating documents yourselves, and have the lawyer or tax advisor review them for any specific provisions applicable to your state or province. Lay people can draft their own legal documents, with the right help. Nolo Press, a publisher of self-help legal books, offers step-by-step books and software on how to form your own partnerships, LLCs, corporations (for certain states), and non-profit corporations in the US, and Self-Counsel Press does the same in Canada. Nolo Press, and Community Associations Institute (CAI), an organization educating and representing homeowners and condominium associations in the US, will both soon publish books on how to create your own community associations.

Beware, however. At least one lawyer told me that doing it this way can cost a community group *more* money, but only if people change their minds several times and request multiple revisions, which increases the lawyer's billable hours.

If you're applying for non-profit tax status, you might want your lawyer or tax advisor to review your federal (and if applicable, state) tax exemption application form too. Arrange it so that your lawyer will answer your specific questions and review — not rewrite — the forms you have prepared. (You can file your applications with the state yourselves as well.)

Why not just do everything yourselves and skip the legal fees? An experienced lawyer can spot potential problems and suggest solutions. He or she might be familiar with other, similar cases, and will make sure that any problems that befell one group won't happen to *you*. A good lawyer is well worth the money, but if your group is as informed as possible at the outset, you'll need far less of his or her time.

I suggest using Chapters 15 and 16 as an overview of the range of legal entities commonly used by intentional communities. Your group can then follow up with in-depth exploration of the legal entities that appeal most. You can do this with specific books and software, certain service organizations, and a consultation with a local tax accountant. (See author's website for resources.) Once you know more, choose two or more legal structure(s) for owning land that seem most likely for your group. Then choose a lawyer to help you make your final choice. To save more money, draft your documents yourselves and have your lawyer review them.

How many people in your group should become familiar with legal issues? Can one person do it? Theoretically, yes. Dave Henson did the legal legwork for Sowing Circle/OAEC, as did Velma Kahn for Abundant Dawn. Yet Dave suggests that you don't leave it up to a single individual, but form a small committee. After doing the basic research, he says, the committee should present to the whole group the best options for the community's legal entities. Encourage extensive discussion. If there are still questions or concerns, let the committee go back and do more research and report back to the group.

Whichever legal entity (or entities) you end up choosing, I recommend that *all* community members — not just those experienced in business and finance — be as informed as possible about these matters. Community-wide knowledge and understanding helps the group function more intelligently and, more importantly, helps equalize power relationships within the community. It can prevent the common dilemma of power being concentrated in the business/finance intelligentsia, with all the attendant resentment and potential conflict that this can engender.

Finding the Right Lawyer

You'll want someone experienced, yet open-minded and flexible enough to understand what you're trying to do. Your lawyer must be willing and able to help you shape the legal entity, wherever possible, to fit your community's values and needs. The best choice would be a lawyer you personally know and trust, who is experienced in tax and real estate law, particularly as it relates to the legal structures you're exploring. This may be a tall order! The next best choice would be to find intentional communities in your area that are using one or more of the legal structures you're considering, and ask if they'd recommend the lawyer(s) they used. In your wider community, you could ask the same of business people who are using the legal structures you're considering.

If you're using a local legal referral service, I recommend using only those run by the local bar association or a local non-profit association, rather than private, commercial referral services. And use only those that refer lawyers experienced in this kind of law who offer a free or discounted consultation as part of the referral program. Avoid those that simply refer lawyers on a strictly rotating basis. And what about low-cost law clinics? They usually bill for services at a higher rate than their initial consultation rate, their staff turnover is usually high, and their experience with the legal and tax issues of the entities you're exploring may be low. I suggest using a low-cost clinic only for general information, and use a more specialized lawyer for your actual legal work.

When choosing a lawyer, it's best to contact several lawyers, interview them and get references, and after choosing one, create a written agreement about all fees and contracted services.

Sometimes the right choice will be obvious. When she explored potential legal entities for Abundant Dawn, Velma Kahn spent several days in a law library researching case law relevant to her forming community's tax issues. She finally found a case that seemed to set the right precedent, and called several tax attorneys to feel them out. But none seemed to understand what she wanted, or get it that a non-lawyer like herself could have discovered something new.

Except one. "What's the case number?" he asked, interested. "I'd like to look that up myself.

"Ah," she said. "We've found our lawyer."

As mentioned earlier, you should set up your legal entity *before* buying property. However, it will be easier to visualize and compare various kinds of legal entities if we use examples of communities you've become familiar with. So let's first meet those communities and learn how they bought, financed, and developed their land. (Later, we'll examine the legal entities they used to accomplish this.)

For many founders this next step is the "juiciest" part of starting a new community — the great land-buying adventure.

⮞ Chapter 9 ⮜

The Great Land-Buying Adventure

IN 1995, WHEN THE SIX cofounders of Dancing Rabbit set out to find property for their ecovillage, they ran into the typical challenges core groups often face at this point. (In this book, the words "property" and "land" are used interchangeably to mean the property your community will buy, whether it's raw land, developed or partially developed property, or a house or apartment building.)

Dancing Rabbit had begun in 1993, when a dozen friends and environmental activists at Stanford University in California decided to create an ecovillage to learn about, demonstrate, and teach others what they called "radical environmental sustainability." They envisioned a small, locally self-reliant settlement of 500 to 1000, with subcommunities of smaller income-sharing groups, cohousing communities, and individual households.

Many of the activists lived in a student housing co-op at Stanford, and had already had a taste of shared living and consensus decision-making. Fueled by community living experience and environmental goals, they launched Dancing Rabbit as an incorporated association. Through monthly potlucks, a newsletter, and an e-mail bulletin board, they eventually became a group of nearly 20 at their monthly potlucks, and of about 100 on their e-mail network, primarily in northern California's university towns of Palo Alto, Berkeley, and Davis. By 1995, when many of the group had graduated from Stanford, six of them moved into a shared household in Berkeley and began researching what it takes to create an ecovillage.

One of their group, Cecil Scheib, had graduated earlier and had spent the last year or so traveling around the county to learn more about intentional communities, visit possible communities to join, and gather information about natural building and possible regions for their ecovillage. Another Dancing Rabbit activist did the same, focusing mostly on desirable areas in northern California.

The first hard realities the Dancing Rabbit founders encountered were county zoning regulations, building codes, and health department regulations that didn't allow sustainable developments.

Legal Barriers to Sustainable Development

They learned, for example, that just owning property doesn't mean you can do whatever you want with it.

In many cities, towns and counties, zoning regulations regarding population density prohibit building more than a certain number of dwellings per acre or clustering houses together and leaving much of the property open space, requiring instead that each house sits on its own same-sized lot. In the Southwest and parts of the Great Plains, where rain is scarce and the level of snow melt or underwater aquifers determines density, zoning regulations often permit no more than one house per 35 acres. Areas on the West Coast with no summer rainfall often allow no more than one house per five acres, while many townships in the Northeast allow no more than one house per 50 feet of road frontage. (The issue in the Northeast isn't water, but money. A township's revenues come largely from property taxes, and budgets for municipal services are usually estimated as one household per lot. While allowing higher density on one lot wouldn't break the budget, if such density allowed many property owners to increase their populations, it could overwhelm the township's school, fire, police, or other services.) To increase population density on a property or to cluster houses usually requires petitioning the city council or county board of supervisors for a zoning variance or special use permit, which generally means holding a public hearing with potential neighbors. As many forming cohousing groups have learned, neighbors' opinions can make or break a project.

Most towns and cities — and an increasing number of rural counties — have adopted the Uniform Building Code (or the Southern Building Code), or have their own local building code which mandates which construction methods and materials can be used. This is an attempt to protect local governments from lawsuits brought by people injured because of faulty construction or to prevent homes from deteriorating too quickly, which could adversely affect banks and other local lending institutions with mortgages on those homes. Thus, time-tested natural building techniques such as rubble-trench foundations or load-bearing strawbale or cob construction, straw-clay infill, earth-based floors, living roofs, or earth-plastered walls, are often illegal because few engineering specifications are available for the load-bearing capacities, durability, or moisture-repelling aspects of these techniques. Most counties that allow this kind of construction do so by default because they are sparsely populated; either they have little or no zoning, or they lack sufficient property tax revenue to pay inspectors to monitor or enforce building codes. And while increasing numbers of counties have been allowing natural building methods under "experimental" permits (usually requiring an engineer's sign-off, protecting local government from liability), not many counties allowed these when Dancing Rabbit's founders were conducting their search. As of this writing, it's still often difficult to impossible to get such buildings approved.

Although it makes no logical sense, roof water catchments are disallowed in many regions in the West, since any rain that falls over a given locale legally "belongs" to the water table beneath it, and shouldn't be messed with by interfering humans, even though such rainfall may only run through people's sinks or vegetable gardens before joining the ground water below.

In most counties, graywater recycling or constructed wetlands are either illegal or, at the very least, illegal as the sole source of waste water drain-off. A county health department may allow these methods but still insist on a septic tank and leach field, regardless that these are considered unnecessary by graywater experts. Composting toilets are also rarely allowed by county health departments. Sometimes counties will allow only certain makes and models of composting toilet, such as those with electric fans, and often, only with the full additional back-up of a septic system and leach field — also considered superfluous by microbiologists familiar with the composting toilet process.

The Dancing Rabbit folks also learned that counties with colleges or universities often per-

mit no more than four or five unrelated adults per house — an attempt to protect homeowners' property values from dropping in case rowdy college students move in next door. Even though most communities won't be like "animal house," rules like this can still greatly restrict a group's ability to form community in such counties. (Chapter 11 will examine ways communities have dealt with these challenges.)

Shopping for Counties — Zoning Regulations, Building Codes, Sustainable Homesteads, and Jobs

At first, Dancing Rabbit's founders were drawn to northern California's beautiful Mendocino and Humboldt counties. But no counties in California, except relatively unpopulated counties on the eastern, desert side of the Sierra Nevadas, allowed the kind of population density they sought, not to mention clustered housing, strawbale buildings, composting toilets, and constructed wetlands. This was true of most areas in the country, especially those near progressive university towns or urban areas where community members could most likely find jobs. The only exceptions seemed to be various rural areas with low populations in the Midwest and Southeast. But although two members worked as software designers and could essentially telecommute from anywhere in the county, not every community member could do that. How could they attract new members if they weren't in an area with locally available jobs?

This was their second hard reality — the trade-off between living sustainably and the ability to make a living. Rural counties in which sustainable building might be possible (because the population was so low they didn't have zoning limitations, traditional building codes, or certain health regulations), offered few potential jobs.

WHAT CAN WE DO ABOUT IT?

I believe culture and laws will inevitably change. The more often that local and state elected officials, planners, and zoning and building officials are exposed to successful, sustainable intentional communities, the sooner they'll realize such communities help them meet their region's locally mandated environmental goals. I believe they will increasingly allow and even advocate special use permits, zoning variances, and more liberal zoning laws and building codes. In the meantime, we can educate officials. We can meet with and get to know local elected officials, planners, building department and health officials. We can tell them what we know, show them studies, give them facts and anecdotes and information. We can solicit their advice, and make them partners in our visions for more cooperative sustainable places to live and work.

Sociologist Paul Ray, who researched values in our population and co-authored the book *Cultural Creatives*, estimates that one-fourth of the US population, 50 million people, have alternative, sustainable values and support such practices. How many of these bankers, planners, and government officials might just be people like ourselves disguised in a suit? How many of them yearn to help create green, sustainable culture too, and simply need our citizen support to justify doing what they want to do anyway?

And in more environmentally-aware areas, such as counties near university towns or cosmopolitan cities on either coast, where potential jobs were more available (and where you'd think sustainable building would be valued), the higher population put greater pressure on county officials to adopt laws about density, housing construction, and sanitation issues, making building sustainable homesteads there impossible. In fact, the more "progressive" the area, from Eugene to Boulder to Ann Arbor, the higher the population and the more likely local regulations made one-house/one-lot, stick-frame construction with flush toilets and a leach field the only kind of development possible.

For a while the group contemplated settling in the same area as Ecovillage at Ithaca, in New York state, a project of three planned cohousing communities with energy-efficient, passive solar homes and an affiliated Community Supported Agriculture farm. One of the first built-from-scratch ecovillage projects in the country, Ecovillage at Ithaca was a tempting model, and it was near a progressive university town with possible jobs. But back in 1995, composting toilets and strawbale homes were out of the question in that location as well.

The third hard reality the Dancing Rabbit founders ran into was trying to find a physically inspiring location with access to alternative culture that wasn't exorbitantly expensive. Living in northern California, they'd become accustomed to seaside cliffs and crashing surf, redwood groves and snow-capped mountains. The farther north they drove, the more ruggedly wild and beautiful the land became. And every college town they stopped in offered familiar culture, from health food stores and vegan restaurants to coffeehouse bookstores. Yet the more beautiful the land and the closer its proximity to a desirable town, the more expensive it was, not to mention the fact that the towns were already thronged with more over-educated folks than there were available jobs.

By now the Midwest was sounding pretty good in terms of land affordability and zoning, and building code freedom. But Mennonite families, and aging soy, corn, or cattle farmers didn't seem like they might offer a familiar and stimulating culture. And the Midwest certainly offered no seaside cliffs or mountain vistas.

After a year of researching land costs and zoning regulations, and impatient to get started, the six Dancing Rabbit founders took off across the country to find rural counties with affordable land prices and few regulations. They looked at the area around Carbondale, Illinois, which offered a beautiful setting and an appealing urban area, but they found land there to be relatively expensive. They checked out the area around Knoxville, Tennessee, which was attractive in its own way but didn't draw them. They also visited a county in northeast Missouri with relatively low land prices, which was also the home of Sandhill Farm, a long-established intentional community whose members had offered to help.

Camped at Sandhill Farm and wondering what to do next, the six founders had long, passionate meetings voicing every opinion — from those who wanted mountains to those willing to take the flats; from those committed to modeling every aspect of sustainable living to those beginning to wonder whether such a project were even possible.

They realized it boiled down to three choices. They could, if they found a way to afford it, buy a small parcel of land in a beautiful, inspiring setting such as Northern California, and, as many communities had done before them, break all kinds of zoning, building, and health department regulations in order to create the sustainable systems they wanted, while remaining so small and low-key that no one would notice.

Or they could work within the system, forming their community in a progressive area like Ithaca, New York, which was regulated by standard zoning and other regulations, and work over the years to change those regulations by persistently trying to educate local officials.

Third, they could form a community in a place so unpopulated that zoning and building codes hadn't arrived yet, and build exactly the kind of model demonstration site they had in mind; to live just as they wanted, somehow finding enough local jobs to get by. (They also wondered, if they chose this option, how rural to be. If they were too far off the beaten path would people want to join them? Would they be too far away for anyone to even visit them?) Burning with a desire to "push the envelope" of environmental activism, and unwilling to either compromise their principles or break laws and remain too safely invisible to accomplish their mission, and realizing that they were willing to live deep in the country, they chose the third option. They planted themselves right in the heart of the Midwest.

The Proactive Land Search

The Rabbits rented a double-wide mobile home near Sandhill Farm. Two members continued telecommuting to Silicon Valley, and two got part-time clerical jobs at the Fellowship for Intentional Community's headquarters at Sandhill Farm.

Continuing the meetings they'd begun in Berkeley, they drafted documents and decided policies, and kept in touch with the wider group of Dancing Rabbit members via e-mail and their website. They created a 501(c)3 non-profit

research and educational organization for Dancing Rabbit. To own the land as a Community Land Trust, they created a 501(c)2 title-holding non-profit, with themselves comprising one third of the Trustees and the other two-thirds drawn from Dancing Rabbit members elsewhere. They created a lease document for land-based residents.

But finding land was their highest priority. They got a plat map from the county, copied down the owners of almost every farm parcel within a three-mile radius of Sandhill, and looked up their telephone numbers in the phone book. They called elderly farmers, farmers' widows, and retired cattlemen, asking if they knew of any land for sale, and once into the conversation, finding out if the landowners might be willing to sell a portion of their own property.

After six months of calling and driving around to look, they ended up with several options. The most promising was a 280-acre parcel of tall-grass prairie with a meandering stream and five ponds. The stream and its branches were lower in elevation than the fields, and the sloping banks were dotted with oaks, black walnut, hickory, and maple. The property also had a short dirt road, a one-story barn with two open sides, a maintenance shed, and a few corrugated metal grain silos. Of the property's 280 acres, 200 had been soybean fields, and were part of the Department of Agriculture's Conservation Reserve Program (CRP). The CRP program paid property owners (in this case) $60 an acre not to farm certain acres so the land could recover from a hundred years of topsoil erosion. The landowner was absentee, and the asking price was $190,000. The group could establish gardens, build passive solar homes, and grow grain in some of the fields not in the CRP program, and slowly restore the prairie ecology of the rest.

They decided to go for it. This would be the site of Dancing Rabbit Ecovillage. The only remaining hurdle was to finance it.

Friendly Loans from Friends and Family

They had the land appraised for $500 an acre, so they made an offer of $140,000 to the absentee owner. He countered, and they negotiated for awhile. Income from the CRP program had artificially inflated the price; however, payments on 200 acres represented a potential annual income of $12,000 a year. Spread out over the next decade, this income would make the price more like $350 an acre — considerably less than the appraised value. So, they decided to offer $678 an acre ($190,000), and the owner accepted.

With two members' high-paying jobs in the computer industry, the group could get a bank loan to buy the property, but only for $150,000. They wanted lower interest rates and friendlier terms than a bank could offer, to protect themselves from repossession in the event of cash-flow problems. They also wanted to raise more money than the $190,000 purchase price, so they'd have the funds to begin developing roads, utilities, and buildings.

The Rabbits got the first of their three low-interest private mortgages from a long-time member in California — $90,000, to be repaid over 15 years at 5 percent interest, with no payments for the first three years. The second mortgage was $50,000 from one founder's parents, also to be repaid over 15 years at 5 percent interest. Their third mortgage was $50,000 for 10 years from the Federation of Egalitarian Communities' (FEC) health insurance fund, at 8.5 percent interest. (When the group had first arrived in Missouri they formed Skyhouse, an income-sharing sub-community of Dancing Rabbit, which joined FEC.) These loans totaled $190,000. Their monthly mortgage payments would be $1,017 a month for the first three years, and $1,730 a month thereafter.

For their land development fund, they combined Dancing Rabbit's treasury, which had accumulated $2,000 in members' dues, and a founder's no-interest, 15-year loan of $33,000, to be paid back only after the first three loans were paid off. Thus, the Dancing Rabbit founders raised $225,000; enough to pay $190,000 cash for the land and establish a $35,000 development fund to begin building infrastructure. They bought the land through their 501(c)2 title-holding non-profit, and placed the property in the Dancing Rabbit Community Land Trust.

They didn't want their primary loans to be first, second, and third mortgages, but wanted their lenders to be repaid concurrently, with pro-rated amounts already determined in case it ever became necessary to sell the property to pay back the loans. So they placed three simultaneous liens on the deed, with their $90,000 lender owed 9/19ths of the proceeds of any future sale and their two $50,000 lenders owed 5/19ths each. The member who made the $33,000 loan didn't have any percentage of pay-back recorded on the deed. (Although the property was in a Community Land Trust, it wasn't paid for yet. The trustees of a land trust property with an encumbered title like this can still sell the property to pay off the debt, if necessary.)

The six founders rented a mobile home across the road from their new property, and because it had a kitchen and bathroom, designated it the temporary community building. Their first tasks were to create a campground, a composting toilet, and outdoor showers, and turn their two-sided barn into an outdoor kitchen. They invited other Dancing Rabbit members, friends, and supporters to visit and help them start their organic garden and build their first strawbale cabins.

The Rabbits' experience illustrates many issues community founders must deal with when they look for and finance land. Most groups who want sustainable development must make the same kinds of difficult trade-offs when choosing their location. They often also learn to approach property owners directly, including owners of land not currently for sale. And, with the exception of cohousing communities, most choose not to get loans from banks or other mainstream lending sources, but seek them instead from family, friends, or organizations aligned with their values.

Onerous Owner-financing (Better than None at All)

In 1990 in Asheville, North Carolina, people began meeting to discuss their common vision of a sustainable ecovillage and begin their land search. To create as self-reliant a village as possible, they assumed they'd need at least 150 residents to provide the range of skills and services required to feed and house themselves and create an active village economy and culture. These goals determined their site criteria — at least 100 acres within 45 minutes of Asheville, with a diverse landscape, abundant water (originating in its own watershed), areas suitable for agriculture, and enough south-facing slopes for at least 40 to 60 home sites and other community buildings. Ideally, the property would be partially or mostly

TABLE 3: DANCING RABBIT'S LAND PURCHASE AND DEVELOPMENT FINANCING

Loan Source	Amount	Terms	Percent of Lien on the Deed
Friend & Supporter	$90,000	15 years to pay; 5% interest; no payments for the first three years	9/19ths
A founder's Parents	$50,000	15 years, 5% interest	5/19ths
FEC	$50,000	10 years, 8.5 % interest	5/19ths
D.R. Treasury	$2,000	—	—
Another founder	$33,000	15 years; no interest; to be paid back after first three loans are paid off	—
TOTAL	$225,000		

cleared land with buildings and utilities, and owner-financed.

Over the next four years the group's land-

search team visited hundreds of properties, shooting video footage of the most promising ones and bringing the whole group out to see

FINDING LAND, LOSING MEMBERS

It's not at all uncommon for a forming community to lose members just as it's about to buy land.

Sometimes the exodus occurs because it's just not the right piece of property for some, or the right location. One of the most enthusiastic members of Dancing Rabbit's original founding group, for example, had her heart set on forming an ecovillage in California. Try though she might to get used to the Midwest, she found she couldn't bear to live in such a place: a flat expanse, few trees, and neighbors who were pleasant enough but mostly focused on rural farming matters. She tried several times to make it work, and eventually realized that Dancing Rabbit might be her tribe, although their new home wasn't hers. While she decided not to move to Missouri, she will always have a second home there, and like many people in the Dancing Rabbit network, has found other ways to contribute to and enjoy the community's progress. Another founding member with many of the same concerns traveled back and forth between California and Missouri for several years, trying to reconcile the vision and values and people she loved with a location that didn't draw her. The pull of love and friendship eventually won, and now, committed to life at Dancing Rabbit, she is one of the many pioneers helping it grow and thrive.

The stress of trying to place an option on, investigate, and finance expensive property can also force interpersonal conflict to a head. Sowing Circle/OAEC had begun as about a dozen people, but when it was time to put up money, the group dropped to seven. And just as they were about to nail down the last details of buying the former Farallones Institute prop-

erty, two couples in the group broke up, and one person in each partnership left the group, and then at the last minute another couple joined them. Besides being devastating personally, this kind of last-minute turnover can be nerve-wracking financially — wrenching people back and forth between different amounts of money they must contribute towards the down payment.

In North Carolina a group met regularly to plan the community that eventually became Earthaven. After searching for property for four years, when some members wanted to buy a particular property and others did not, some persistent personality conflicts and an essential difference in vision were forced to the surface. The conflict was so strong that it broke up the group. Earthaven came into being because four original members, along with some new people interested in forming a community created a hybrid group to purchase the property.

Sometimes people leave because the reality of buying land makes the prospect of living in community all too real. They realize they can't afford it after all, or it may not be the right time in their lives to spend that much money, or they discover they're not really ready to change their lives that much.

If this happens in your group, it doesn't mean the end of your community dream. You may need to buy the property as a smaller group; however, others may come along to join you before the purchase. And certainly people will join you *after* the purchase — there's nothing like a group with a beautiful vision and an appealing property to inspire new people to leap into the adventure with you.

them. They eventually narrowed their search to an area southeast of Asheville, near the town of Black Mountain. As mentioned earlier, one of the founders, Valerie Naiman, got real estate sales and broker's licenses in order to learn more about real financing and local land values, and took a job with a real estate agent in Black Mountain so the group would know about properties as soon as they came on the market.

In 1993, they found a mountain property of three converging stream valleys 45 minutes southeast of Asheville. It had abundant water — two major streams, many smaller streams, and 16 springs — and a quarter of the land was arable. Its slopes and bottom lands were covered in a relatively new forest of pines, locust, poplar, oak, maple, beech, and hemlock. A gravel road and an ancient hunting cabin were its only human-made features. The owners believed it was 368 acres, although they hadn't surveyed it and weren't certain of this. They were asking $1,200 an acre, or $441,600 for 368 acres, with ten percent down. They were willing to owner-finance.

The group originally rejected the property because its uncleared forest represented considerably more work to develop than the mostly-cleared land they'd envisioned. It also had poor soil, depleted during decades of unsustainable farming through the 1930s. While the land search continued, however, a few members of the group returned to reconsider the site. The property seemed to call them back.

"The land was attractive for a number of reasons," recalls cofounder Chuck Marsh. It shared common boundaries with two older intentional communities, Full Circle and Rosy Branch, whose members were supportive of the project. While the entrance to the property was in the more populated county that surrounded Asheville, thus offering good telephone, police,

and ambulance service and well-funded schools, most of the property lay within a considerably more rural county. "That meant we would be subject to less stringent building and development ordinances," recalls Chuck, "and the tax rates would be lower than they would be if we were 100 yards farther north. Our development costs would be significantly lower and we'd have greater flexibility in meeting our ecological goals."

As happens with many forming community groups at this point, the pressure to make a decision about a particular property, and the need for members to come up with significant funds to buy it, forced the issue on long-standing personality conflicts and basic differences in community vision. Some wanted to live in a simple community with friends; others wanted to create a model ecovillage with an educational mission. The group couldn't resolve these differences, and over the next year fell apart in conflict and disappointment.

Valerie broke the impasse by making an offer on the land herself in September 1994, offering $100,000 down, with a clause in the contract allowing her to exit the deal if she couldn't get other people to join in the purchase.

She invited the group members who favored the ecovillage vision, and many new people interested in community, to a "founders meeting" at her house. She handed pledge cards to each guest, explaining that each person or household who pledged $10,000 towards the down payment would get a roughly quarter-acre home or business site in the new community. Those pledging first would get first choice of sites, those pledging second would get second choice, and so on.

That afternoon 11 people, four from the first group and the rest new people, made seven $10,000 pledges for home sites and one for a business site. A twelfth person pledged $20,000 for both a home and business site, and they had their $100,000.

Now that they'd agreed on property and financing, the heat was on. The hybrid group of 12 cofounders settled on the name "Earthaven" and began meeting weekly. Between September and December of 1994, they drafted agreements, membership procedures, and bylaws, and incorporated as a non-profit Homeowners Association. Even though they had the money for the down payment they continued raising money. They increased the site fees to $11,000 and let it be known that site fees would be $12,000 the following year. Through word of mouth, they found friends and other interested people to pledge for additional sites. Some contributed the full amount; others put half and agreed to pay $150 a month at 10 percent interest. By December 11, more people had joined them, and the 21 cofounders had raised a total of $150,000.

They decided to keep $22,000 aside for initial development costs, and so offered the owners $128,000 down, with seven payments towards the unpaid balance over the next seven years, at 8.75 percent interest. The owners stipulated that they would release the property to the group incrementally, upon payment of each of the annual payments. The down payment would guarantee Earthaven ownership of 80 acres, but only 40 of them would be available for the group to develop.

But the total number of acres wasn't clear. If the Earthaven group was willing to pay for a post-purchase survey to determine the actual amount of acreage, the owners were willing to reduce the price commensurably, but no more than 40 acres less than the original asking price (or $48,000), no matter what the survey might show. Thus, if the Earthaven founders wanted this property, they had to agree to buy at least 328 acres, no matter how much smaller the property might actually be. (The later survey showed it was nine acres smaller — or 320 acres — so at $1,200 an acre they ended up paying an extra $10,800 as the cost of doing business.) The owners also stipulated that, after the down payment, Earthaven couldn't pay off much more than $100,000 a year without incurring a ten percent penalty.

These weren't great terms, but at least the sale was owner-financed. Earthaven closed the deal in December of 1994. The property, or part of it anyway, was theirs.

TABLE 4: EARTHAVEN'S OWNER-FINANCING

Actual No. Acres & Final Purchase Price	Total Money Raised	Down Payment & Terms	Amount of Development Fund
320 acres, $396,577	$150,000	$128,000 down; 7 annual payments of principal & interest, at 8.75%. Releasing 40 acres with each payment	$22,000

Do-it-Yourself Refinancing with a "Shoe Box Bank"

The founders knew they would need to raise more than $72,000 the next year for the first annual principal and interest payment, so they decided to refinance as soon as possible. As we've seen earlier, Valerie learned about small-scale, self-financing methods from the E. F. Schumacher Society in Massachusetts and proposed that the group create a private "shoe box bank." This they did, calling it the EarthShares fund, and asking people to transfer money from CDs and savings accounts into it, and encouraging those with other assets to turn them into cash to invest in the project. They offered 8.5 percent interest, a slightly higher rate than many people were receiving in their banks and CDs at the time. Contributors would be paid back in annual payments over the next seven years with money from the membership fees and site lease fees of incoming Earthaven members. The first year, 1995, would be an interest-only payment to the EarthShares fund.

As a "shoe box bank," the EarthShares fund was a seven-year private loan agreement between community members and their own Earthaven Association, allowing them to raise enough money to pay off the sellers as soon as possible and gain control of their own property, so they could develop more than just the first 40 acres.

By December 1995, when the first principal and interest payment would have been due, 18 Earthaven people had transferred money to the EarthShares fund, raising a total of $232,000.

They used a promissory note as the legal instrument for the EarthShares fund, with the signatures of all 18 investors as the Lenders, and the Earthaven Association as the Borrower. The EarthShares fund then placed a lien on the property deed. This meant that no future creditors could force the sale of the property to collect any outstanding debts unless the EarthShares investors themselves, as the first creditors in line, agreed to it, which of course they wouldn't. This created a layer of legal protection around the property.

The $232,000 in the EarthShares fund was more than enough to pay off the rest of the principal and most of the interest for 1995 still owed to the owner-financers. But because of the owner-financers' stipulated ten percent penalty for early pay-off, Earthaven paid them off over four years instead.

By 1997, four Earthaven members invested $61,000 more in the EarthShares fund, and with these funds, as well as with income from site lease fees from new members, they were able to pay off the owner-financers that year. Because of acreage adjustments from the survey, they ended up paying $396,577 to the former owners, along with $28,423 in interest, making their total purchase price $425,000. Of this, $128,000 came from funds raised during their founder's meeting and in the last months of 1994, $24,000 came from membership and site-holding fees, and $293,000 from the EarthShares fund.

Establishing the EarthShares fund had benefited the community in three ways. First, community members themselves became the financers of the project. If for some reason they couldn't make an annual payment one year, there would be no danger of foreclosure. Second, they reduced their annual interest from 8.75 to 8.5 percent, saving several thousand dollars. And third, once they had paid off the former owners, Earthaven members owned the property outright and were free to develop all of it.

Although their land was now financially secure, the community was not out of debt, since the Earthaven Association still owed principal and interest payments to EarthShares investors. Given the principal and interest payments required to pay off the EarthShares fund, they will end up paying several hundred thousand dollars more than $425,000 for their property.

As we've seen with Lost Valley and Dancing Rabbit, it's not uncommon for some founders to have considerably more money or more access to money than others. Sometimes it's only this fact that allows the group to buy property at all.

When One Person Buys the Property

In early 1998, social justice activist Hank Obermeyer began looking for likely properties in Oakland, California to create an intentional community focusing on activism and the arts, with some kind of limited equity for owners. He wanted property with at least two houses and several housing units in a tree-lined neighborhood not far from public transportation, preferably in north Oakland.

In November of that year, he and some friends found three two-story houses with eight units on a double lot in a neighborhood in north Oakland with these features. The asking price was $505,000, a fairly reasonable price for the Bay Area at the time.

Hank's offer of $485,000 was accepted, but only if he paid it in 30 days. Hank had to liquidate many other investments to raise the $485,000 plus an estimated $100,000 for repairs and renovations. But 30 days wasn't enough time to accomplish this, so he got short-term personal loans, which he paid off over eight months.

Hank and the first people who planned to live long-term in the community, now named Mariposa Grove, began what ultimately became a three-year renovation project. They repaired a sagging foundation and replaced wood that had dry rot and termites in one house, and redid much of the wiring and plumbing in another. They tore out walls and rearranged living spaces, eventually creating six two- and three-bedroom apartments and a large apartment to serve as a community common area, containing a kitchen, dining area, large living room, and guest room.

TABLE 5: HOW EARTHAVEN PAID OFF THEIR OWNER-FINANCERS

Year (month)	Money Raised in 1994 for Payments	Total Invested in Earthshares for payments	Money Owed Owner-Financers	Principal Payments to Owner-Financers	Interest Payments to Owner-Financers	Remaining Balance Owed to Owner-Financers
1994	$150,000	---0---	$396,577	$128,000	---0---	$268,577
1995	---0---	$232,000	$268,577	$105,701	$22,299	$162,876
1996	---0---	---0---	$162,876	$99,671	$359	$63,205
1997 (May)	---0---	$61,000	$63,205	$50,202	$5,765	$13,003
1997 (June)	---0---	---0---	$13,003	$5,246	---0---	$7,757
1997 (July)	---0---	---0---	$7,757	$7,757	---0---	---0---
Totals	**$150,000**	**$293,000**	--------	**$396,577**	**$28,423**	**$425,000**

Other planned common areas include office space, laundry facilities, and possibly art and music rooms. They dug up a concrete parking lot and planted a vegetable garden and fruit trees.

The property is in a mixed African-American and white neighborhood, and from the beginning Hank wanted Mariposa Grove to offer affordable housing and be socio-economically and racially diverse. So as soon as apartments were ready he rented the first one to a friend, and they chose the third tenant, and the three chose the fourth tenant, and so on, until they had eight members (while expecting 12-13 eventually). They do in fact represent a diverse group — people who attended Ivy League schools, people who never went to college, and people who came from working-class backgrounds. Most are white; one is African-American.

At first, when the project had just a few short-term members, it was really a one-man show. But Hank didn't make any important decisions or begin any major construction projects until other long-term members became involved. Although everyone made consensus decisions together about long-range matters, Hank carried out their decisions, mostly because he knew how, and because ultimately he was financially and legally responsible for everything. But the increasing load of responsibilities grew so heavy that he finally burned out in exhaustion. He told the group he couldn't continue doing this work by himself. Others would have to share the load. At that point leadership shifted from Hank to the group as a whole, and everyone began serving on one or more committees — finance, construction, governance, new-member outreach, and so on — sharing more equitably the responsibilities of establishing a new community.

"A crisis like this is pretty common in new communities," he says, "when leadership shifts from the founder (or founders) to everyone involved."

As of this writing, Mariposa Grove is in the process of researching the legal and financial requirements to become a limited equity housing co-op under California law. If they choose this form of limited equity housing, it means Hank will sell the property to the housing co-op for approximately $750,000 (the $485,000 purchase price plus what will be more than $250,000 in renovation costs, plus six percent interest). While he could sell for twice that amount since the market value has more than doubled since he bought the property, it would no longer be affordable housing. By the time the group buys the property, the accrued six percent interest will compensate Hank to some degree for his efforts and his business risk, yet keep the units affordable.

In a limited equity housing co-op, each member owns shares in the co-op and is a member of its board of directors, and has the right to live there through a proprietary lease with the co-op. If Mariposa Grove chooses this form of ownership, each shareholder, including Hank, will pay a down payment and monthly occupancy fees to the co-op, which will pay the mortgage payment to the bank, and any maintenance or other costs.

In Chapter 1 we saw how Lost Valley's founders acquired fully developed "turn-key" property for intentional community. Here's how Sowing Circle/OAEC faced similar challenges.

Acquiring Fully Developed "Turn-Key" Property — Confidence, Persistence, and Negotiation

In the mid-1980s, a group of around 25 social justice and environmental activists and artists in the San Francisco Bay Area met regularly to celebrate

Summer Solstice and New Year's together in beautiful rural settings. Many of them had lived together at various times in urban group households. They enjoyed these experiments in community so much that in the late 1980s and early 90s a dozen of them began to periodically look for property near the Bay Area to form an intentional community and activist and arts center.

By 1991, about a dozen members of the group got more serious about creating what would eventually become Sowing Circle community and Occidental Arts and Ecology Center. They acquired the General Plans and county maps for several counties around San Francisco that interested them. Like Dancing Rabbit's founders, they used the maps and county tax records to contact the owners of likely properties, even if the properties weren't for sale. They narrowed their search down to two counties and mailed a form letter to every real estate agent in those counties.

They chose a couple of real estate agents in these two counties from among the responses to their letters, and visited more properties.

In 1993 they learned that an 80-acre parcel fitting their description had just come on the market near the town of Occidental in Sonoma County. The site of the former Farallones Institute, it had been a living/teaching center whose staff had researched and taught classes on

SOWING CIRCLE'S FORM LETTER TO REAL ESTATE AGENTS

Dear Realtor,
Greetings. We are a group of couples and individuals looking for rural or semi-rural land, with or without structures, in Sonoma and southern Mendocino counties.

We're looking for property large enough for and zoned for multiple homes, barns, and other outbuildings. We would ideally like land that could accommodate our building a small retreat center there.

What we're looking for:

- Between 20 and 300 acres
- Zoned to build four or more homes on the property, plus outbuildings
- Within one to three hours' drive of San Francisco
- Less than $500,000 (we'd consider paying more if the property were already a well-developed retreat center with homes).

Ideal:

- Old church camps, summer camps, rural schools, or retreat centers zoned for multiple dwellings and multiple use
- A large parcel of undeveloped land or several contiguous parcels zoned for multiple dwellings (i.e., sub-dividable, perc-tested for several homes, etc.)
- An already-developed property with many older structures needing a lot of work.

Pluses:

- Year-round river or creek and/or a pond
- Mix of forested land and open areas; hilltops and valley or canyon
- At least two acres of arable land
- Privacy.

TABLE 6: SOWING CIRCLE/OAEC'S LAND PURCHASE AND DEVELOPMENT FINANCING

Number of Members and their Contributions	Total Money Raised	Down payment and Terms	$850,000 Purchase Price Amount of Owner-Financed First Mortgage	Amount of Development Fund
Plan #1: 10 people each contribute $20,000	$200,000	$50,000 down; 6.7% interest; interest-only payments for first 5 years	$800,000 Owner-Financed First Mortgage	$150,000
Plan #2: 7 people raise $100,000	$100,000	$50,000 down; 6.7% interest; interest-only payments for first 5 years	$800,000 Owner-Financed First Mortgage	$50,000
Last-Minute Plan #3: • 7 people each contribute $20,0000 • $40,000 2nd Mortgage (5% interest); interest only payments 1st five years • $25,000 3rd Mortgage (same terms)	$205,000	$150,000 down; 6.7% interest; interest-only payments for first 5 years	$700,000 Owner-Financed First Mortgage	$55,000

passive solar design, appropriate technology, and organic gardening. When the Farallones Institute folded in 1990, a private environmental foundation acquired the property and used its organic gardens for a seed-saving project to preserve heirloom vegetables, fruits, and flowers.

When the group drove out to Occidental to take a look, they found rolling hills, meadows, sweeping views, stands of oak, redwood groves, a swimming pond, and, on the north and south sides of a small hill, two of the most beautiful and prolific gardens they'd ever seen. Around the top of the hill were 16 redwood buildings, including a kitchen/dining building, an office complex, a workshop, classroom space, five small vault-roofed passive solar cabins, and another half-dozen intern cabins. The property had a use permit for up to 26 residents full time, with up to 50 people allowed to live on the site for workshops 60 days of the year. The foundation that owned the land was not necessarily looking for the highest bidder, but for a buyer with a similar vision and values to theirs. They were asking a million-plus for the property, and were willing to owner-finance for five years. They offered a $200,000 discount for a buyer who would continue their seed-saving work.

It was a community founder's dream.

It was clearly the ideal property for this group, and they saw themselves as ideal stewards for the property, no matter that it had a million-dollar price tag and none of them had much in the way of financial assets.

But now the pressure was on. The group began meeting 15 hours a week, working on three major tasks. One was organizing their future community life — who would do which tasks, who would live where, and so on. Another was public relations — countering the potential hostility of local residents towards whomever might buy the old Farallones Institute property. They knew county residents would want to know who it was that presumed to buy this very special property, and what they intended to do with it. So representatives of the group met with neighbors and other county residents and explained, in person and through local reporters, how they intended to continue the seed-saving project and initiate similar projects to those of the Farallones Institute, through workshops and classes in organic gardening, permaculture design, and other aspects of sustainable living. The third major project was the legal and financial aspects of acquiring the property.

They realized that this third project would take full-time work. So Dave Henson, a member of the group with extensive experience fundraising for non-profits, and who had gone to law school (although he was not a lawyer), quit his environmental activist job to devote himself full-time for eight months to the project. The group thanked him by giving him the best cabin. (They considered pooling funds to pay him a salary if the land purchase were to take any longer than eight months.)

The first task in acquiring the property was to find out if it was as ideal as it seemed, so Dave looked into the usual issues of property suitability: whether there was enough water and septic system capacity for the amount of peak use they envisioned; if the soil would perc-test well enough for any additional septic systems; what potential hazards might be upwind or upstream of the property; how any future developments planned for the area might affect their use and enjoyment of the property; and the amount of repairs or renovations the buildings might need.

Most of these questions were answered to their satisfaction, but they discovered that almost all the roofs needed repair and that most of the septic systems and some of the foundations needed replacing. They figured out it would take approximately $150,000 to make these and other needed repairs, remodel and enlarge the cabins, and build new accommodations for workshop participants and interns. Given the amount of work the property needed, they decided to offer $850,000 — a full $150,000 lower than the asking price of over a million, even after the first $200,000 was discounted for buyers who'd continue the seed-saving project.

If at First You Don't Succeed ...

For the many months leading up to the purchase, a dozen group members attended meetings, but when the time came to choose to be in the community or out, only seven people stepped forward to commit to the purchase.

They sought three more cofounders, thinking that if ten members could raise $20,000 each, they'd have $200,000. With this amount they'd pay $50,000 down, request an owner-financed mortgage of $800,000, and use $150,000 for development. But they didn't find three more people with $20,000.

They next decided that the seven of them would raise $100,000, pay $50,000 down, request an owner-financed mortgage of $800,000, and use just $50,000 for development, which would stretch out their planned renovations over a longer period. This was the offer they submitted in May 1994. They described how the intended Occidental Arts and Ecology Center was aligned with the foundation's own vision for the property's best use, and agreed to continue the heirloom seed project. A business plan outlined how they'd raise the down payment and make interest and principal payments. They proposed terms quite favorable to themselves — 6.7 percent interest (at a time when banks were charging 8 percent) and relatively small interest-only payments for the first five years — in exchange for signing a contract with the owner-financers that would bind the group to doing repairs and improvements to the buildings and infrastructure, thereby improving the value of the property over the first year of occupancy. They backed this up by describing how they would repair each building, a timetable for the improvements, and another business plan showing how much money they'd use for that purpose and where they'd get it.

"This is an important point for forming communities to keep in mind," advises Dave. "Many owner-financers are reluctant to sell to groups who say they can meet the down payment and mortgage payments, but whom might be so financially strapped in the future that they'd default on payments and the owner would have to repossess the property. If the property hadn't been properly maintained, the owner could get back property that might then be worth less what it had sold for because its buildings were rundown or falling apart. But if potential buyers can demonstrate that they will maintain and even improve the property, and can document the source of their funds for doing so and how they will accomplish the upgrades, the landowner may not only be willing to sell to them, but also willing to reduce the down payment, the interest rate, and/or the amount of monthly payment. If a group with this arrangement defaulted and the original landowner repossessed and got the property back," Dave says, "it would be worth considerably more than when the owner first sold it, over and above any increase in land values."

The foundation accepted their offer and terms.

Because they were too overwhelmed by financial stress at this point to establish a more complex legal entity to buy the property, they drew up a simple partnership, called the "Sowing Circle."

They later learned that the foundation had received over 200 other offers, some of them offering more cash than they had. But their offer was most likely chosen, they believe, because their intended use was probably the most aligned with the foundation's goals for the property, and they had presented the most coherent financial model of how they'd pay for the property and what they would do with it. It also helped that Dave and others in this group had credibility and good reputations nationally as environmental activists.

But at the 11th hour they had serious setbacks. Two of the couples broke up, and as a result, two members left the group, leaving just five people to raise the money. Fortunately a new couple joined a few weeks before closing, bringing their number back to seven.

But that wasn't the worst. Several days before closing the sale, and after they'd all quit their jobs and given notices on their apartments, as they were all relaxing and celebrating at a friend's cabin in the country, they got a phone call.

"The deal's off," the foundation director said, "unless you pay $150,000 down. We can't go with $50,000 down, and we can't offer you any extra time to raise it. We'll need it at closing, five days from now." The group was stunned. They later learned that the foundation's New York lawyers were horrified to learn that this million dollar property was about to go for just $50,000 down, and put pressure on the foundation director to somehow stop the sale. The group assumed the additional $100,000 down was intended to be a deal-breaker, a demand they couldn't possibly meet on such short notice so the foundation could get out of the sale.

Half packed, no longer employed, and about to lose their homes to incoming tenants, the partners decided all they could do was try to raise the additional $100,000. They created large fold-out brochures with color-photocopied photos of the property and descriptions of their agreements and goals. Some of them flew home to their parents, and, using the brochures to help explain what they hoped to do, asked to borrow enough money to come up with $20,000 each. Meanwhile, Dave and some of the others called several close friends and family members to ask for loans. In a few days they had each secured $20,000 for seven down payments totaling $140,000, and had arranged for two friendly loans: a $40,000 second mortgage and a $25,000 third mortgage, each at 5 percent interest with

interest-only payments for the first five years. This $65,000 in additional mortgages, plus the $140,000, gave the group $150,000 for the down payment and $55,000 in reserve for repairs, renovations, and new construction. When one of the seven couldn't come up with the whole $20,000, the group dipped into the $55,000 development fund to give her a temporary loan of $5,000.

Five days after the phone call the founders were able to hand the director of the foundation a certified check for $150,000. The old Farallones Institute property was theirs.

For the first eight months after their August 1994 move-in, six of the partners worked day and night repairing roofs, upgrading utilities, renovating the cabins, and building two yurt dormitories and a new bathhouse. The seventh person, who had just begun a new job in the area, brought home enough pay to keep them in food and other necessities during the renovation. By March 1995 they'd completed enough to launch the Occidental Arts and Ecology Center. (They had arranged to operate OAEC first through the non-profit Tides Foundation, planning to create their own 501(c)3 non-profit two years later.) They created a series of programs, promoted them locally, and held their first OAEC workshop that summer.

As you can see, the challenges and benefits of buying a fully developed "turn-key" property are quite different to those of buying raw land. While the founders of communities like Sowing Circle/OAEC and Lost Valley must usually jump through more hoops to investigate and finance such properties than those who buy raw land, after about eight months of hard work both Lost Valley and Sowing Circle/OAEC had comfortable living quarters for members and

offered their first workshops on sustainable living. Primitive facilities didn't stop either
Dancing Rabbit or Earthaven from creating
internship programs and offering similar workshops soon after land-purchase, but it will be a
long time before either has facilities like those of
Lost Valley or Sowing Circle/OAEC.

Lost Valley and Sowing Circle/OAEC can
also show us what founders seeking turn-key
properties can encounter. Both core groups found
properties that had previously been used for
almost identical non-profit purposes to their
own. Both properties had not been lived in for
two or three years, and both, especially Lost
Valley's, required extensive repair and renovation.

Both sets of founders acquired their property by making offers far lower than the asking
price. Sowing Circle/OAEC's offer was helped
by the fact that their intended use of the property was similar to the owner's wishes, and their
documentation of how they'd raise the money to
finance the purchase was so thorough. Lost
Valley was helped enormously by the fact that
one founder could afford to offer two $100,000
land-purchase and development loans.

In Chapter 10 we'll look at the step-by-step
process of finding community property.

⪜Chapter 10⪜

Finding the Right Property

IN THE LAST CHAPTER WE SAW various communities buy raw land, developed land with buildings and utilities, and fully developed "turn-key" properties. Each of these communities found property with pretty much everything they wanted, perhaps with the exception of Earthaven, whose hybrid founders' group didn't choose the developed land with open space envisioned by the original founders. There's much we can learn from these and other groups about finding the right property — realistically determining site criteria; how the land-search process works; and the importance of researching properties ahead of time.

Choosing Your Site Criteria

One of the keys to getting what you want is to have clear, realistic expectations from the beginning about your chosen location and any limitations on property available there. Here are five basic questions to ask yourselves.

1. Which region or city would your group like to live in, and why?
2. How much land are you looking for?
3. Do you want raw or developed land?
4. How much do you want to pay for property? On development and construction?

5. How much and what kind of financing is available for your land purchase?

How Much Land Do You Want?

The amount of land you're looking for will probably depend on the purpose of your community, how many total members you plan to have, the population density allowed by local zoning regulations, and, in the West, the amount of available water.

Of course, everything can change once you begin the land search. The amount of land or the cost of available properties you find might induce you to change your plans. Sowing Circle/OAEC originally planned to spend no more than $500,000, but paid nearly twice that because they found fully-developed property. An increase or decrease in the size and/or the cost of property could make you decide to increase or decrease your planned number of households. Many cohousing communities, for example, have increased their number of units by ten or more because they underestimated the cost of land (or the cost of development or construction), so to keep their homes affordable, they spread the cost over a larger number of people.

Raw Land — Lower Initial Cost, Years of Effort

Dancing Rabbit and Earthaven bought essentially raw land, though each had one road and one or more outbuildings, and both faced the same set of advantages and disadvantages.

Advantages of Buying Raw Land

- Within the limits of local zoning regulations and building codes, with raw land you can design your site to express your community's values or sustainability goals. For example, like Dancing Rabbit and Earthaven you could cluster your buildings and design your site to enhance community interaction; use permaculture design to create mutually reinforcing shelter, energy, water, and vegetable gardens; or build passive solar homes. Raw land means you won't have to try to counter the effects of a poorly designed site or bring poorly designed or shoddily constructed buildings up to speed.

- You can infuse your group's particular energy and "vibes" into the site and express your own aesthetic taste, instead of working with a site that's already "set" in its energy and aesthetics.

- You'll pay less initially. If your group has limited funds and enough time to develop infrastructure as you can afford it, raw land may be ideal. While you'll need much more money than the land cost to turn the property into a place where all of you can live, at least you'll have a start (and a place to show interested potential new members).

Disadvantages of Buying Raw Land

- Developing the property — roads, off-grid power or bringing in power lines, wells or piped water, septic tanks and leach fields or sewer hook-ups, and building homes and community buildings from scratch, takes much more money (twice as much? three times?) than if you'd bought fully developed property with all the same facilities, because everything costs more now than when properties were developed even just a few years ago.

LOCATION, LOCATION, LOCATION

Location is a critical factor for many reasons. For example, do zoning regulations there allow the kinds of activities you envision (farming, market gardening, light industry, animal husbandry?), or the degree of density you plan (apartment living, single-family dwellings on separate lots)? If not, how likely would it be, and what might it cost, to get a zoning variance?

Unless you're bringing already successful community businesses to the land, or most or all of you will telecommute, does the area offer potential jobs? What are wages and salaries like there? Consider commute times to jobs, gasoline and other transportation expenses, and whether the distance to jobs resonates with your community's values.

Consider your needs for proximity to towns or cities, an airport, and health care facilities. If you'll have community-owned or individually owned businesses, what about local markets for your products or services or access to trucking or other delivery services or a post office; if some of you will telecommute, what about access to phone lines and the quality of local phone service? What about access to farmers markets, CSA farms, food co-ops, or health food stores? What about proximity to schools, high schools, continuing education facilities, and recreational opportunities; or to art, music, and culture?

- Development and construction usually means full-time work for several people — paid professionals or community members. If you plan to do it yourselves, can several of you afford to take leaves of absence from (or quit) your jobs for six months to a year? Does your development fund include money for labor?

- Developing and building on the property can take far more time (three times longer?) than you anticipated. You may have to wait a year, or several years to simply live in community. If your community has an educational, service or other purpose, it may take years to actually start fulfilling that purpose.

Earthaven's founders, for example, bought land in December 1994. By the end of the next year they'd cleared an area and built an open-sided pavilion for workshops and meetings, and three small huts for interns, none with electricity or running water. By the third year they had cleared more land and built a second road, a kitchen-dining room with solar electricity and running water, a composting toilet, and more huts for interns. By the fourth year they had built more roads, more huts, and increased their amount of off-grid power, but only interns and a few members lived on the land. By the sixth year they'd built more roads and a community building that was usable but not finished. More members had moved to the property, living in huts and temporary shelters. By the end of 2002, fully seven years after land-purchase, while several permanent homes were under construction, only one was finished. It'll be years before Earthaven's founders live in the thriving village of 150 they envisioned in the early 1990s.

- The development and construction phase can be exhausting and can lead to burnout, conflict, relationship break-ups, and even loss of members. Consider the statistics regarding couples breaking up while building a new house — and multiply it!

Developed Land — Electricity, Toilets, and Showers

Abundant Dawn in Virginia, Zendik Arts Community in North Carolina, New View cohousing in Massachusetts, and Higher Ground cohousing in Oregon all bought old farms. Eden Ranch in Colorado bought a former "flying ranch" and airport runway (turning an airplane hangar into their community building). A community I'll call Pueblo Encantada (see Chapter 18) acquired the former servants quarters and surrounding acreage of a former estate.

Urban cohousing communities have done it too — Doyle Street in the California Bay Area bought an urban warehouse; Monterey Cohousing in Minneapolis purchased a Georgian mansion; Old Oakland Cohousing chose a historic downtown market building; Southside Park in Sacramento and Temescal in Oakland bought Victorian homes; Terra Firma in Ottawa acquired six 19th-century row houses; and Trillium Hollow in Portland got an upscale executive's home built in the 1980s. There are as many ways to buy and remodel community buildings as there are existing buildings out there.

Abundant Dawn's founders considered undeveloped land at first, but later were aghast that they thought they might form a community that way. "We thought we were going to buy property without *buildings?*" recalls Velma Kahn of Abundant Dawn. "Without showers and a flush toilet? What were we thinking?"

I've been involved in two small-group development projects on about ten acres each: one starting with raw land and the other with an existing house and utilities. In the first instance we paid $10,000 for a pipeline to the local water co-op and thousands more to bring in electricity and build a road. We spent the first seven months dealing with permits, inspectors, roads, utilities, and hooking up an ancient single-wide mobile home, which four of us then crowded into for three years (with me sleeping in a tent) while we very slowly built our house. In the second instance we moved right in, and by about 18 months had dug a second well, installed a solar system, enlarged the garden, and built two storage buildings and a second, four-bedroom house.

Advantages of Buying Developed Land

- With buildings, running water, and electricity you'll have a "base-camp" on the property. One or more people or households can live there as early caretakers. People can have a place to eat and sleep as they build their homes. A house (or garage, or barn) can be turned into a community building with a common kitchen, bathroom, meeting room, and laundry facilities for everyone.

- You can save money in the long run, since the property will probably cost less than if you built the same improvements from scratch.

- Because you will probably add more buildings, you have many of the same advantages as buying raw land — you can design some of your site and buildings with your group's energy, values, and aesthetics.

Disadvantages of Buying Developed Land

- You have to raise more money initially.

- Because you'll mostly like do additional construction, you'll have many of the same disadvantages as buying raw land — expense, time, and potential burnout.

Fully Developed Turn-key Property — Move Right In (With a Big Financial Bite)

Let's say that you set out to buy fully developed turn-key property which will already have most of the infrastructure you'll need for an intentional community.

You could look for old YMCA camps, church camps, Boy or Girl Scout camps, conference centers, schools, or church complexes. "Often you can get a good deal on properties like these," says Dave Henson of Sowing Circle/OAEC. "Especially if the property is devalued because the buildings are funky or small, or the property consists of one or more small or odd-sized lots, or if there's no view."

Many forming communities have bought and remodeled properties like these. As we've seen, Sowing Circle/OAEC bought and renovated a live-in teaching center, and Lost Valley did the same with property that had once been a large intentional community. Shenoa Retreat and Conference Center in Mendocino County, California bought a former children's camp. Hank Obermeyer bought eight apartments in three existing buildings for Mariposa Grove.

Advantages of Buying a Turn-key Property

- It will cost you less in total expenditures than if you developed the property from scratch.

- After whatever degree of repairs or remodeling may be necessary, you can move right in and begin your lives in community; if you have an educational, service, or other mission, you can begin it right away.

Disadvantages of Buying a Turn-key Property

- You can create a cash-flow problem for your first few years of operation, as it will cost far more at the outset.

- In some instances, the cost of renovating damaged buildings and remodeling would be so prohibitive it would be cheaper to build from scratch, unless, like Lost Valley's founders, you bought property with huge potential for a fraction of its current market value.

- You may inherit a site which is poorly designed for social interaction and community glue; for example, the buildings are too spread out, or are not facing each other, or are not contributing to any kind of central commons. It can be poorly designed for sustainability; for instance, the flattest and most arable land is used for buildings or parking lots, the gardens are far from the living areas, or the homes are on top of a ridge instead of part-way down the slope.

- You may inherit poorly designed buildings with energy-hog appliances, low to no solar access (built on a north slope), or thin to no insulation with poor heat retention in winter and too much solar gain in the summer. Lost Valley, for example, bought property with a counter-intuitively planned septic system, which broke down every time it rained, and uninsulated steep-roofed wooden cabins in a forest which, though storybook charming, grew mold and mildew in the wet season.

- If the property hasn't been lived in for awhile you can find termites, rodent infestation, frozen or otherwise damaged water pipes, leaking roofs, or water-damaged interiors.

- You must live with someone else's infusion of energy and "vibes," or aesthetic taste.

- You can get yourselves in debt to the hilt, dividing enormous mortgage payments among too few people, and being eaten alive by interest payments while barely chipping away at the principal. This can cause you become so desperate for relief that you consider new community members not for shared vision and values, but with a financial gleam in your eye, assessing how much their monthly payments could lift the financial burden you've buried yourselves under.

Buying Property like the Professionals Do

As you've already seen, no matter what kind of property you seek, the process of finding land and shopping for financing can be a full-time job for someone. It's a good idea to elect one or two of your members to do this, since commercial developers — your competition — spend full time seeking properties just like those you're looking for. The property that would make a great site for a community would also make a great site for a subdivision, from a developer's point of view. So if you can afford it, do as Dancing Rabbit, Earthaven, and Sowing Circle/OAEC did and arrange for one or more members to make this work their sole occupation for awhile.

Commercial developers and real estate professionals use the following tools and strategies to get the best value for their money; there's absolutely no reason you can't use the same ones.

- **Find out how much money your group can borrow.** Whether you'll be seeking owner financing, private loans, or a mortgage from a local bank or lending institution, knowing your borrowing power ahead of time can help you determine your price range, and whether you'll want to add more people to your group to raise more money (and more borrowing power).

RAW LAND AND "PAPER LOTS"

Why do some parcels of raw land cost three or four times more that other parcels of similar size? The price of undeveloped property is affected not only by its size, but by how it could potentially be developed.

First, if it's in an area the city or county has zoned for intensive development it will be worth more than if it were in an area zoned for more restrictive development. Second, if the owner has already secured approval for subdivision and development — with approvals for streets, utilities, or other infrastructure, and an approved "tentative map" showing the boundaries of the new lots to be created — while the land physically looks the same, it's now in the "paper lots" stage and worth considerably more to potential developers because the time-consuming and expensive process of getting these approvals has been completed.

If your group finds desirable land like this but you don't want to subdivide or develop it as it's currently approved, keep looking. There's no point paying two or three times the price for approvals that won't benefit your future development.

- **Master current property values and "the market" in your chosen area,** so you'll recognize a high price and a low price when you see one — whether or not you plan to work with a real estate agent to find property.
- **Armed with this knowledge begin the search** — and consider all properties that meet your criteria, whether or not they're currently on the market.

Assessing Your Potential Borrowing Power

Experienced real estate brokers recommend getting preliminary information from local banks and lending institutions about how much you can borrow before conducting your search (even though you may not borrow from these sources).

To do this, each group member or household adds up four sets of figures:

1. Total monthly income
2. Total assets
3. Total amount of debt owed
4. Total monthly payments for these debts

With this information in hand, make introductory information-gathering visits to the senior officers of banks and lending institutions in your chosen area. Ask for information on rates, loan alternatives, and if they would consider loaning money to a group like yours (since not all lenders make all types of loans). Be sure to refer to yourselves as "a group of families" or a "group of households" — not as a "community" or an "ecovillage." There's no point conjuring up images of "hippie commie cult" in the minds of the (probably conservative) bankers.

Here are two do-it-yourself methods for making rough estimates of your potential borrowing power.

Add up the total annual gross income of everyone in the group who might cosign on a loan, then double this amount. This is roughly how much a bank would loan you. One percent of that amount would be the approximate amount of your monthly mortgage payment. Let's say you're a group of six people, and everyone's total gross annual income adds up to $250,000. Using this formula, you could (roughly) borrow $500,000 as a group. Your monthly mortgage payment would be roughly $5,000, or $833 a month each.

Let's say you found desirable property with an asking price of $460,000. Knowing in advance that you have this amount of borrowing power, and if you had at least $45,000 in cash already, you could offer $445,000, with 10 percent ($44,500) down, seek a $400,000 mortgage, and set aside $100,000 of the loan for repairs, renovation, and new construction.

The second method is based on monthly income. Add up everyone's total monthly gross income. Twenty-nine percent of this amount represents the maximum monthly land payment you'd be able to maintain (including principal, interest, property tax, and insurance). Now add up everyone's total monthly debt payments. Most commercial lenders consider ten percent of your monthly gross income to be the maximum you should be paying out to maintain other debts. If your monthly debt payments add up to more than ten percent of your total monthly income, the amount you'd have available for monthly land payments would be reduced proportionately. For example, if your group's gross monthly income is $20,000, that allows for a land payment of $5800 per month, and $2000 for other debts. If your group's other debts amount to, for example, $2500, then your land payment amount will drop accordingly, to $5300.

It's a good idea at this point, before starting the search, to find out the credit rating of each group member that may be co-signing on a loan, or otherwise contributing to monthly land payments. You can do this by getting credit reports on each member and reviewing them as a group. If one of you has bad credit, you might ask that person to bring his or her credit into good standing now, before your group begins trying to obtain a loan.

Method A: Working with Real Estate Agents

When it comes to finding land for new communities, there are three possible routes to take. You could work with one or more real estate agents, you could work on your own, or you could work on your own with help from an agent some of the time.

Let's look at how realty companies work.

Real estate agents enter into contracts with property owners for three to twelve months to find a buyer (called "listing" a property). The real estate agent markets the property with For Sale signs, ads in the newspaper and local real estate publications, a description in the local Multiple Listing Service, and by driving potential buyers out to visit the property. If the property sells during the contract period, the agent who listed the property gets the amount of commission agreed upon with the buyer, usually four to ten percent of the final sales price. The commission is paid to the agent whether the agent actually sells the property, or the owner sells it directly to buyers who just happened by, such as your group. Therefore, if you approach a property owner directly whose property is currently under contract with an agent (or, in most cases, was under contract within the previous six months to a year), the agent's commission will still be a factor in any sales price you and the seller may agree on. Of course, you can still negotiate with both of them about the commission.

Let's say your group decides to work with one or more real estate agents because they know the market and available properties far better than you do, and you don't have the time or energy to devote to mastering the local market as is suggested below. The first thing you should know is that, since agents list properties for the property owners, they are contractually obligated to get highest price and the most favorable terms for the sellers, rather than the lowest price and most favorable terms for the potential buyers.

One option, however, is to sign a "buyer's agent" contract with one agent for one to three months or longer. This means the agent now works for you, not the seller, and will try to find you property at the lowest price and best terms, for either a flat fee or a percentage of the final sales price, depending on what you and the agent negotiate. Look at the contract to see whether it contains a clause which says the fee goes to the agent even if you find and buy property on your own after the contract expires. If so, you may want to strike that clause. All clauses and fees in any contract with a real estate agent are negotiable. Experienced real estate buyers (and many community founders), strongly recommend paying a real estate attorney to look over any contracts before signing.

While some agents will work with your group as buyer's agents without any proof of your ability to buy property, other agents will not unless they, or a local lending institution, have pre-qualified you financially, and your group has a preliminary commitment for a mortgage from a lender. The agent may also want to first see the net-worth statements and credit reports of each individual in the group before working with you.

The kind of service you get from a real estate agent and the fee you pay for it can depend on what you and the agent agree upon ahead of time. You might agree on a full service package in which the agent takes you out on half-day or full-day property tours, or on a simpler service, in which the agent gives you relevant printouts from their Multiple Listing Service database and a map, and sends you on your way.

You'll need to find the right agent for your group, and one who specializes in the kind of property you're seeking. If you're looking for a rural location, start with agents who specialize in farm and ranch properties; if it's an urban location you're after, look for agents who specialize in commercial or multi-family properties.

You may want to do as Sowing Circle/ OAEC did, and write a form letter to all the agents affiliated with the local Board of Realtors or Multiple Listing Service, as well as any other local agents listed in the phone book. Dave Henson of Sowing Circle recommends adding in bold letters at the bottom of the letter: "Please do not contact us unless you have property that fits this description." Sowing Circle/OAEC didn't do this, and got calls about three-bedroom homes in suburbia. He also suggests that you introduce yourselves as "a group of families" or "a group of families and individuals," rather than as an "intentional community" or an "ecovillage." You don't want to confuse, prejudice, or scare them. (See Chapter 9, "Sowing Circle's Letter to Real Estate Agents.")

Whether you shop for an agent by sending letters or by visiting many realty offices, when you find one you like and trust, and who resonates with your values, tell the agent enough of what you want and why you want it, so he or she can truly help you.

Mastering the Local Real Estate Market on Your Own

Bob Watzke, a real estate dealer and developer in Milwaukee who has long been involved in intentional communities, encourages community founders to do it on their own; however, following his advice below can also empower your group and make you more savvy property buyers if you *are* working with real estate agents. He advises thoroughly learning property values in your desired area so you'll recognize a good deal when you see one, and acquiring and studying the following kinds of local marketing data.

1. **Market value reports on recent sales in the area.** Prepared by a realty company, a market value report demonstrates that the asking price of the particular property the realty company has listed for sale is in line with local market values, through a comparison of the prices and features of other similar properties recently sold in the area.
2. **Comparable sales books.** Compiled by the local Multiple Listing Service, these books itemize properties in similar or "comparable" categories, showing their prices and features. (Because market value reports and comparable sales books are prepared by real estate agents, you may need to pay a realty company for them, unless you're working with an agent who provides them.)
3. **Record of all realty properties recently sold.** This information is usually available in the office of the County Registrar of Deeds.
4. **Databases of recently sold properties and their sales prices, and current properties for sale and their asking prices.** Compiled and owned by local real estate appraisers for their own use, these can be made available for a price.

WORKING WITH A REAL ESTATE LAWYER

"Real estate lawyers can be invaluable — use them!" says experienced real estate dealer Bob Watzke. Your attorney can prepare and review your sales offer and any subsequent contracts prior to submittal, advise you on negotiations, prepare loan and deed documents, order title work from a title company, and advise you at the closing. "Pay your lawyer 30 to 50 percent in advance and he or she will give you even better service," Bob adds. "But follow up with him or her frequently, since 'squeaky wheels' still get the best service."

In some states, closings are handled by a lawyer who represents both buyer and seller in place of a title company, and the closing is held in their office. In other states, attorneys can act as brokers.

Bob suggests keeping your attorney in the background unless the seller has one too. "Ask your attorney to review everything you're supposed to sign *before* you sign it, not after," he cautions. If you find yourself in a position where you must sign a contract by a certain time and your attorney hasn't seen it, Bob suggests you insist on inserting the clause: "This contract is subject to my/our attorney's review and written approval within forty-eight (48) hours after acceptance or this contract shall become null and void, at the buyer's option."

5. **Comparable Sales Study.** This is a description, including sale price, of all the properties similar to the kind you're seeking that have been sold in the recent past (usually the last six months) in your chosen area. This is prepared especially for your group by a professional real estate appraiser, for a fee. (Appraisers are real estate evaluation experts who determine the current market value of properties by comparing the features and final sale price of other similar properties sold in the same area.) A comparable sales study will probably cost more than the usual

kind of appraisal (which determines the current market value of a specific property), but if you can afford it, this analysis will offer valuable insight into current property values in the area.

Most counties and municipalities have a zoning map of the county or municipality which shows how each area is zoned (meaning what kinds of development can take place within those areas), whether such zoning might be changed, and how to go about doing so. You can also look up tax maps, which show the boundaries of every property in the county or city. Through the tax numbers of each property, you can also get the names and contact information for each property owner.

Study your marketing data. By examining the tax records and zoning designations for various areas, and by driving around and looking at properties, you'll learn promising areas to consider within your chosen location. You'll also get an idea of the average cost per acre or per square foot in these areas, and which factors in these areas may be most significant in determining price — for example, the size of the property, location and zoning, views, access to water, type of soil, trees, and proximity to major roads. You'll learn which are the most desirable properties for your purposes, how they're zoned, and who owns them.

By continuing to add information to your comparable sales study, Bob says, you will eventually come to know more than the local professionals themselves about what's going on in the area during the time of your search. (You'll also have back-up material to support your proposal to lenders, appraisers, and sellers when you make an offer.)

"A well-informed negotiator — knowing whether any given piece of property is priced too high, too low, or at the going market rate — can save you thousands, even tens of thousands of dollars when you buy at the low end of the value range," Bob says. "Not to mention that you can save more when you are informed enough to negotiate your price and an owner-financed loan under your terms."

Conducting the Search — On Your Own or with a Real Estate Agent

Besides the obvious places to look for properties such as local newspapers, free real estate publications, "For Sale" signs, and any local for-sale-by-owner organizations, be sure to do what developers and real estate agents do —scour every road in your desired location by car. Correlate the map with addresses you see on mailboxes. Get out of the car, climb on top of it if need be, or bring a ladder to stand on so you can see better or get a sense of a property's view. Ask neighbors about various properties that seem interesting. "Do you know how large it is?" "Does it go all the way to that fence over there?" "Do you know who owns it?"

At city hall or the county courthouse, check on various properties; find out when they last sold, and how much they sold for. This is time-consuming work, but it does give you expertise on property in that area, and puts you on a near-equal footing with developers, who know the land as well or better.

Like Dancing Rabbit and Sowing Circle/OAEC, you might write letters or call owners of properties that interest you, or the owners of properties next door to those that interest you, if you can't find the current owner. You might say something like, "May I speak with you? You have a beautiful farm/homestead/piece of property here. We're seeking something like this for our group of families to farm/grow organic vegetables/build passive-solar houses (or whatever it is you'd like to do). Do you know of any other farms/homesteads/properties like this in the (whatever general area you're looking in), where the owners might consider selling to a group like us?" This kind of approach can open the door for property owners to invite you in, show you around, and possibly consider selling to you themselves. But maybe not. While you'll meet some nice people this way, and learn a lot more about the county, also be prepared to experience some cool or angry dismissals. Don't be discouraged; just keep going.

Like Dancing Rabbit, you may find property with an absentee owner. "Say, do you know who takes care of that property over there?" you might ask some neighbors. Or, "Do you happen to know how I might be able to contact the owner?"

Once you've found a few likely properties, it's time to start researching them a bit more thoroughly.

Investigating Likely Properties

With or without the help of real estate agents, let's say you've found several likely properties that meet most of your criteria. Just because a property looks good doesn't mean it will be suitable over the long run, so you must do further research, primarily involving water issues (if it's rural land), potential dangers to the land from natural causes or other people's plans, zoning and land-use issues, neighbor issues, and financing options for that particular property.

For properties you're seriously considering, make sure you get an Owner's Disclosure Statement (now required by many states), or a similar list, showing any problems with appliances, wiring systems, structural aspects, environmental factors, or legal issues that could affect the property.

Most experienced real estate buyers do a preliminary feasibility study like this on every property that fits their criteria, narrow them down to the most promising properties, and pick one that seems like the best choice, given the information they uncover. I suggest you do the same. Here are some issues to look into in order to narrow your search. Gathering this information can also help you negotiate a price with the seller.

Zoning. What activities, and what population density, are allowed on this property by local zoning regulations? What is the likelihood of getting a zoning variance, special use permit, or other kind of exception, and what might it cost? This is such a significant issue we take it up more thoroughly in Chapter 11.

Water. If it's rural property, is there enough water for your purposes? What are county regulations regarding the amount of available water relative to the number of houses you plan to have and the number of people who will live there? Are any springs, streams, or ponds year-round? What's their water quality? Have weather patterns been changing in the area? Have creeks been drying up? Have wells been running dry? You could talk to neighbors in the area and local well drillers, or pay a local well driller or a dowser to assess in a general way where they think ground water would most likely be, in case you'll need to dig any future wells. Does your development fund have money for drilling wells and installing pumps? Are roof water catchments allowed in this area? Does the county health department have rules about it? What would it cost to bring in piped water?

Roads. If it's rural property and you'll need to build your own roads, are there likely places for roads, or does it have too many steep slopes? What would be the likely costs for building gravel roads

ZONING AND THE GENERAL PLAN

Contrary to popular belief about individual property rights, county, town, and city governments have broad legal powers to regulate the use of all land within their boundaries in order to protect local residents from potential health and safety impacts of new developments. Local governments regulate land use primarily through a General Plan and through zoning regulations.

A General Plan is a document which creates an image of what the local area will be like in the foreseeable future. It describes policies and goals, and designates what land uses, population densities, and public facilities will be permitted or encouraged in each area.

Zoning regulations enforce the General Plan's land-use policies and goals by dividing the county or municipality into various use districts, such as rural, rural-residential, residential, commercial, industrial, and agricultural. Zoning primarily regulates density (the number of residents allowed per acre), building mass, setback from property boundaries, and parking.

Subdivision ordinances of the state, county, or city are a separate set of codes from the normal zoning regulations. Property owners wanting to subdivide property into smaller parcels and sell some or all of them must meet the conditions of the subdivision ordinances, which usually require specific setbacks, building size and dimension restrictions, density, and specific kinds of improvements such as roads, utilities, and so on.

Many local governments offer various levels and types of exceptions or changes to zoning regulations. These include rezoning, zoning variances, conditional use permits or special use permits, non-conforming use permits, and other kinds of exceptions. These must be specially applied for and approved by planning departments, city councils, planning commissions or county boards of supervisors. Exceptions are granted if the new development meets certain special requirements, helps the county or municipality meet the goals of its General Plan, or offers certain benefits to the area such as additional parking, preserved open space, a protected wildlife corridor, and so on.

Sometimes exceptions to zoning regulations are granted directly by local officials, but they usually involve a public hearing, where potential neighbors to the proposed development are invited to express their support for or concerns about it. Since the officials making the decision are elected, the neighbors, as potential voters, have a great deal of clout. They can make or break a community's proposed development project and affect whether or not the founders will pursue buying a particular parcel.

(which must be redone every five to seven years), or much more expensive asphalt roads?

Utilities. If it's rural property, do telephone lines or power come that far? If not, what would it cost to bring them to your property? What would it cost to dig a well? How much power would you need to operate a pump? Is the site appropriate for generating your own power through micro-hydro, wind, or sun (or some combination)? If it's semi-rural or suburban property, what would be the cost to hook up to power, gas, and sewer lines? Having utilities readily available to a site or having to extend lines to your property or create them yourselves can make an enormous difference in the amount of money you must put aside for land development.

Septic systems. If it's rural property, what are county health department requirements about septic systems and the amount of people living on the land (usually based on your expected number of bedrooms)? How well does any current septic system work? Does the soil perc well enough for additional leach fields if you'll need them? You could pay a soils consultant to walk the property and give a visual assessment of likely percability, and likely places for leach fields, and estimated costs. Or you could pay for perc testing before buying the property to find this out.

State of existing buildings. Most professional inspections take place during the closing period. However, if you're seriously considering a property with buildings, you can always arrange for an earlier inspection, to find out if there are any potential repair costs that would be so prohibitive as to lower your offer, or change your mind about the property entirely. What would it cost to repair or replace any foundations, roofs, or wood damaged by termites or dry rot? Does any plumbing need to be replaced? Do any buildings need rewiring? Are there problems with radon? (And while we're at it, do dowsers find any problems with geopathic zones? Can they be mitigated? And, going further out on a limb, is the place haunted? And if so, can you get it cleansed?)

Building codes. What kinds of building construction is allowed in this county or city? Could you build the kinds of buildings you want on the property? (See Chapter 13.)

Possible future problems. What might be any potential dangers in the area? Have there been floods? Where would flood waters flow on this property, and what might be damaged? Would floodwaters flow where you'd ideally like to build? Are there fire hazards, such as dry brush downhill and downwind from structures? Are there any ponds that would be dangerous for small children? Any marshy areas or ponds that breed mosquitoes? What has the property been used for in the past? Have hazardous waste materials been dumped there? Should it be tested for environmental contaminants? What would be the cost? Does the property have sensitive wetlands, or is it home to an endangered species that must be protected at the buyer's expense? Is the property downwind or downstream from cattle ranches, pig farms, or poultry operations with manure polluting the watershed, or from manufacturing plants or commercial agriculture fields with toxic outputs? What future development is planned for the area, or for next door? If it's rural property in a western, open-range state, how much would you need to spend to fence your neighbors' livestock out? (And if it's property in a wilderness area traditionally used by hunters, will you continue to let them hunt on your property? If you don't want hunting, is there any safe way to prevent it? Could you afford to fence hunters out?)

Possible legal issues. Must any legal hurdles be cleared before the property can be purchased? For example, is it owned in trust by a family, where all members must agree to sell it? Is it owned by a non-profit with internal agreements that it can only be sold to another non-profit? Is it part of a larger development project whose owners are placing design or other constraints on whomever develops it? Will any of this require negotiation with lawyers, and if so, what will it cost?

Neighbors. What would your neighbors be like? Are they progressive, "alternative," politically or religiously conservative? Would they welcome a group of families or households moving next door? If they heard the term "intentional community," would they feel apprehensive? Would they assume "hippie commie cult?" What is their lifestyle? Are they into loud parties, drinking, or drugs, and if it's a rural area, noisy trucks, barking dogs, hunting, or shotguns? What structures or activities can you see and hear from your property, and what structures or activities of yours would they be able to see and hear from theirs? (See Chapter 11.)

Amount of offer. What's a realistic offer to make on this property? Once they've found a promising property, some groups pay for an appraisal of that property to get a realistic sense of its current market value. If you've done your homework, with all the marketing data you've collected this may not be necessary.

Financing. If you're not paying the full sale price with the group's assets, can you arrange private financing, owner-financing, or bank financing for this property? (See Chapter 12 for more on financing.)

Taking Property Off the Market While You Do Further Research

After researching the most promising properties and comparing the results, experienced real estate buyers pick one that seems to be the best choice. The prospective buyer takes the property off the market in one of two ways; either by making an "offer to purchase" with contingencies in the sales contract allowing one to three months (or more) to conduct a more detailed feasibility study, or by offering to purchase the property using an "option to purchase."

If the prospective buyer chooses an "offer to purchase" and during the contingency time discovers that the property doesn't satisfy the contingencies, the contract can be voided and the sale doesn't go through. The prospective buyer loses no money, and tries again with the next most promising property, if it's still on the market.

Making an Offer with Contingencies

Let's say your group chooses a likely property and you decide to make an offer with contingencies. How much to offer depends on what you learned from your research of current local property values, how desirable this property is to you, the condition of the property, your guess as to needs and circumstances of the seller, and how much money you have to spend on this property to do any repairs, renovations, or further development.

Your offer proposes your sales price, amount of down payment and other financing terms, the date of closing, and all terms of the contract and contingencies of the sale. It may be accompanied by a check for a certain amount of "earnest money," usually a nominal amount that is negotiated between you and the seller, usually ranging from a few hundred to a few thousand dollars. "Never give more than you are willing to walk away from and write off," advises Bob Watzke.

The contract states that your group will buy the property dependant on your finding out and/or accomplishing certain things during the contingency period. This permits you, the buyer, to make sure the property is appropriate for your needs.

The seller may accept or reject your group's offer or make a counter offer. You can agree to buy the property at this new price, or make a second offer. After you and the buyer have negotiated the price and terms, you sign a sales contract, which (unless the seller doesn't agree) takes the property off the market for the agreed-upon contingency period.

Although contingencies are specific to a particular buyer and a specific property, a typical printed sales contract form (depending on the state) offers check boxes for many of the following items. Whichever items the buyer checks off (or writes into the contract) must be accomplished or learned to the buyer's satisfaction in order for the deal to go through:

1. The buyer's ability to secure financing.
2. A property inspection, if called for by the buyer, who pays for it.
3. A boundary survey, which, if the seller doesn't already have, the buyer pays for.
4. Determining any easements, liens or unpaid taxes that exsist, usually taken care of by the title company or real estate lawyer.
5. Tests for radon and hazardous wastes, if called for by the buyer, who pays for it.
6. The status of any mineral leases previously placed on the land, which the seller must divulge, as these constitute an encumbrance on the title (a limitation of rights to use the property).
7. Additional pieces of information or concerns which the buyer must know and be satisfied about in order to buy the property. For example, if you're subdividing the property into smaller, separate units that members will own individually, one of these write-in contingencies should be having your subdivision map approved by local planning officials. If this involves having a request for a zoning variance approved, that must be a written contingency as well.

Assuming all your contingencies are met, the sale closes. (If contingencies are met but you change your minds about buying the property and refuse to close, you may either forfeit the earnest money and/or face additional claims for damages.)

Offering an Option

Let's say you plan a large community with many members living on a large or otherwise expensive property, and so much money is at stake you'd like a longer time to research it. Or let's say you'll need a special use permit or zoning variance to build what you want on a particular property, and/or you plan to subdivide your land so that members will have deeds to their own lots, and you need more time to learn whether you can get the use permit or the variance or if your proposed plat map will be accepted. Either because so much money is potentially at stake, or it's not certain that you'll get the use permit or the variance, you may decide to take the property off the market for a longer period so you can research these issues by making an offer in the form of an "option to purchase." This means you pay a negotiated amount of option money for the exclusive right to purchase the property at an agreed-upon price during an agreed-upon period of time, such as six months to a year or more. This gives you additional time to conduct your feasibility study. If your group decides the property won't work for your purposes, you forfeit the option money. If you decide to buy it, or "exercise the option," the option money may or may not be applied to the purchase price, depending on what you or the seller negotiated.

The money you pay to learn whether a property is right for you — the option fee and any costs for permits, fees, and professional surveys or reports — is high risk. If you don't buy that particular property you won't recover it. You'll need to consider these funds part of the cost of conducting a property search and be willing to walk away from the fee if necessary.

You, your attorney, or a real estate broker may draft an option. There are standard printed forms for them too.

Two of the most crucial challenges for community founders are resolving any zoning issues and securing financing. We'll examine these in Chapters 11 and 12.

Chapter 11

Neighbors and Zoning

IN 1998, DOZENS OF PEOPLE from around the county began meeting on the Internet in response to Luc Reid's call for cofounders of an income-sharing community in rural New England. After figuring out a way to do the Formal Consensus process online, and meeting every few months to get to know each other and make more significant decisions in person, the group deputized two of their members to find property in Vermont. They wanted at least 125 acres near a town with attractive culture and a healthy economy. The property needed good southern exposure for passive solar buildings, accessibility to roads and utilities, possibly enough water for micro-hydro power, woods to ramble in, and areas where they could keep live-stock, do some organic farming, and operate community businesses. They decided to call their community "Meadowdance."

How Zoning Issues can Impact Community Plans

In 1999, the Meadowdance group found 165 acres of raw land with almost everything they wanted, just outside a progressive college town in Vermont. The property had woods, an old apple orchard and plenty of berry bushes, a large stand of maple trees for making maple syrup, lovely meadows, and a hill with south-facing slopes, and best of all, a jaw-dropping view.

They had intended to have about 20 group members before they bought property, but at this point only eight were willing to commit, so they forged ahead with a much smaller group, spending the next year in the land-purchase process.

The asking price was $250,000. They raised $130,000 from their own contributions (in $5,000 and $10,000 increments, with one family putting in the lion's share), and knew they'd need to get a bank loan as well, using their combined borrowing power. With the loan and their cash, they would make a down payment, bring in util-ities, build their community building, buy mobile homes as temporary housing, and start their software testing business, keeping enough cash in reserve to make mortgage payments until their business took off.

They created a Limited Liability Partnership to own the property, and put down a $10,000 option to take it off the market for a year. They spent another $10,000 researching the property, getting surveys and various soil, water, and other tests, and acquiring a state septic system permit and an Act 250 permit (a Vermont requirement that addresses a new development's potential economic, ecological, and social impacts). Their next step was to apply for a conditional use permit for a Planned Residential Development (PRD).

They had also spent some time designing their large three-story community building — which they considered central to their functioning as an income-sharing community — with apartments, office and other business space, recreational space, a large kitchen and dining room for community meals, and rooms for learning, the arts, and music.

And, since Meadowdance wasn't hiding their plans, when a local newspaper approached them to do a series of articles, they agreed. They later wished they hadn't though, since each of the three articles contained serious inaccuracies, and repeatedly referred to the group as a "commune."

At their first public hearing some neighbors didn't want them to get a conditional use permit, saying that the group's large community building would negatively impact their view. One of the planning commissioners also objected to the building's high profile on the hill. Concerns were also expressed about the amount of traffic that their project might generate. So over the next few months group members visited with and heard the concerns and ideas of as many potential neighbors as possible, and shared their vision for Meadowdance. They redesigned their community building to have a lower profile and sit lower down on the slope, and showed their redesigned plan to neighbors and the planning department, as well as giving specific assurances of their anticipated impact on local traffic. By the time of the second public hearing they had garnered so much public support that the chairman of the planning department commission

declared his enthusiasm for the project, and prominent local citizens stood up to speak in favor of it.

But another member of the planning commission now raised objections to the building's multiple functions. "To approve the conditional use permit," Luc says, "she required us to hack up our community building into three separate buildings, and accept stringent limitations on what could go on in any given building." The group was stunned; these requirements were unusual. Traditionally, the planning commission could either grant a conditional use permit or not, but they didn't actually have jurisdiction about what activities might take place in its buildings.

Over the next few weeks the Meadowdance group considered their options. By this time they really liked the location and had fallen in love with this particular property. They had conducted an enormous amount of research on it, invested $20,000 in the option and permitting process, and figured out how they could swing the purchase and create temporary housing for themselves.

It came down to having three choices. First, they could agree to the restrictions, and chop up their community building. Not only would this cost significantly more, it would disrupt the flow of social and economic connections and community "glue," which, because they understood the relationship between architecture and human interaction, they had painstakingly designed into the building. Second, they could appeal, and would probably win, given that this commissioner offered the only opposition, and she didn't have a substantial case. Third, they could just walk away from the property.

After much discussion, they decided on the third option. "We didn't want to fight the town," said Luc. While the commissioner was alone in her objection, the other commissioners weren't particularly outraged by it, and seemed to accept her new conditions. It was as if the town, through one if its officials, had said "No." Even if the founders could win an appeal, they didn't want to begin their community life on such a negative basis. So they walked away, leaving their investment of money and time, and their heartfelt connection to the property.

As an interim measure they bought a large house in another Vermont town, moved in, and kicked off their community businesses there. ("We later realized how hard it would have been to develop the property *and* start new community businesses," says Luc.) At this writing, several years later, Meadowdance has found and bought an even better property, and are willing to try again.

Zoning Issues and Your Property

The General Plan and zoning regulations of a county or municipality are aimed at regulating new development, and most intentional communities fall into that category. Therefore, the same regulations designed to limit the excesses of large commercial developers also limit what community founders can do. Zoning regulations can cover building size and impact on the landscape, as we've seen with Meadowdance, but most affect communities in terms of density and house clustering. And while increasing numbers of counties and municipalities now allow clustered development, the total number of houses usually must not exceed density requirements. If a core group of 20, for example, wanted to buy 200 acres in an area that allowed clustered development but was zoned for one house per 40 acres, the group could cluster no more than five houses on the property. Building more would require

getting a zoning variance, a conditional use permit, or some other kind of zoning exception.

Density is usually the central zoning challenge for community founders, since the greater the number of members they can spread their costs between, the more likely they'll be able to afford to buy their property and develop their community. (Communities founded in the 1970s and '80s didn't jump through these hoops because many more counties had few or no zoning regulations then. Ma and Pa counterculture could just buy an old farm and move in.)

As mentioned earlier, in the progressive areas where you'd think it would be easier to buy land for a community, it's often worse. Many city planners in environmentally aware areas such as Boulder or Amherst are already advocates of sustainable development, and would love to see more clustered development with open space, shared housing, passive solar design, pedestrian pathways, and so on. Appalled by the urban sprawl and acres of parking lots, environmentally oriented citizens in such areas often elect officials who promise to enact and enforce stringent "no growth" or "slow growth" policies. While such policies effectively restrict commercial developers from churning out more housing subdivisions or strip malls, the same policies also stop community founders from creating the very kinds of sustainable developments local planners and officials would most like to see.

One practical way to deal with zoning regulations is to do as Dancing Rabbit did and shop for counties that have little to no zoning and bypass the issue altogether. But, as we've seen, this can decrease the likelihood of members' finding local jobs, setting up the new challenge of how members in such a low-population area might make a living. Another way is to buy property that's already zoned for your planned use

WHAT IGNORING ZONING CAN COST YOU

In the 1990s a group of seven founders planning a spiritual community I'll call Ponderosa Village bought 210 acres in the high desert of Colorado. They tried to get approval for higher density than five houses, since their particular parcel had enough water for 15 houses. After being refused, the founders considered subdividing their property into six 35-acre triangular parcels that all met in the center like the slices of a pie, then building a large house on each parcel around the center where the parcels met. They would use one as a common house, and, after the building inspectors went home, they'd remodel five of the houses into triplexes. While they toyed with this idea for awhile, they didn't end up doing it, since they really didn't want to break the law. They eventually disbanded as a forming-community group and subdivided the parcel into six rectangular lots which they sold to others.

What happens when a property owner violates zoning regulations or building codes? Nothing —unless their violations are visible from the road, or if a neighbor turns them in. Counties and municipalities don't have the manpower to scour every back road and drive onto every property to enforce zoning and building code compliance. But they're duty-bound to respond to a neighbor's complaint, since the person lodging the complaint is most likely a voter and public officials must respond if they want to be re-elected. If Ponderosa Village had gone ahead with their idea they would have been vulnerable to any neighbor over the years blowing the whistle on the secret triplexes in each house.

A well-known story in the communities movement concerns Morningstar Ranch, a famous commune north of San Francisco in the 1970s, where a hundred or so residents lived in tents, tipis, and tar-paper shanties. Their over-the-top density and substandard housing worked for awhile, but after a neighbor complained the county gave notice that the buildings must be dismantled and the excessive population must disperse. When Morningstar Ranch refused, early one morning county workers rumbled out to the property in bulldozers, and as everyone watched, smashed into rubble every one of their illegal homes.

and density. While some cohousing groups and urban communities like Mariposa Grove have done this, it's not a likely scenario for your community if you're seeking rural or semi-rural land, since you're probably planning a higher density than such properties are normally zoned for. It's more than likely your group will be dealing with non-ideal zoning. Some things to keep in mind:

1. Often the goals and policies of a General Plan don't match the current zoning map. Newly enacted zoning regulations may not be distributed, understood, or implemented yet, or local officials may not agree on them.

Experienced real estate investors advise buyers not to believe anything they read in a General Plan or see on a zoning map, but get an official opinion about a property's zoning from local planning or elected officials *before* buying the property. Keep in mind too, that different public officials can interpret their documents differently, and in all sincerity may tell you completely different things. To protect yourselves later, get their opinions in writing.

2. You can research the history of a property at the County Courthouse or City Hall to see if it had a previous use permit that allowed more density than is currently allowed.

Sometimes a prior use carries weight with current officials. Would it have more density if it were an educational center? Was permission ever given for a subdivision? Was it ever zoned agricultural, and hence now be permitted additional people if they were agricultural workers? (And would organic gardeners qualify as agricultural workers?)

3. You can sometimes buy property with an expired conditional use permit, or one the county decided to discontinue, and work to get it reinstated.

Gambling with Former Use Permits

In the more liberal zoning atmosphere of the 1970s, the Farallones Institute secured an educational use permit allowing up to 50 permanent residents and up to 150 at a time for workshops and classes. When Sowing Circle/OAEC founders researched the property local officials said the permit would remain in effect for only three more years to give the county time to decide whether or not the new owners' use would warrant continuing the permit. The founders thought this was a reasonable gamble because they planned on hosting the same kinds of educational events the previous owners had, and they bought the property without knowing the outcome. Three years later the officials lowered the density to 26 permanent residents, with up to 50 allowed for courses and workshops, but granted the use permanently as what's called a "nonconforming use." (A nonconforming use is one the county or city allows as an exception to the rest of the zoning in an area, because it was established before current zoning use for that area took effect.)

Sometimes, hiring professionals such as a private land-use planner and/or real estate lawyer can make all the difference in keeping or restoring a use permit that's in question.

One of the first things Kenneth Mahaffey and Dianne Brause did before buying the Lost Valley property was to research the status of its former conditional use permit (called a "special use permit" in their county) to see if it could be re-established as a nonconforming use. They intended Lost Valley to be a community of 20 or so, with hundreds of conference and workshop participants yearly. They had learned that in the early 1970s, the previous owners received an extremely liberal conditional use permit for hosting public events — up to 50 full-time residents and up to 3,000 visitors over a year's period, as well as permission to build 25 buildings. While conditional use permits are usually attached to the property deed and follow from owner to owner, in this case its was discontinued because the former owners lost title when the property was seized by the IRS. The county had certain requirements for use permits to remain valid, including that there should be no gap between owners for longer than 12 months, and the property's density had reverted to the county standard — one household on a parcel that size, or up to five unrelated adults if they were doing reforestation.

Kenneth and Dianne learned that everyone who had wanted to buy the property before them had failed to secure the continuation of the conditional use permit. But as an experienced real estate investor, Kenneth knew you could sometimes challenge a county in zoning matters, and prove that a permit should be reinstated. So, even though buying the property with no certainty about the use permit was an enormous gamble, they did it anyway. (Experienced founders do *not* recommend this, since your group could be stuck with an expensive property you can't use. Kenneth and Dianne's back-up plan, in case they didn't get the permit, was for Kenneth to use the property as a family home.)

The two hired as their advocates a private land-use planner who'd formerly been employed by the county planning department, and a real estate lawyer familiar with the property. Neither had ever lost a case, and said they weren't planning to lose this one. The advocates said that, probably in three of four months, the county would cite them for having too many people. To prepare for it, they offered the following advice:

1. Don't ask the county directly if they're aware of the expired use permit, but test their knowledge of it by requesting something small and innocuous instead. This they did, asking if they could put a mobile home on the land, and learned that the county was indeed aware of the issue.
2. Don't approach the county asking for a non-conforming use, since the burden of proof would then be on Lost Valley to demonstrate that the county's ordinance about the required year of continuous use was invalid.
3. Wait for the county to approach the community, which meant the county would have the burden of proof to demonstrate that no similar-use activities had occurred during the 13 months between owners.
4. Lost Valley must gather documents to demonstrate to the county that the community's intended educational uses of the property would be similar enough to the previous owners' to match the terms of the former conditional use permit, and that those same kinds of uses had occurred on the property in the 13-month period between their ownership and the former owners'. Fortunately, the property's caretakers had hosted a Greens meeting, a men's sweat lodge, and several other minor events on the land which could be construed as public events.
5. Be as open and public as possible about their conference center plans and activities, since, after all, this demonstrated they were continuing to host events that benefited others and involved guests on the land, just as the previous owners had.

This is just what they did, holding large public conferences, workshops, and classes, as well as opening a youth hostel. They always made sure to collect and pay the county's required room tax on overnight guests. The county accepted their tax payments — a tacit implication of approval the group could use in their documentation. A year after they'd arrived there was wave of local media coverage of their activities, which also served to publicly document their use of the property for educational and public activities. Finally, two years after the land purchase, the county contacted them, and nine months later, after reviewing Lost Valley's excellent records of the former caretakers' public events and their own public events, the county granted them nonconforming use status. Up to 35 families or 160 people total could live there year-round, with up to 3,000 total visitors over a year, and they could build more buildings. The gamble had paid off.

Seeking a Zoning Exception

If your group finds property that looks promising but doesn't allow as much density as you want, you'll need to apply for a zoning variance or conditional use permit (depending on the terms used in the area). If your community plans include a retreat center, guest facilities, a healing center, or other type of service facility, you'll need to apply for a conditional use permit, unless the property you're considering already has one. And if you're planning to buy land and subdivide it so that members will hold title to their individual lots or housing units, you'll need to comply with the state, county, or city's subdivision ordinances, including approval of a plat map for your proposed development, and assurance that you'll build all the required roads, etc. Depending on the location, any of these will most likely require a year-long process costing $10,000 to $20,000 or more in permit fees, tests, surveys, and consultants (and probably far more for a subdivision), and involve at least one public hearing. And you won't know until the end of the process whether your application will be approved. Like Meadowdance founders, you may want to consider funds like this "the cost of doing business," and be willing to walk away from it if the property doesn't work out.

Depending on the state and the area, applying for a conditional use or noncomforming use permit, and possibly getting permission to subdivide, can require various tests and permits. These can include one or more of the following:

1. An archaeological survey to make sure the building and development sites don't contain artifacts.
2. A traffic study to determine the impact of increased traffic on access roads.
3. A test well or wells to find out if there would be enough water for the proposed project.
4. A septic and soils survey to discover whether the property's soils are compatible with large-scale septic systems.
5. An Environmental Impact Report to determine the effects of the proposed use on wildlife, wetlands, or forests.
6. A study to find out whether road width, grades, surfacing, and water storage would meet fire codes.

7. A report by the local building department about whether the property's existing buildings meet health and safety standards.

As we've seen, county officials and neighbors tend to consider use permit applications more favorably when the property was previously used to serve the public. "It's becoming increasingly difficult to develop a public facility from scratch on property with no public use history or zoning," observes Stephen Brown, cofounder of Shenoa Retreat and Conference Center in California.

The specific process of getting approval for and subdividing your property is considerably more complex and expensive than simply getting a zoning variance or a use permit. As such, it's beyond the scope of this book, but there are plenty of resources for communities seeking to subdivide.

Your first step in any of these scenarios is to write up an outline of what you have in mind. Visit with an official in the planning department, a planning commissioner, or county supervisor, or if the property is in a municipality, a city council member, to see whether your proposed exception is likely to be accepted. Ask their advice for how you can adjust your proposal to help meet the goals of the General Plan, and for the names of any other local experts you might consult. Meeting as many zoning officials as you can and seeking their advice far in advance of your public hearing is, along with meeting the neighbors, the best thing you can do to influence a positive outcome. At the public hearing you won't be an unknown group out of the blue, but one whose interests and goals are familiar to them, and whose members have already demonstrated respect for their authority and for the goals of their General Plan. They might just become the best allies your project could have. (With one exception — if the change you're seeking would actually change the zoning law itself, in many states you're not allowed to meet with any officials beforehand.)

Negotiating for What You Want

You can negotiate with the county to try to get what you want. In 1991, when Sharingwood community in Snohomish, Washington decided to become a cohousing community, they wanted a narrow pedestrian pathway to connect their group of homes and encircle their central commons. The community had legally transformed their form of private and shared land ownership to that of a condominium association, and when they applied for a building permit to build their common house, the county said their new status required that they couldn't have a pedestrian pathway but must build a regular city street with plenty of room for parking. Sharingwood members negotiated, saying it would alter their community's safe and friendly atmosphere to have a wide street circling through it. So to get a narrower road they offered the county two concessions — they'd forbid street parking (visitors would park in a nearby field), and they'd allow speeds no higher than five miles per hour. The county agreed, and shaved four feet of width off the road requirement. Now Sharingwood has a rather thin asphalt road with three large speed bumps, which is used as a footpath, children's play area, everyone's basketball court, and very slow-driving car access for members. It's not a pedestrian pathway, but it's close.

You can also negotiate a variance, conditional use permit, or other kind of zoning exception by considering what you can offer in return, based on the policies and goals of the General Plan. Does it call for clustered housing, open space, or what it defines as "sustainable development?" Tell the officials how your community's planned development will do this, and use their terms, even their phrasing, from the General Plan. If your property is in an urban area, can you offer public parking, public open space, creekside access, or extension of any urban trails or bike paths? If it's rural, do you have a wildlife biologist willing to testify as to how your plan will protect a wildlife corridor? Can you protect an endangered wilderness, wetland, or species habitat, or preserve open space and views, or keep an area permanently devoted to agriculture? One legal device which allows you to do this is a conservation easement, which is an irrevocable use restriction attached to the deed and binding on all future owners. Another is a declaration of restriction, a use restriction which does the same but is revocable. (Some counties give property-tax reductions in exchange for conservation easements that help land fit into their General Plan.) When Sowing Circle/OAEC founders were negotiating to preserve the high density of their property's educational use permit, they put their two locally famous hillside gardens into an organic easement, so that they and any future owners must keep the gardens organic forever. (See Chapter 16.)

Again, hiring a private land-use planner and/or real estate lawyer to help, as Lost Valley did, can be invaluable.

James Hamilton, cohousing resident and project manager of Stone Curves cohousing in Tucson, advises founders to remind local elected officials that members of an intentional community put so much time, energy, and heart into developing their project that they're likely to live there for many years and invest themselves in the neighborhood. This is highly desirable to elected officials, since, in our highly mobile society, in each election many people who once voted for these officials have moved away and the candidates must woo new voters.

Zoning Exceptions, Neighbors, and Public Hearings

Because the concerns of neighbors will most likely affect how local officials may respond to your request, you'll probably need to seek out neighbors, as the Meadowdance group did: listen to their concerns, and make a good-faith effort to gather all reasonable information to answer their questions, and even modify your plans, if possible.

Not all founders have known this. In the early 1990s, a group of meditators in northern California wanted to offer meditation retreats to their fellow meditators in the wider area. The group, which I'll call Valley Oaks Sangha, bought a five-acre rural property and renovated the house to accommodate retreat participants. They didn't seek the required conditional use permit for their periodic high-density use because they were afraid they might be turned down. So to call the least amount of attention to themselves, they interacted as little as possible with neighbors. Soon they realized they needed to build more dorm facilities, which required a building permit, which in turn required seeking approval for a conditional use permit and a public hearing. Again, to protect themselves from possible objections, community members said nothing to neighbors about their plans and were silent about the upcoming public hearing. At the hearing the county supervisors were quite willing to grant the conditional use permit and overlook past infractions, but not the neighbors, who had turned out in force. Although they would have had little objection to the use permit originally, they now vehemently opposed it, resenting the community for being so secretive and unfriendly, and for trying to slip the public hearing past them unnoticed. The supervisors bowed to public opinion and rejected the use permit. (Valley Oaks Sangha later established another center elsewhere.)

A similar fate befell a community I'll call High Mountain Meadow, whose founders wanted to establish an educational center for spiritual and environmental practices on a former ranch in the Colorado Rockies. They needed their rancher neighbor to approve a request for higher density and clustered housing on one part of their property. Although their relationship was delicate — the ranchers were suspicious of environmentalists, and the founders didn't like the ranchers' target practice on coyotes and prairie dogs — they had reached an agreement. Workshop participants would park in town and carpool out to the site, drive slowly on the area's dirt roads to keep noise and dust to a minimum, and keep their workshops relatively quiet; the ranchers wouldn't shoot off rifles during workshop weekends.

One summer in their second year of operation the founders rented their facilities to a group that led workshops on spiritual-emotional healing work that involved a lot of "express and release" yelling and screaming. While the group promised the founders they'd keep the noise of their workshop to a minimum, they got carried away, and soon the howls and yowls of long-buried childhood wounds went careening down the mountainside and bouncing off the cliffs. Three days of what was effective healing work for workshop participants was nothing but unearthly caterwauling to the ranchers. So, while the founders' conditional use application was backed by an inspired vision, an enviable cash-flow, and a committed group of members, at the zoning hearing the ranchers squashed it flat. High Mountain Meadow didn't get their use permit. (They succeeded with another plan several years later, however.)

In 1993, the four young Phoenix-based founders of a community I'll call Anasazi Ecovillage were all set to buy 147 acres of piñon and sagebrush in a remote county with few zoning restrictions and no building codes in the Four Corners area. Their property was near two towns — a hip tourist destination, and in the more remote county, an old-time ranching town. The founders mailed out a flyer describing their plans to friends and acquaintances in the area, and posted a flyer in each town. Although the response was overwhelmingly positive from the tourist town, one county supervisor and several people from the ranching town called a meeting to express their alarm about the project. To them, the flyer's terms "composting toilets" and "constructed wetlands" conjured up visions of stench and unsanitary conditions that would lower their property values. "Ecospiritual" meant the group probably worshipped rocks and trees. "Ecovillage" meant they were damned tree-huggers that would try to shut down the town's only industry, a plant that ground up aspen trees to make swamp cooler filters. At the meeting, the county supervisor said they could bring the group to its knees financially if the county insisted that the state's subdivision law applied to the project. This would require the founders to widen their access road to standard subdivision width, which would cost them between $35,000 and $500,000. "I know how we can stop 'em faster," vowed an irate rancher. "And I'll supply the kerosene!" Unwilling to deal with this level of prejudice and misinformation, the founders abandoned their plan.

It doesn't have to be this way. In 1994 when few people had heard of cohousing, the first public hearing for a zoning variance was held for Greyrock Commons Cohousing in Fort Collins, Colorado. After the core group described the cohousing concept and presented the group's proposed site plan, neighbor after neighbor stood up and expressed fears about increased traffic, "big developers" coming in to build houses that would block views of the neighborhood's open meadow, and apprehension about a "snooty close-gated community" ruining the ambiance of their friendly family neighborhood. The City Council didn't grant the zoning variance, but scheduled a second public hearing several months later to give the Greyrock Commons founders time to meet with neighbors and see if they couldn't work something out. This they did, making appointments to visit and sending representatives door to door to meet their neighbors and listen to their concerns, answer their questions, and describe what the founders had in mind. By the time of their second public hearing, like Meadowdance, they'd won over most the neighbors and the City Council granted the variance.

A year later, after Greyrock Commons had become a neighborhood which local officials proudly showed off to visiting dignitaries, an actual "big developer" in Fort Collins made plans to turn a vacant ten-acre parcel adjacent to riverfront park into a housing subdivision. The neighbors of the park wanted none of it, and sent a delegation to City Hall, saying if a development was going to come into their neighborhood and block their access to the park and the river, they'd rather it be that new kind of development "like they have over at Greyrock Commons." And that's just what they got. A new core group formed, and River Rock Commons cohousing

YOUR RELATIONSHIP WITH NEIGHBORS

Even if you don't need the support of local residents to change any zoning, you'll certainly want their support as neighbors and potential friends. The greater the contrast between your community culture and theirs — if they're farmers, ranchers, or other politically and religiously conservative country folk — the more important this is.

Successful community founders advise giving your neighbors every opportunity to learn that you're friendly, hardworking, and respectful; that you pay your bills; that you treat your children well. Ask your neighbors' advice, find out how you can help them, get them to tell you about their farm or ranch operation and about local history. Join local civic endeavors — the Volunteer Fire Department, the Women's Auxiliary of the VFD, the 4-H club, community theater groups, friends of the library, the local hospice. Offer to feed and water their livestock and pets when they go on vacation. When they're planning a construction project, go over there with carpentry tools. When they're going to pour concrete, show up with shovels. Don't preach to them about organic food or a vegetarian diet or what's wrong with the government. When they preach to you, listen graciously. If there's a fire or other local disaster, they'll be the best friends you have on Earth.

In 1971, when the founders of The Farm community near Summertown, Tennessee arrived in a bus caravan from San Francisco, their distinctive hippie appearance triggered alarm and hostility in local residents. So the newcomers behaved as respectfully and responsibly as possible with neighbors and townspeople, and made sure their checks were sound and they paid debts promptly. Although community members didn't smoke tobacco or eat beef, they helped neighbors bring in a tobacco harvest, and donated pulp from their soy dairy to help livestock-raising neighbors get through a rough winter. After a few years Farm members had earned such a good reputation in the area that rumor had it you could cash a check anywhere in those parts if you just wore tie-dye and had long hair.

was built there instead — maybe the first time ever that folks in mainstream America clamored to have an intentional community move in next door.

If your group needs a zoning variance, conditional use permit, or other kind of exception to zoning regulations before you buy your property, you will also need to meet and listen to your future neighbors. Don't send your group's most serious or businesslike members; send your warmest and most engaging. Follow Stephen Covey's advice and "Seek first to understand, rather than to be understood." First ask what the neighbors might want for the field next door before you lay your community rap on them. Don't bombard them with information or scare them off with environmental or sustainability jargon. Use the word "community" sparingly if at all, and avoid altogether terms such as "intentional community," "spiritual," "sustainable," "ecospiritual," or "ecovillage." It may be far better to simply say you're a group of families and individuals who want to make life easier and more enjoyable by sharing some resources and creating a friendly, wholesome neighborhood where everyone knows and helps one another, and where children and elders are safe again, like in your grandfather's day. If you're environmentally oriented and have sustainability goals (depending on what you're planning), you could say you plan to heat your homes partly by the sun's heat, or save money by generating your own power instead of paying a big company for it, or grow your own vegetables like your grandmother did. How could any old-time rancher, conservative executive, or Fundamentalist believer object to that? (But if your group is also into vegan diets, raw foods, meditation, emotional healing, shared parenting, cross-breast feeding, shared love partners, or channeling archangels, aliens, or entities from the Causal Plane — please keep it to yourself!)

Keep in mind that any local media coverage could be a double-edged sword. A sympathetic reporter with similar visions and values can help your case; but if the reporter (or the editor) is suspicious, ill-informed, or simply prejudiced against "communes," an article with snide comparisons or inaccurate information can negatively influence local citizens, future neighbors, and/or the elected officials who'll consider your request for a zoning exception. To benefit from any potential media coverage and mitigate against the effects of a potential negative spin, prepare a press release describing what you hope to do and hand it to any reporter who seeks you out. Keep it short and use your Vision Statement in the first paragraph. Don't write a self-congratulatory PR puff piece, but a matter-of-fact article in classic newspaper style. (If you don't have a group member who knows how to write newspaper style, hire someone who can do this for you — it's money well spent.)

When it's time for your public hearing, be prepared for the fact that, as in Meadowdance's case, some of the deciding officials can be inexplicably for or against a project, or officials who formerly offered support can suddenly change their minds for no reason you can fathom. Even if you've done everything you could to stack the deck in your favor — meeting officials and neighbors beforehand, getting opinions in writing, and hiring a land-use planner — you could still be turned down. If this happens, remember that, like Meadowdance, Valley Oaks Sangha, and High Mountain Meadow, a community can still follow their dream if the first property they wanted to buy, or the first zoning exception they tried for, didn't work out.

In Chapter 12 we'll look at the many ways you can finance your community property.

~Chapter 12~

Financing Your Property
(Loans You Can Live With)

WHEN BUYING PROPERTY for a communi-ty, it's clearly more advantageous not to borrow money at all but to pay cash, owe nothing, and be done with it, as Hank Obermeyer did with Mariposa Grove.

The major disadvantages of borrowing money to buy property are risking its loss if you can't make the payments, and the cost of interest. Interest is like rent. If you rent an apartment you're actually "borrowing" its use from the landlord. If you rent it for $1,000 a month, after a year you've paid $12,000. If you live there 10 years, you've paid $120,000. If you borrow money you're "renting" its use for some period of time, and the interest payments are the rent. Depending on the interest rate and the length of payback time, you'll pay considerably more than the purchase price when you include the interest. You can figure this out in advance by looking up tables of principal amounts, interest rates, and payback times in an amortization loan schedule book, available at office supply stores.

But since few forming-community groups can afford to buy community property with donations of cash from personal assets, borrow we must. In this chapter we'll look at how per-sonal loans, owner-financing, and bank financing apply to communities in which the property is not subdivided and members will not have title to individual lots or housing units.

(A good resource for financing and developing community property in which members will hold individual title is Chris Hanson's *The Cohousing Handbook*. We'll touch on this briefly in "Drawing on the Cohousing Model" later in this chapter.)

About "Renting Money" — What You Should Know

The combined borrowing power of your group means you can theoretically borrow money to buy your property as well as for a contingency fund for making payments, development (which can include repairs, renovations, and new construction), and land development. (Some banks may discount your borrowing power, reducing it by 10 to 20 percent, because of the inconvenience of dealing with the net worth statements and credit reports of a whole group.)

Banks and most owner-financers will want all group members to sign the loan repayment guarantee, along with anyone else willing to co-sign, such as family members and friends. While many people co-signing the loan helps your group increase its borrowing power, it's a double-edged sword. If for some reason you can't make the payments for a few months, banks (and most owner-financers) will repossess your property and sell it to get their money back. If they can't sell the property at a high enough price to repay their loan, they'll go after the assets of everyone who's co-signed the loan to recover the loss. It won't matter if you've paid 90 or 95 percent of the loan before missing a few payments. Banks (and some owner-financers) will still repossess your property; in fact, it's more lucrative for banks to repossess your property when it's almost paid off.

Here are some tips for borrowing money.

1. **Know your group's borrowing power ahead of time.** As discussed earlier, you should have figured out your group's potential borrowing power before you began the land search. This will help you determine whether your desired property is within the means of your borrowing power.

2. **Know each other's credit rating ahead of time.** You'll need to know about each other as credit risks. Ideally, you got credit reports for group members intending to be co-signers on a loan before looking for land. Look at the reports as a group and learn whether anyone has bad credit. If so, arrange for that person to re-establish or improve their credit before you seek a bank loan. If that's not possible, don't have that person co-sign the loan. Perhaps he or she could contribute to the group's cash needs by arranging a small private unsecured loan, which that member pays off personally.

3. **Get the property appraised ahead of time.** The amount you offer on the property will be based on its current market value, your assessment of the needs and circumstances of the seller, and how much you estimate you'll need to spend on any repairs, renovations, or further development. Hire a local appraiser to get the current market value of the property before you make an offer on it (unless you're already convinced of its value), and before applying for a loan. You'll want to know what a reasonable purchase offer would be, given the current market values in the area, and knowing that will give you a better idea of what an owner-financer or bank would consider a reasonable amount to loan you. Bob Watzke suggests that if there's a chance you'll seek a bank loan, use the appraiser your bank usually works with. Ask them who they use; they'll tell you.

Since the bank will arrange an appraiser anyway, why pay again for the same service? In order to get the highest loan amount (since banks will make a loan based on a percentage of the property's value), you'll want the property appraised at the upper limits of its current market value. You have the best chance of this if you know local market values, get your appraisal ahead of time, and pay the appraiser yourself. Also, if you already have an appraisal, instead of charging you a second appraisal fee, the bank may charge you no more than a minimal "recertification fee" — 10 to 20 percent of the original appraisal fee.

"Imagine how confirming it could be to the bank when they see that your appraisal supports your requested loan," says Bob, "and the signature on the bottom is one of it own appraisers." The bank will then have marketing data and an appraisal of your intended

RAISING MONEY FOR DEVELOPMENT

The amount of money you'll need to renovate or develop your property will depend on whether you're buying raw land, developed property, or a fully-developed turn-key property, and whether you'll do simple repairs, minor to major remodeling, or begin at square one with roads, utilities, and buildings. It will also depend on how many members you have, how much money you can raise, and how long you're willing to wait for your community to function as you've envisioned.

Lost Valley raised $100,000 to buy their turn-key property and another $100,000 to repair and renovate it. Sowing Circle/OAEC raised $150,000 for the down payment on their turn-key property and $55,000 for repairs and new construction.

Hank Obermeyer paid $485,000 for the Mariposa Grove property, and by the time repairs and renovation are complete, will have spent at least $200,000 more.

Buying raw land is quite different. Dancing Rabbit raised $190,000 for their land and $35,000 for their contingency fee and first expenses of physical infrastructure. Earthaven raised $128,000 as a down payment for their raw land, and an initial $22,000 for their first development expenses. Again, the cohousing model is a bit different; cohousers who buy raw land develop it all at once and then move in.

At both Lost Valley and Sowing Circle/OAEC, once the founders had spent their initial development fund, they were able to live on their property and begin their educational center businesses. And while additional income over the years has been spent on further renovation and new construction, most of it was completed early on. Mariposa Grove's renovation will be finished three years after purchase. At Dancing Rabbit and Earthaven, income from new members adds to the development process which will take many years to complete.

property that represents and supports the amount of your loan request.

4. **Don't get loans with penalties for early repayment, if at all possible.**

5. **Seek only fixed-rate loans.** Bob advises getting 15 to 30-year, fully amortized mortgages with fixed interest rates, and fixed mortgage payments. If a land purchase deal is so attractive that you've got to accept a variable rate mortgage, then do it — but refinance the loan as soon as possible to a fixed rate and fixed term mortgage.

6. **Negotiate for no payments or interest-only payments for the first few years.** If you're founding your community with fewer people than you ultimately plan to have, then you won't have as much money for monthly or quarterly payments as you will later, when more people have joined you. If at all possible do as Lost Valley, Dancing Rabbit, and Sowing Circle/OAEC did, and negotiate for no payments or interest-only payments for the first three to five years.

7. **Establish a contingency fund.** Bob Watzke and other real estate investors strongly advise that you create a contingency fund for times when you can't make your land payment through your normal means. "The last time in the world that you want to seek money from a lender is when you need it — especially when you're behind in your payments," Bob says. "From your preliminary market research, find out how much you are likely to need before you start looking for property. Establish a purchase plan and a budget that provides enough money to buy the property, and enough money to operate with, plus a contingency reserve; say, six to 12 months' cash reserves to cover both fixed and variable operating expenses for that period."

Private Financing

Lost Valley, Dancing Rabbit, and Mariposa Grove founders used their own funds or private loans and paid the sellers cash to buy their properties. Kenneth Mahaffey of Lost Valley and Hank Obermeyer of Mariposa Grove paid the whole purchase price from personal assets. Dancing Rabbit's founders raised two personal loans from within their own membership, one from a founders' family, and another from colleagues in the communities movement. Earthaven's founders raised money mostly from within their membership to pay off their owner-financers and hold their own internal mortgage. (For information on creating your own "shoe box" bank, as Earthaven did, see E.F. Schumacher Society in Resources.)

The obvious advantage of borrowing from founders, family, and friends instead of banks or owner-financers is that no money is owed to outsiders. If the new community has a financial shortfall and can't make payments for a few months or a year or so, there is far less danger of foreclosure. Presumably founders, family, or friends who loaned the money would be willing to wait much longer before it became necessary to ask for repayment or force the sale of the property.

When approaching community founders, friends, and family members for a loan, offer them what private lenders usually need to see — a clearly written, well-presented explanation of your community's vision and goals, a strategic plan for how you'll accomplish those goals and your intended timeline, and how you'll manage and care for your property. Create an agreement, such as a promissory note, that covers all the standard aspects of a loan.

- What is the amount of the loan?
- What is the length of the loan?

- What is the interest rate and terms of repayment? Will payments be monthly or quarterly? Is the interest to accrue and become due along with the principal? Is the interest simple or compounded?
- Will the money be secured by real estate or a promissory note with a personal guarantee from your group? Will you place a lien on the deed? If the loan is secured by real property or other assets, is there sufficient equity to guarantee the loan?
- If the note is unsecured, how will your group repay the loan if the community isn't successfully created as planned?
- Have you notarized the loan and/or recorded it with the county?
- If there's more than one lender, how have you arranged that each lender be repaid — proportionally, or first one, then another?

Here's where your real estate attorney can serve you again. Dancing Rabbit's founders wanted to make sure that each of their three private loans were in fact mortgages, so the lawyer not only recorded the loans with the county, but created the wording in the promissory notes and placed liens on the deed showing that the loans were secured with 9/19ths, 5/19ths, and 5/19ths respectively of any proceeds of the sale of the property if the community were to disband.

When One Member Buys the Property

Sometimes the best way — or even the only way — for a group to acquire property is for one or two members who can afford to do so to just up and buy it. Every community profiled in this book that paid cash for their property did so because one or two founders had the money. The clear advantage here is that the person with means secures the property immediately, freeing the group from spending months trying to raise the money while another buyer with ready cash snatches it off the market. The founder buying the land functions like a bank, financing the property for the group at a presumably reasonable rate of interest and being reimbursed over time until the loan is paid back.

This is what Kenneth Mahaffey and Lost Valley did, with members reimbursing his $100,000 purchase loan and $100,000 development loan over the years through income from the conference center business, and later by refinancing the property. And Hank Obermeyer will be reimbursed all but his own ownership share when the Mariposa Grove property is refinanced as a limited equity housing co-op. Dancing Rabbit is paying off its founder, family, and friend lenders quarterly, through rents collected by the increasing numbers of members living on the land.

Protecting Your Sole Owner with a Triple Net Lease

Many founders who could afford to buy the property for their forming community group hesitate to do so because they're wary of the potential problems inherent in sole ownership. For example, if the founder buying the property were to make all decisions affecting its property value (since he or she took a personal financial risk), other members would resent the power imbalance — a sure set-up for structural conflict. On the other hand, if decisions affecting property value were made by the whole group, the founder who bought it could resent it since his or her equity could be diminished by people

who'd risked nothing. The sole property owner would also be liable for any lawsuits or damages and financially responsible for maintenance, taxes, and insurance, with no legal recourse to induce others to pay a share of these expenses if there were a dispute.

If a forming community finds a desirable property and one or two of them could buy it, the group could bypass these problems with a Triple Net Lease (also called a Net Lease). This is a device that spells out the rights and responsibilities of landlord and tenant in commercial space rentals. However, it can also be used to protect a sole property owner from undue financial or legal burdens and spread the responsibilities of property ownership fairly throughout the group. A community can use a Triple Net Lease as a legally binding document between the person who buys the property (the Lessor) and all the other community members (the Lessees). It can declare, for example, that certain named community members (including but not limited to the property owner) have certain property use rights and restrictions, and are equally responsible for paying the cost of maintenance, utilities, taxes, and insurance. It can indemnify the property owner from sole responsibility for these as well as from any other legal or financial liabilities (although the legal entity through which the group buys the property should offer liability protection as well). A Triple Net Lease can include clauses that cover any kinds of rights and responsibilities unique to intentional communities but not found in commercial property landlord/tenant issues, and stipulate any default scenarios or remedies in the event anyone violates the terms of the lease. A lawyer familiar with both commercial real estate law and a group's values and goals can check over its proposed Triple Net

Lease document to make sure it thoroughly protects the property owner as well as all community members.

Owner Financing

In owner-financing, the seller is willing to forego receiving the entire sale price at once, and instead will receive a down payment and earn interest on the balance due. Normally the seller will want 25 to 30 percent down, monthly payments, and interest at a negotiated rate. The terms could be equal to, or greater than what a bank would charge. Rural properties are commonly financed this way.

But owner-financing can differ as widely as the circumstances of the sellers themselves. For example, Sowing Circle/OAEC had a reasonable down payment of 17.5 percent of the purchase price and generous terms (although, if you recall, the owner-financer demanded triple the down payment five days before closing). Earthaven's founders paid 32.5 percent of the purchase price and had to deal with unusually difficult owner-financing terms.

In contrast, the founders of Abundant Dawn had a far more straightforward owner-financing arrangement. In 1996 they found 90 acres of fields and woods in a rural county in southwestern Virginia for $130,000. The property was in a U-shaped bend of a river, with gently rolling wooded hills and meadows, a road, an old farmhouse, a cabin, and an open-sided barn. The owner was willing to take $13,000 or 10 percent down, and owner-finance a 15-year mortgage at 8.3 percent interest. Abundant Dawn's seven founders each contributed slightly more than $1,800 apiece for the $13,000 down payment.

If your group plans to seek owner-financing, take the same steps you would as if you were seeking financing from a bank and get an appraisal of the property *before* you make an offer. (In which case, unlike when seeking a loan, you'll want an appraisal at the lower end of the value range for the property's current market value.) Owner-financers will probably want to see each of your group member's net worth statements and credit reports just as a bank would.

If you're buying developed property and plan to improve it anyway, you might do as Sowing Circle/OAEC's founders did and negotiate for a lower down payment or better terms in exchange for a contract promising to do certain repairs and improvements on the buildings and infrastructure within a certain period of purchase, backed up with a business plan showing how much money you'd use for that purpose and where you'd get it. This assures the owner-financers that the property value will increase with your ownership and lowers their risk, since if your group defaults on payments they would probably repossess a property with a higher market value than it had before.

If you're bidding on developed property and you suspect your offer may be less than other bidders, you can use the same principle. Remind the owners that it's not just money they'll need, but many people on site most of the time to maintain and protect the property, which is something your group uniquely can offer.

Your real estate attorney should see all documents relevant to the property to make sure any note to the previous owners has been paid off, and that the seller has the right to sell the property without paying the note off first. You'll need a boundary survey, title search, and title insurance. Don't skip these in an attempt to save money. The owner could have made an honest mistake, and you'd have to live with it for the rest of your community life.

NO FUNDS? HOW ONE COMMUNITY DID IT

Let's say your group has few assets and little to no borrowing power. You can still do it. Community activist Rob Sandelin heard the following story from a community founder he met at a shared campsite.

In the early 1980s this man and his friends dreamed of creating a community in rural Oregon, but none of them had any money. They all had jobs of one kind or another, but each household was only meeting its expenses, not saving anything, and the group couldn't imagine coming up with enough money to buy land and start a community from scratch.

Then they had a very simple idea: Why not all move in together, and use the amount they'll save by sharing expenses as a starting stake? They drew up a simple financial agreement saying they'd put the money they saved every month by sharing rent, food, utilities and other household expenses into a savings account. Although each household could withdraw their share of the money if they decided to leave, in time, their accumulated savings would be their stake to buy property in the country.

They found a large rental house in their small Oregon town, remodeled the garage as a kids' dorm and play area, and took the plunge — eight adults and four children all moved in together. They saved money by buying food and household items in bulk, and by splitting rent and other living expenses. They quickly discovered that they really only needed three to four cars between them, so they sold their extra four cars and put that money into the account as well. While they learned many lessons about how to live together as a community, they managed to put away a little over $2000 a month. To their surprise and delight, in two years they had accumulated $50,000.

However, by that time their vision had changed, and they decided they liked living in their small town. So they formed a legal entity and bought a large home. They remodeled it to fit their needs and turned the yard into a large organic garden with chickens and two milking goats.

The amount they owed on the house was low enough that after seven years they were able to pay off the mortgage. Their friends all thought they had a great thing going, so when one of the families moved out, two others bought in as new members. The community continued sharing resources and saving money and bought an RV and a boat, and even took vacations together.

Not a bad life for folks who started off with nothing!

Bank Financing

Bank financing (meaning both banks and other commercial lenders), is probably the last choice of most forming community groups, for two reasons. The development plans of most communities don't meet most banks' criteria for loans. Further, if your property will be owned as a non-profit, keep in mind that most banks prefer to loan to for-profit legal entities such as corporations or LLCs. And, unlike private lenders friendly to the community, banks will repossess the property if the group can't make payments for a few months. Some founders, like Earthaven's, also didn't want bank financing because they intended to demonstrate workable alternatives to conventional development, including a sustainable, home-grown financing method.

Banks don't often want to loan to intentional community groups, as they're wary of financing non-standard or alternative development. Banks evaluate a loan application with the possibility that they may have to repossess the property to get their loan money back, so they want property that's attractive to the average home buyer and thus simple and easy to resell. This doesn't usually include projects with several houses on one unsubdivided property, natural building techniques, off-grid energy, composting toilets, and so on. The more sustainable, natural, and environmentally sustainable your planned development, the less likely a bank will be interested in it. An increasing number of banks are financing cohousing communities, however, which offer subdivided properties with individual housing units, and as such are considerably more marketable as possible resales. To get bank financing therefore, most cohousing founders have created standard housing units with conventional construction and utilities.

Meadowdance founders, however, were willing to get a bank loan for their intended property in Vermont. If private loans or owner-financing aren't an option, your group may want to do this too.

Most people buying property allow the bank to determine the value of the property as well as the amount of the loan. This is less than ideal because you have little to no control over the process. But Bob Watzke and other experienced real estate investors strongly recommend you learn as much as possible about the practices of local banks ahead of time. Approach them as fellow business people who already know the current market value of your desired property and the amount you want to borrow, and compare. "Here's the current market value of the property we want to buy; here's the amount we want to borrow; here's documentation on exactly how we'll spend the loan; here's financial and credit information on each of us. Can we do business?"

Unfortunately there's still another difficulty in seeking a bank loan. As the economy began declining in the late 1990s, many banks began having less money available for loans. This means that they increasingly depend on selling their loans to the secondary loan market — large-scale "bankers' banks" that buy whole groups of loans in bulk from local banks in order to free up money to loan out again. (One of the most well known is the Federal National Mortgage Association (FNMA), or FannieMae.) This way, local banks grant loans, keep them a short while, sell them to the secondary loan market, and get their money back to loan again. Unlike previously, many banks are increasingly holding only short-term loans in their portfolios — those they can sell to the secondary loan market — and hold fewer and fewer long-term loans.

This results in two problems for community groups seeking loans. First, banks are reluctant to grant loans FNMA won't buy from them, such as small loans or loans for nonstandard properties, because it means it becomes a long-term loan; they have to hold the loan in their own portfolio until maturity (like a retail business having too much capital tied up in inventory instead of cash). It's likely that the kind of property a community will buy, and its plans for development, would require a loan that's too odd for the secondary loan market, and thus not a profitable enough loan for the local bank to grant. (By the way, if you think it's possible you'll seek a bank loan when you create your legal entity, don't state in your bylaws or other documents that your decision-making method is consensus. FNMA doesn't accept consensus as a reasonable decision-making process, although they do accept super-majority voting of 66 or 75 percent.)

The second problem is that while banks used to tell a customer fairly soon that they'd approved a requested loan, increasingly they can only give preliminary approval while they wait for final approval from FNMA or another bank in the secondary loan market. The wait can be weeks or even months, although this varies in different areas of the country. It's possible that a community group can put an offer on property, seek a bank loan, get preliminary approval, and find out the morning of the closing that the loan's not approved, with enormous negative consequences to both buyer and seller. This has happened to several people I know, and it happened to me. If your group plans to seek a bank loan, make sure you get final approval of the loan — in writing — before making any plans to pack, move, quit your jobs, or otherwise change your lives.

But let's assume a bank loan is your only option. Besides the basics — that you know your group's borrowing power, each other's credit ratings, and the appraised value of the property — here are additional steps Bob Watzke recommends.

1. **Make sure your legal documents support getting a bank loan.** Banks will want to see corporate Bylaws, an LLC's operating agreements, or other documents of your community's land-owning legal entity. They'll also want to examine documents relating to the property for details about property insurance, permission for zoning variances, approval of any plat maps for subdividing, and to make sure nothing would devalue your property or make it hard to later resell.

2. **Research local banks.** Call a loan officer at each bank, and without specifically identifying the property or yourselves, find out whether the bank is making loans on the type of property you're interested in. Narrow it down to those banks making this kind of loan, and ask them about their loan rate and lending practices so you'll know the terms, policies, and procedures of each bank in advance. You'll especially want to know their preferred ratio of loan to property value. Request a copy of the annual report of these banks and view the profit and loss statements of the last year and the current year-to-date. Do they hold any long-term loans (that is, those unlikely to be resold to the secondary loan market)? If so that's good, since your requested loan may fall into this category. Examine the size and assets of each bank and learn who their directors and operating officers are. With this information, choose the bank or banks you'd most like to approach.

3. **Determine the amount you want to borrow and write up your own loan application.** The amount you'll request will be based on:
   - the appraised property value
   - the bank's preferred loan-to-value ratio
   - how much cash your group has and its likely borrowing power
   - how much you'll want to spend on a down payment
   - how much you'll need for repairs and remodeling or development and new construction
   - how much you've chosen to set aside as a contingency fund.

Bob Watzke recommends creating a one-page loan application document which describes to the bank the amount you want to borrow and the terms you want. He recommends using the name and street address or the rural route box of one of your founders, rather than a post office box, and not using your community name. Keep it brief, using the terms in the sample loan request, below: Borrowers, Guarantors, Purpose of Loan, Loan Security, Length of Loan, and Means of Payback.

SAMPLE LOAN REQUEST

Loan Request — $200,000
May 25, 2004

John Smith
1563 Northwest Skipper Lane,
Nathansville, ME

BORROWERS: John Smith, Jane Smith, Susan Jones, Cindy Brown, Ned Brown
GUARANTORS: John Smith, Jane Smith, Susan Jones, Cindy Brown, Ned Brown
PURPOSE OF LOAN: To buy property for our neighborhood
LOAN SECURITY: Property at 3563 Ancient Forest Way, Old Town, ME
LENGTH OF LOAN: 30 years
INTEREST RATE: 9%
MEANS OF PAYBACK: Monthly payments of $1,609.00

The appraisal of your intended property should be at least equal to, and preferably greater than, your intended purchase price. Therefore the ratio of your loan request to the appraised value should be better than what the bank normally requires, thereby adding to their margin of safety. This could make a substantial difference in the bank's giving final approval to your request.

4. **Create a document showing, in detail, how you plan to use the loan funds.** If you're seeking funds in excess of the amount used to purchase the land, to do repairs or create improvements, describe the repairs, renovations, and new construction, the expected costs for each, and your timetable for doing them, as Sowing Circle/OAEC did. You might want to identify the contractors you plan to use.

5. **Collect resumes, net worth statements, and credit reports for each person co-signing the loan.** The resumes should be brief and concise, describing each member's background and accomplishments. Don't include your community's vision documents or description of purpose or goals, which could distract, annoy, or turn off the bankers. Tell them only what they want to know and no more, focusing on your individual strengths and your ability to pay back the loan.

Use the bank's own form for your individual net worth statements.

Find out which credit agency or agencies your chosen bank (or banks) use, and from each of these credit agencies get a copy of the credit records of each person who'll co-sign on the loan, as well as for the legal entity of your group. Why provide banks with credit information they'll procure on their own? It will help you to know what credit agencies are going to say about you before the bank knows, which enables you to correct any discrepancies — since studies show that 20 percent or more of credit agencies' information about people can be false.

6. **Meet with the bank's executive vice president.** Bob Watzke advises that you dress the way the way the loan officers in the bank

dress, and ask to speak *only* with the executive vice president (or to the president in the absence of the executive vice president). If the executive vice president is busy, wait or come back. If a secretary wants to shunt you off to one of the bank's loan officers instead, insist in a nice way on making an appointment with the executive vice president, saying it's about a business loan.

What's the significance of the executive vice president? This is the person who runs the place, Bob says, and if he or she likes your group, you're in. (Remember to avoid terms such as "intentional community" and "ecovillage.") The executive vice president can usually poll the bank's loan committee or board of directors by phone. Besides, the authorized loan-commitment limits for the executive vice president or the president are almost always greater (if not unlimited) than those of other loan officers. And finally, if the executive vice president doesn't want to give you a loan, other loan officers aren't going to get it approved either.

When you meet with the executive vice president give him or her:

- Your one-page loan application document
- The appraisal for your intended property and other comparables and marketing data that supports the appraisal
- Documentation on how you'll repair or renovate the place (estimated costs, timetable, etc.), if applicable
- Documents for your legal entity
- Any approvals or permits from the county or municipality about zoning variances, use permits, or subdivision

- Brief resumes, net worth statements, and credit reports for everyone who'll co-sign on the loan.

7. **Negotiate simultaneously with more than one bank.** Some banks dislike this, feeling they are being "shopped," and they are. Nevertheless, you are taking a position of power. A bank will know you're talking to other banks because they'll order credit records of each co-signer (even though you've given them copies), and they'll see in these records that other banks have recently sought credit information also. You might avoid this by applying to all banks on the same day and providing all the documentation that each bank needs.

If you believe that these steps may be overly assertive, Bob Watzke points out that the your bank will most likely require that everyone in your group, and perhaps even your family members and/or officers of the companies any of you work for also become co-signers and guarantee the loan. This means if you were unable to continue making payments for some reason and the bank couldn't recover its loan by selling your property, it could go after each community member's other assets, or those of anyone else co-signing the loan. If you're risking this much to buy your property, you might as well tailor the loan to your specific needs and requirements. "Move as assertively as you feel comfortable without being overbearing," advises Bob.

Drawing on the Cohousing Model

Unlike the founders of most non-cohousing communities, cohousers sell housing units on the open market and build all their infrastructure and housing at once. Some cohousing groups have developed their communities themselves, or one or more members of their core group has served as their developer. But an increasing number of cohousing core groups have partnered with professional real estate developers, and such partnerships are often quite successful in acquiring, financing, and developing their property. In exchange for a percentage of profit (usually relatively small, compared to the profit margins developers are used to), the developer supplies expertise, an entrepreneurial "sixth sense," some of the up-front money, an intimate knowledge of the local real estate market, and established working relationships with local planning officials and lenders, architects, engineers, and building contractors. Group members are actively involved in the design process and in marketing the project.

If your group plans for members to hold title to individual lots or housing units (whether you plan to sell them on the open market or only to your own members), you might benefit from adapting some of these cohousing methods or working with a cohousing developer. (See Resources.)

Here is a brief overview of one version of this model, based on how groups have worked with Wonderland Hill Development Company in Boulder. The groups use three sources of financing: funds raised by themselves and the developer, the construction loan, and individual mortgages.

1. Funds raised by the group and the developer. Before the project breaks ground, the group raises at least ten percent, and sometimes considerably more, of the total cost of the finished project from assessments to themselves (with new people joining and contributing money at all stages of the process), sometimes supplemented by short-term loans from members of the group who might have

more money, or from cohousing lenders. The developer usually also contributes funds, management, and overhead, and will be reimbursed later. These up-front funds are used for what Wonderland Hill calls the feasibility phase and pre-construction phase of their process.

In the feasibility phase, the group creates site criteria, a preliminary budget, and a legal entity for buying the land (usually an LLC). Group members each get pre-qualified for mortgages on their individual housing units. The group chooses a likely property, puts a 60- to 120-day option on it, and arranges a feasibility study to determine whether this parcel of land will work for them. They pay for legal fees, promotional expenses, land-search costs, and the option fee.

In the pre-construction phase, they conduct the feasibility study, pay for any tests, surveys, permits, and fees, and get any necessary zoning changes. If they decide to buy the property, they usually pay a certain amount down and arrange with the seller to pay the balance when they secure a construction loan, which can be up to a year later. Some sellers are willing to owner-finance this pre-construction phase. (If a seller requires all cash, the group usually doesn't pursue the property, but keeps looking until they find one whose seller could work with these terms.) The group hires architects and engineers to design the site plan and buildings specifically for this property, tests the market to see if the housing units will sell at the projected prices per the current budget (and adjusts the prices and/or the budget accordingly); and advertises and promotes the project in order to attract additional group members and continue raising money.

2. The construction loan. This loan pays off the seller and funds the "hard" development costs — grading the site, hooking up utilities, and building roads and parking lots — as well as all construction costs for the common house and individual housing units.

A construction loan is granted only after the group has acquired property and met all legal requirements to develop it, has produced professionally-designed site and building plans, and has had everyone in the group pre-qualified for a mortgage. To get a construction loan the group approaches local banks with their developer partner. "Banks are much more likely to give construction loans if a well-known local developer is leading the charge," notes cohousing consultant Zev Paiss.

3. **Individual Mortgages.** These are usually standard 30-year mortgages at current interest rates, set into motion when construction is complete. Money from the individual mortgages pays off any private loans from individual group members or cohousing funding organizations, the developer's contribution (plus profit), and the construction loan. Money credited towards everyone's mortgages immediately pays off any private loans for the up-front costs and any money contributed by that developer plus a certain amount of profit. Each individual member household now owes the bank the balance of the sale price of their own housing unit, which they

IS COHOUSING CHANGING THE WAY WE FORM COMMUNITY?

As of this writing, cohousing is not cheap. As of 2002, buy-in fees for studios to two-bedroom units and a share in the common infrastructure can range, depending on property values in the area, from the low $100,000s to the high $200,000s. Three-and four-bedroom units and detached homes with shared common infrastructure are often in the $300,000 to $400,000-plus range. And yet, while cohousing communities are usually the most expensive of all communities to join, since the housing units are individually owned, banks do give homeowners loans for them. And developer-assisted cohousing communities do get construction loans. So, paradoxically, buying in to a cohousing community can sometimes — in terms of initial cash outlay anyway — be comparable to buying in to a non-cohousing community with shared land ownership, if you consider the cost of joining fees, site-lease fees, and building your own house without a bank loan. (See Chapter 14.)

As of 2000, there was one Christian cohousing community in North America, at least two with straw-bale houses and off-grid power, and in the forming stages, a vegan cohousing group, a Jewish cohousing group, and a group exploring self-financed, exceptionally affordable buy-in costs. I believe that increasing numbers of forming communities with specific shared lifestyles or common purposes like these — with spiritual, religious, or ecological goals; even aspiring ecovillages — will choose the cohousing model, rather than attempting the arduous, do-everything-yourself model we've seen in these pages. These forming community founders will prefer private ownership of their individual housing unit and shared ownership of common facilities, developer involvement, and bank loans, rather than trying to leap the land-purchase, zoning, financing, and development hurdles entirely by themselves. The successes of the developer-assisted cohousing model might just be influencing forever the way we go about creating intentional communities.

pay off like any other mortgage holder, through monthly payments of interest and principal.

Other developers who partner with cohousing groups do it somewhat differently. Chris ScottHanson of Cohousing Resources recommends that the core group first acquire the property and get the site and buildings designed, then work with a developer to build it for them. "The *only* reason to use a development partner," he says, "is to have the developer locate, acquire, and guarantee the construction loan financing."

What about Grants and Donations?

A common misconception among forming community groups is that philanthropists or grant-making foundations would want to fund a group's land purchase, but this isn't usually the case. Wealthy people and foundations do, however, often give money to groups or organizations whose vision and mission for a better world matches their own, who have a demonstrated track record of accomplishing their goals, and whose principal players have shown through past accomplishments that they use money responsibly. If your group is just starting out and you have inspiring plans to benefit the environment or serve people or serve spiritual goals — but so far no history of accomplishments as a group — it's unlikely you could get grants or donations to help you get started.

But by all means seek grants and donations after you've bought your property, have created a 501(c)3 non-profit for receiving tax-deductible donations, and have demonstrated for several years how you've benefited the environment or people, or achieved some service goals. Seek grants and donations for a particular project with a particular budget, timeline, and measurable goals. If you're an aspiring ecovillage, for example, and you want to teach others about alternative building construction or off-grid power, seek a grant for construction funds of your classroom teaching facility, or for work-scholarship funds, so that potential students can come as interns and offer free labor to help build the facility. If you get a grant or donations, spend the money the way you said you would, and keep accurate records. Send photos and the records of how you spent the money to your donors, with thanks. If your donors like what you've done, they may consider you for future funding requests.

Sowing Circle/OAEC got private loans of $40,000 and $25,000 with generous terms, because the founders were well-known to the philanthropist lenders, and were their colleagues in environmental activism. For getting grants, donations, and friendly loans, there's nothing like knowing your donors or lenders through shared activist work and having a good reputation with them already.

Refinancing Your Property

If you don't think it will be easy to live with your financing terms but it's the only way you can secure the property, consider how you might refinance it later. (Remember, avoid loans with early repayment penalties.) You can't live too long with high monthly payments, or with interest-only payments that will skyrocket as soon as you begin paying the principal, or with onerous terms and lenders who'd readily repossess. Earthaven, Lost Valley, and Sowing Circle/OAEC all successfully refinanced their properties and their members are now breathing easier because of it.

We saw how Earthaven's founders refinanced the year after they bought the property, creating the EarthShares fund to pay off their owner-financers and get control of their entire property. It was a good thing they did. The founders overestimated the number of new members who'd join in the next few years, and the resulting cash shortfall meant that for the next three years they couldn't afford to both develop the property and make their interest-and-principal payments. So they made interest-only payments for three years in order to build

HOW FINANCING AFFECTS OWNERSHIP AND DECISION-MAKING

Presumably, months before you seek financing, you'll have decided whether founders will make financial contributions toward the purchase, and what the relationship will be of each member's contribution to basic aspects of community ownership and governance. Here are some points to consider in determining these issues:

1. Will each founder be required to contribute an equal amount towards the purchase?
2. Will founders be allowed to contribute different amounts toward the purchase?
3. Will the amounts each founder contributes confer equity in the property, and is the amount of equity commensurate with the contribution?
4. Will the amount of contribution be tied to ownership rights and responsibilities, and to decision-making rights?
5. Will some make loans to the community that others pay back over time?
6. Will incoming new members contribute the same amount as the founders did? Will they contribute more, based on increasing property improvements and rising property value? How will founders be reimbursed?
7. Will the founders' (or members') contributions be reimbursed if they later leave the community? Where will the money come from to reimburse them?

In every community whose purchase we've examined, founders have had equal rights and responsibilities for the entire property and equal decision-making rights. But it doesn't have to be so: for example, a community could have contributors to the property purchase, but not others, make decisions affecting property value, with all members making all other decisions together. If the original contributions were loans, other community members could pay the loans back over time, and thus earn the right to make decisions affecting property value. But while this scheme would solve issues of some contributing money and others not, it raises issues of possible resentment or imbalance of real or perceived power in the group. As we saw earlier, Hank Obermeyer, as sole founder of Mariposa Grove, paid for the property himself. However, when it's refinanced as a limited equity housing co-op, each shareholder/member will have ownership and decision-making rights.

Dancing Rabbit and Lost Valley, in which only some founders contributed loans or gifts, different ways have been worked out for non-contributing founders and new members to reimburse the contributing founders. Dancing Rabbit members don't pay a joining fee, but pay a fee for the amount of square footage they lease from the property, which pays back their loans. Lost Valley members pay a joining fee and pay rent to the community for their cabins or housing units, which reimburses the community for their current (refinanced) loans. Incoming Earthaven members pay a $4,000 joining fee, and a site lease fee, which has increased by $1,000 every year since the founding. In 2002, the site lease fee was $17,000.

the necessary roads and buildings. They could never have done this with their original owner-financers.

And as we saw in Chapter 1, for its first two years Lost Valley made no payments on its two $100,000 loans from founder Kenneth Mahaffey, and for the next four years reimbursed him $30,000 annually — $20,000 in interest and $10,000 toward the principal. This meant that by 1995 they'd paid $120,000 total, but had reduced the loans by only $40,000. At this point, Kenneth was far less involved in the community and no longer living there, and preferred to be cashed out if at all possible. So in 1995 the community secured a $125,000 loan from Cascadia Revolving Loan Fund, and a private loan for $150,000 from friends who were members of their board of directors. With this $275,000 they paid off part of the $160,000 in principal they still owed Kenneth, and used the rest to make additional improvements on the property. In 1998, they refinanced a second time, borrowing $161,000 from three friends and supporters, and paid off the balance they owed Kenneth as well as the Cascadia fund. They still made annual payments, but their loan was in the hands of people who thoroughly supported what they were doing and were unlikely to repossess the property if the community ran into hard times. Since that time they've borrowed more funds for development and renovation. As of 2002, they owe $360,000 in total to approximately 15 different lenders, and pay $3,500 monthly in principal and interest.

Sowing Circle/OAEC began with a $700,000 owner-financed first mortgage at 6.7 percent interest, and two private loans of $40,000 and $25,000 at 5 percent interest each.

All three loans allowed interest-only payments for the first five years. For four years, the community paid approximately $37,500 a year on these loans, but as they approached the fifth year they realized they'd better refinance before their annual payment increased dramatically in 2000. They got an appraisal and learned the property had increased in value to about $1,400,000 (by 2002 it was probably double that amount). By this time OAEC had been offering classes and workshops for four years in organic gardening, seed saving, permaculture design, and other aspects of sustainable living, and had gained quite a loyal following in the region. Many workshop participants returned frequently, and some became friends of the center and regular volunteers for their monthly garden tours and biannual plant sales. Dave Henson asked one of these friends about the possibility of becoming more closely involved by providing a refinancing loan. The friend was glad to do so, and she and Dave worked out a refinancing loan of $1,000,000, to be paid back over 30 years at 6.85 percent interest. The community used this money to pay off the $765,000 still owed on all three mortgages, and designated the remaining $235,000 for further capital improvements and a contingency fund. Their monthly land payments were then $5,565 a month, split between 11 people, so after refinancing they paid $515 per person per month towards the refinanced mortgage.

In Chapter 13 we'll look at the common challenges of the development process, and how some communities developed their land.

≈ Chapter 13 ≈
Developing Sustainable Human Settlements

AS SOON AS THEY BOUGHT their property, Earthaven's founders wanted to began the permaculture design process and create a site plan. But in their particular circumstances this process would take a year or two, partly because of the rugged terrain and partly because they needed to get a boundary survey, since the former owners didn't know the exact number of acres or the actual location of all the property lines. At the same time the group wanted to initiate at least some rudimentary physical infrastructure in order to move their vision forward, but which wouldn't conflict with the site plan still to be developed.

Here's what they did.

Earthaven's Development Process

Earthaven's mountain terrain made creating a site plan and developing the property more challenging than for most new communities. Their property consisted of three converging stream valleys, flood plains, bottom land, lower terraced slopes, and steeper ridge slopes and ridge tops. (Unlike Abundant Dawn's forested mountain properties, Earthaven had steeper slopes, no clearings or meadows, a phone line but no other utilities, and except for a tumbled-down hunter's cabin, no buildings.) The property's once-fertile soil had been depleted by the unsustainable agricultural practices of its previous inhabitants, a small Appalachian farming community. The area had apparently been settled fairly densely, as a post office stood at the confluence of Earthaven's two major streams, and people had even settled in the small side valleys and cultivated the steep slopes. Uninhabited for the past two generations, the land had reverted to forest, and was in the secondary stages of forest succession when Earthaven's founders acquired it in 1994.

The first thing they did was invest about $6,000 in a boundary survey and about $2,000 in aerial photos and a contour map.

Map in hand, and led by Peter Bane and Chuck Marsh, two Earthaven founders who are also permaculture designers, the group walked the land to identify sacred sites, springs and stream courses, flood plains, erosion gullies, plant communities, land suitable for agriculture, potential pond sites, and potential home and business sites. They also wanted to get a sense of the optimum carrying capacity of the land and limit their future population to match it. The concluded that if they grew most of their own food their land could support about 120-160 people.

After several seasons of observing the land and getting to know its nuances under various conditions, they overlaid key components of their intended ecovillage onto their contour map. They identified sacred sites; land that would remain forested; areas for gardening, farming, and orchard; potential locations for ponds and hydro-power stations; the center of their village and future sites for community buildings; the existing road; and future roads and paths, and they mapped out residential neighborhoods for clustered housing with likely road access. They decided they would build only on slopes, and save their flat bottom land for agriculture.

With this knowledge, and led by their vision of "a planned permaculture ecovillage," they decided to develop the following physical infrastructure:

- A village center with a Council Hall, a large kitchen/dining room/conference facility, a media center and library, possibly shared workshop and commercial space, and possibly high-density apartment-style housing.

- Ten (later, 11) neighborhoods of three to eight passive solar homes on quarter-acre or eighth-acre sites, clustered on gentle south-facing slopes, each site potentially terraced in home gardens, and each neighborhood sharing a common agricultural area of bottom land, benches, and/or lower slopes.

- To help restore the soil's fertility and create food sustainability, they would keep as much water on the land as possible, through roof water catchments, swales, and ponds, rebuilding the soil in specific areas with layers of organic matter.

WHAT WE MEAN BY "PERMACULTURE" AND "ECOVILLAGE"

Permaculture is a set of techniques and principles for designing sustainable human settlements, with plants, animals, and buildings — and especially the relationships between them. It's guided by a set of ethical principles, such as "care for the Earth," "care for people," and "sharing the surplus." (See Resources.)

Here's Robert Gilman's widely used definition of an **ecovillage:** "A human-scale, full-featured settlement in which human activities are harmlessly integrated into the natural world in a way that is supportive of healthy human development, and can be successfully continued into the indefinite future."

Although the term was coined in the early 1990s, increasing numbers of intentional communities are attracted to the ecovillage concept. Some older communities have retrofitted various aspects of sustainability (such as building with natural materials or adding off-grid power) and now call themselves "ecovillages," while others, including some cohousing communities, are attempting to create full-scale ecovillages from scratch. Most ecovillage activists agree, however, that no true ecovillages exist yet (since we can't yet know whether these settlements are sustainable "into the indefinite future"), so they call these communities "aspiring ecovillages."

- An initial "base camp" settlement near the center of the property in which people could try out experimental natural-building construction techniques before settling the neighborhoods.

- Member-owned businesses on business sites in the village center and throughout the neighborhoods.

- Fields with larger-scale agriculture or livestock.

- Bridges across each of the three streams for cars to get to the center of the property.
- They agreed not to build on ridge tops, to protect their identified sacred sites, and to preserve their most tranquil and beautiful valley as a wilderness area, to remain undeveloped.

The process of mapping and observing the land, creating a proposed site plan and agreeing on it as a group took three years, and occurred while they simultaneously raised the money to pay off their owner-financers and undertook the first stages of physical infrastructure development.

Here's what their process looked like chronologically:

1995: This first year, they contracted for the boundary survey, aerial photos, and contour map, and began the process of walking the land and observing its subtleties in various seasons, adding to and correcting the contour map.

They investigated the process of creating a "shoe box bank," and created the EarthShares fund to raise the money to pay off the owner-financers more quickly and gain control of the entire property. (See Chapter 9.)

Most of the founders lived and worked in Asheville, 45 minutes away, so through weekend work parties and with the help of interns, they created a campground and cleared a south-facing slope at the center of the property, where they built an open-walled meeting pavilion and one member built a small hut.

1996: The next year, they continued walking the land and correcting their map. They cleared more land on one particular slope in the center of the property, and built a second road for better access to it. They intended this area, called the Hut Hamlet, to be the "base camp" cluster of small experimental passive solar dwellings of about 300 square feet each, which would serve as temporary housing until people could build permanent homes. The founders wanted to try many different construction techniques in these huts in order to learn how to work with locally-available, inexpensive natural materials. They also wanted to make their mistakes on a small scale first, before attempting larger buildings.

Using lumber harvested from the land with horse-drawn logging and a portable sawmill, they built a small timber-framed strawbale kitchen/dining room/bathhouse for the Hut Hamlet, brought in piped water from a spring, installed a small photovoltaic system to power the pressure pump and the kitchen's lights, and installed a propane refrigerator. They also built a clay-straw composting toilet building, a root cellar, three more private huts, and footbridges across the streams. They brought in organic matter as mulch and began creating gardens. Beauty was important to the founders also; the Hut Hamlet buildings had forest-green metal roofs (for water catchments) and, because of the red clay in the soil, the earth-plastered exterior walls were various shades of peach-pink and apricot. Several had earth-coupled clay floors.

Like Sowing Circle/OAEC and Dancing Rabbit, Earthaven was eager to fulfill its mission of offering sustainability education, so that second year they began presenting classes and workshops in the small open-walled pavilion. By this time, because they had rudimentary housing and other facilities, a few people lived in the Hut Hamlet year round.

1997: The third year, they finished adding details to their map. Their permaculture designers proposed a detailed site plan, and over a series of meetings, the group modified and approved it.

This was the year they paid off their owner-financers and could finally develop their whole property, so they began building roads to their identified neighborhoods. They built more huts in the Hut Hamlet, and logged and milled timbers for their planned 13-sided Council Hall. A few more members moved to the land.

1998: The fourth year, they continued building roads to the neighborhoods, cleared an area in their planned village center, erected the timber framing for their Council Hall, and installed a micro-hydro system in the stream across the road. Several members formed the worker-owned Forestry Co-op to fell and mill timber and do construction, and they set up a portable sawmill and lumberyard in the village center.

The community finally had enough revenue from the joining fees and site lease fees of incoming members to pay not only for ongoing development projects like these, but to start reimbursing principal to the EarthShares fund, instead of paying interest only. By this time about 15 people had moved to the land.

1999: The fifth year, they created a small constructed wetlands to handle the Hut Hamlet's graywater, built a three-story multi-unit dwelling to house couples with young children, and set up a visitor's campground across the creek. They put a roof on the Council Hall and filled in its walls (with strawbale, straw clay, and cob), and began holding meetings there. Several members began construction on their shared community building in one of the neighborhoods.

2000: The sixth year, they remodeled and improved the kitchen/dining room in the Hut Hamlet. More founders and new members moved from town onto the land and built dwellings in the Hut Hamlet and/or broke ground on permanent homes in the neighborhoods. By this time about 25 people lived there.

2001: The seventh year, they finished plastering the interior of the Council Hall, and built another root cellar. One member built and opened a small general store and a lodge which will one day be a members' cafe. Another member raised funds for and organized volunteer labor to build a sauna.

2002: The eighth year, they completed a large water tank above the Hut Hamlet to improve its water supply and extended piped water to other nearby areas. They finished plastering the exterior of the Council Hall and installed its wooden floor. One family built a large house to serve as a permanent home for themselves, and as temporary lodging for visitors and other members who were building their homes. Another group leased adjacent home sites and began building a two-story townhouse-style common-wall building with small individual units and a shared kitchen and other common facilities. And at long last, eight years into the project, they finally had the funds, the labor, and the know-how to build their first bridge across a creek ford.

By this time about 35 people lived full time on the land.

By Earthhaven members' standards, and those of many of its visitors over the years, theirs has been an excruciatingly slow development process, and it isn't over yet. Even though your community may not buy undeveloped mountain land with no utilities, and you may not intend to build a whole village, Earthaven's story illustrates many aspects of the process you'll face in developing your property, or in renovating buildings and adding new construction to it.

Listening to your Land

A community site plan depicts how its buildings and other human-made features (courtyards, common greens, children's play areas, gardens, orchards, agricultural fields, ponds, roads, bridges, pathways, parking areas, and so on) are situated in relation to each other and to natural landscape features such as clearings, woods, streams, naturally occurring ponds, wetlands, and so on.

One of the principles of permaculture design is that for human settlements to be sustainable, they must adapt themselves to the needs of the ecosystems they inhabit. So a permaculture-based site plan also shows how the human-made features will enhance and mutually reinforce the needs of the land, its living creatures, and its human inhabitants.

Permaculture designers and experienced community founders strongly suggest creating your site plan before locating any homes or community buildings on your property, rather than finding a likely spot for the first building and then making up a plan as you go along. And creating a permaculture-based site plan requires getting to know your property intimately first — "listening to the land" over several seasons to understand its needs.

"I have had numerous occasions to work with intentional communities," observes permaculture designer Ted Butchart. "I have been struck by the subtle but important contribution made by the community members who first pierce through to a real connection with their particular land. They have a clear sense of the spirit of that land,

and that guides them in making decisions that will lead to sustainability."

Ted notes that the usual approach to land development in our culture is to see the land itself simply as "an exploitable resource: a blank canvas with a certain topology for us to place our buildings and roads upon." To take a more sustainable approach, he suggests we must first see our community land as a long-term dwelling place both for humans and the other creatures living there. Secondly, he suggests "we must seek out the soul of that land, the spirit of the place. What is sacred, untouchable? What is inspiring or uplifting?" One quick method, he says, is to find the most beautiful place on the property, then build somewhere else. Lastly, he says, "design the built environment with an eye for minimal harm and maximum enrichment of the place." As we've seen, Earthaven founders followed these design principles.

The other communities we've studied have engaged in a similar process. Dancing Rabbit observed their land for several seasons, studied permaculture design principles as a group, and created a permaculture-based site plan for their 280 acres. Even though their properties were already developed, Lost Valley, Sowing Circle/OAEC, and Abundant Dawn created land-use policies and other agreements about how they would sustainably develop the rest of their land and engage in any new construction. Four communities we've studied — Earthaven, Dancing Rabbit, Sowing Circle/OAEC, and Lost Valley — offer classes and workshops in permaculture design or sustainable earth-based building practices, or both.

Creating your Site Plan Yourselves

"How well we succeed in manifesting our vision of a new village culture at Earthaven will be determined by the quality of the work we do as both social and permaculture designers," observes Chuck Marsh. "Most community failures stem from inadequate design, either social or physical. Design takes time, but up-front investment in good design will more than pay for itself in the long-term health of the community and its members."

He notes that while in mainstream culture design and planning are usually relegated to professionals, in communities this can be disempowering to members who are directly affected by the decisions. Like most permaculture designers, Chuck suggests that communities get training in permaculture design principles, and, perhaps with the guidance of a permaculture designer, create their site plan themselves. "Community-based design and planning, while a much slower and occasionally frustrating process, has the distinct advantage of investing the participants in an outcome that is more likely to meet their real needs."

Here's how Zuni Mountain Sanctuary went about the process. In the 1990s, permaculture designer Ben Haggard was hired to help this 315-acre community in northern New Mexico develop a permaculture-based site plan. The group began with an in-depth study of permaculture, then assessed their site for wind patterns, erosion patterns, and evidence of past fires and floods, and learned something about their region's soils and plant and animal communities. "Zuni Mountain residents identified the most appropriate locations for buildings, gardens, agroforestry, sacred places, and wildlife corridors," Ben Haggard recalls. "They listened to the land, allowing its potentials and liabilities to dictate the pattern of development."

He describes a portion of one of their draft site plans: "A single, short, easy-to-maintain road offers access to a tightly clustered village center surrounding agricultural fields and a spring-fed pond. This road gets good solar access, so it's less likely to be icy in winter and muddy in summer. It's on contour, so it can prevent erosion. It's just above the orchard, so runoff from the road surface can be used for irrigating trees. It's perpendicular to prevailing winds and the direction of greatest fire danger, so it's an ideal firebreak. And it leaves the majority of the property free from incursion by automobiles, minimizing potential pollution and maximizing open space and wildlife areas. Zuni Mountain members took on an ambitious and complex project that few could afford or had the experience to build as individuals. Their efforts will leave the land healthier than they found it."

Avoiding "Urban Refugee Syndrome"

"Many of us have been so traumatized by the fast pace of modern life that we feel we need lots of space around us to protect us from a harsh and dangerous world," says Chuck Marsh. "I find that one of the greatest challenges at Earthaven is to find ways to meet people's privacy needs while keeping our homesites compact and not sprawled all over the landscape."

Ben Haggard calls this tendency to spread out "urban refugee syndrome."

"Urban and suburban people, afraid of the potential lack of privacy in villages and close-knit communities, scatter across the landscape looking for a place to hide," he says. "This only repeats in microcosm the worst mistakes of suburban development — destructive, repetitive sprawl. Networks of paths and roads proliferate, requiring maintenance, creating erosion scars, and disrupting wildlife. The costs of distributing water, energy, or wastes go up. Communication becomes more difficult. Often these siting decisions assume that residents will remain young and healthy forever."

Before Zuni Mountain Sanctuary members learned about permaculture, one member had planned his house site far from the community center. Like all Zuni Mountain members, he would have to first build his house, requiring the delivery of construction materials and water (for concrete). Ben Haggard pointed out that a remote location requires its own access road and, in the fragile ecosystem of New Mexico's high desert, even driving over the ground once leaves a permanent scar. And this house, like all houses, would require ongoing work and materials to maintain. And even well-designed solar houses require fuel — firewood or propane for backup heat during the bitterly cold winters.

Ben also pointed out that having a home so far from the center of the community would make life harder in an environment where life is already hard enough. Forgetting a necessary tool, for example, would require a long hike home, sometimes in harsh weather. "I've noticed that in spread-out communities, people simply adjust to not having what they need. The daily effort of getting from one place to another hampers residents' ability to do their work. Individuals and the whole community suffer as workloads become overwhelming and maintenance of people and infrastructure is neglected."

Ben asked the member to imagine the 20 or more proposed members' homes placed as isolated dwellings around the land. "He saw that such a pattern would eliminate the most desirable open space of the community," Ben said. "Anywhere one walked would be someone's backyard." The member agreed, finally persuaded that clustered housing would allow optimal use of the best areas for building and maintain the integrity of the commons.

Creating Privacy in the Midst of Community

Yet the desire to spread out is understandable. The greatest fear of many people choosing community is that they won't have enough privacy. However, Danish cohousing residents, who've been living in densely clustered townhouse-style housing units since the late 1960s, and cohousing architects Kathryn McCamant and Charles Durrett know very well that not having enough privacy is rarely a complaint of people living in this kind of community housing. "People find that once they close their door, their unit is as private as any private housing," says Kathryn McCamant.

"It's much easier to get solitude in the midst of community than to get community in the midst of solitude," observes Winslow Cohousing member Tom Moench.

Since privacy is a real issue, we need to find ways to create sustainable development *and* meet our needs for privacy. Fortunately, there are several things we can do. One is to arrange living spaces so that front doors and front porches (and often, kitchen windows) — the "public" side of a dwelling — face the front doors and public sides of other dwellings, and locate living rooms and bedrooms in the rear "private" side, facing away from other dwellings and into rear patios or back yards (with no public sides facing into anyone else's back yards). Another is careful window placement, so that windows don't look out into other neighbors' windows. A third way is to effectively sound-insulate exterior walls, especially common walls between separate housing units, and use windows and doors that close snugly, to create more sound privacy between neighbors.

"Until your needs for privacy and autonomy are met," says Boulder architect David Barrett, "you can't really do community."

Designing for Conviviality

A community site plan can enhance social interaction and "community glue," what Chuck Marsh calls "designing for conviviality."

"Designing for conviviality involves placing our access ways and buildings in patterns that allow for, and in fact encourage, quality human interactions as we go about our daily activities," says Chuck Marsh. Some of these patterns include:

Visual connection. Designers use "line of sight" to help people feel more connected. If you can see the community building from your front porch or kitchen window, it tends to make you feel more connected to it and inclined to visit and use it. If you can see other members' homes from your front porch or kitchen window, it tends to make you feel more connected to the people who live in those homes and more inclined to visit and interact with them. It creates the feeling of a cozy neighborhood, for example, if dwellings are aligned so that their front porches or patios and kitchen windows face each other, so everyone has views of other members' homes.

Cozy distance. How far away buildings are from a well-traveled common pathway also affects the sense of community. In a study conducted in the 1990s, cohousing architects and members of a Davis, California cohousing community found that the coziest and most charming "felt space" for a front porch from a common pathway was about ten feet.

Prominence. For a shared community building to be well-utilized, and to become a beloved and inspiring symbol of the community, it should be more visually prominent than other buildings and placed in a central area where people can see

it from their front porches and kitchen windows. To take advantage of these "conviviality" patterns, cohousing communities are often designed with their dwellings in rows facing each other across a narrow or oblong central commons, about ten feet from an encircling pedestrian pathway, with their large community building at one end of the central commons in full sight of every home.

Footpaths, gathering nodes, and centripetal energy. The flow of foot traffic can also encourage social connection, and the path of car traffic can disrupt it. Having a limited number of pedestrian pathways between destinations with natural congregating places en route — gazebos, shaded benches, picnic tables, and so on — encourages people to spontaneously encounter each other and have conversations. Locating parking at the edge of the site, having the pathway between the parking area and the homes pass by the front of the community building, and having individual mailboxes and a community bulletin board located in the community building encourage people to stop in at the community building while walking to and from their homes and cars, where they're likely to meet others and connect. Design features like these create a concentrated, centripetal energy, rather than a dispersed, centrifugal energy.

"In good design, conviviality happens spontaneously among the inhabitants of the settlement because the physical spaces are 'tuned' to the wisdom of our bodies," Chuck says. "Buildings create positive outdoor spaces; entrances are prominent and transitions are marked by gateways; paths meander and cross; places to sit or to tarry are frequent, people feel safe to sleep in public or to make love in the woods. Permaculture design should nourish not only the Earth and our bodies, but also the individual's soul and the group soul."

Earthaven's members utilized many of these principles in their site plan. Their roads and footpaths follow the terrain and lead naturally to members encountering one another as they walk between the kitchen/dining room, dwellings in the Hut Hamlet, the general store, or the Council Hall. Home sites in the neighborhoods are clustered. The kitchen/dining room with its

YOUR COMMUNITY BUILDING

Community buildings are as varied as the communities they're part of. They can range from a single structure housing a kitchen/dining area and meeting space, or they can include these functions and more: dance space, daycare facilities, teen hangout rooms, laundry facilities, and workshops, to name a few. Some community buildings feature separate structures for different activities. (A good resource is the "Pattern Language for the Village" in *A Pattern Language,* by Christopher Alexander et al. See Resources.)

A well-designed community building can literally help create cohesiveness, give the feeling of a central "hearth," and be a source of pleasure, joy, and pride for its members. Here are some design tips to help you design such a center.

Put all your eggs in one basket. For better social interaction, to effectively "design for conviviality," as well as to save money, it works best to have relatively small individual living spaces and larger community buildings with many amenities.

Make it prominent. Many communities use architect Christopher Alexander's principles of "building archetypes" in *A Pattern Language* for creating a warm and inviting built environment that invites community spirit. One of his principles is that the primary community building in any given location be taller, bigger, or somehow more visually prominent than other structures around it.

Put it at the "heart." It should also be accessible, both visually through "line of sight," and by footpath, from many other locations around the community.

Make it beautiful. Cohousing architects Kathryn McCamant and Chuck Durrett, as well as Christopher Alexander, insist that for a community building to function well and be used by its members, it must be beautiful. Ideally, it inspires and uplifts the members whenever they see it — a physical symbol of the community to its members.

Build it first. Many founders have learned that constructing the community building first, before any individual dwellings, adds significantly to a group's identity and community spirit. It creates an energetic center for the group's focus — a centripetal energy. In contrast, when everyone is preoccupied with building their own homes first, it tends to create a more dispersed centrifugal energy in the community.

Build it yourselves. Nothing builds community glue like working together, and nothing makes people more proud of their community building than building it themselves. "I see repeatedly that people in general enjoy being a part of, and want to contribute in a fullbody, hands-on way to the physical building of their community," observes Ted Butchart. Ideally, a community building isn't built quickly by professionals or hired laborers, but created consciously, even ritually, and, as Ted says, "placed and quilted and kneaded and shaped by the users themselves."

gable-roofed canvas awning and terraced front patio is larger and more imposing than other nearby structures, and is visible from the main community road and one of the parking areas. The Council Hall is large and imposing and located on high ground, and also visible from the main road.

Developing your community physically is an ongoing process that could take 10 to 15 years to complete. But creating community itself is never really "complete."

"Earthaven is very much a work in progress, a constantly evolving attempt to more deeply inoculate permaculture and ecovillage culture into our bioregion," says Chuck Marsh. "We're working away in the belly of the beast of western civilization to find our way home in the company of kindred yet diverse spirits."

In Chapter 14 we'll look at one of the most crucial issues of your community-forming process — how your internal financing affects your lives in community, and how attractive your community may be to potential new members.

Chapter 14

Internal Community Finances (Can We Afford to Live There?)

GETTING FINANCING TO BUY your property is one thing; living with the financial arrangements is another.

The financing terms of your property purchase — especially the amount of monthly payment — will affect your internal finances as well. Internal finances are the choices you'll make about whether, and how, you'll assess yourselves over time, and/or assess new members when they join. You'll need to account for such expenses as the mortgage payment, property taxes and insurance, utilities, maintenance and repair costs, any remodeling or infrastructure development, or any management costs such as office and bookkeeping supplies, website expenses, and so on. Sources of revenue for communities can include joining fees, monthly and/or yearly assessments, rent from community-owned living quarters, and site lease fees. Your internal community economy also involves members' labor requirements.

As you'll see, the founders of the communities we're examining arranged their internal financing in completely different ways. And most created these unique economies from scratch, without benefit of knowing how any other communities may have done it. But your group does-

n't have to reinvent the wheel. I hope the examples in this chapter will to give your group plenty of ideas for considering how you might (1) raise enough money to pay off loans, pay operating expenses, and build any needed infrastructure; (2) call up enough labor; (3) meet your members' needs for income, housing, and possibly equity in the property; and (4) attract the new members who'll help you do all this.

Thus, when arranging the terms of your financing, you'll need to consider how much the monthly payments will be, and whether the amount you'll need to assess yourselves to make these payments will be affordable — depending on how many of you will split the payments, your income levels, and if your contingency fund is large enough to subsidize part of the payments until enough new members join you. (And will your monthly payments and contingency-fund supplements allow you to choose members based on your agreed-upon criteria, or will financial pressure dictate that you accept people you aren't sure of because you desperately need their cash?)

If you're seeking property in a rural area the challenge escalates. You've got at least three choices:

1. Buy your rural property near a town or small city with a reasonable job market, or within acceptable commuting distance of one.
2. Arrange financing with monthly payments that are low enough so that assessments will still be affordable to members with low-paying or part-time rural jobs, or who are dependent on the uncertain income of individually owned businesses.
3. Create one or more community-owned businesses that will pay members decent enough wages to meet your monthly assessments. (In this case, "business" could include a non-profit organization that, like Lost Valley's or OAEC's educational organizations, generates an income and pays employees.)

Rural Communities — How will your Members Make a Living?

Here's how members of some rural communities make a living.

1. Rural communities near a good job market. Sowing Circle/OAEC is in a rural-residential area surrounded by the cities and towns of Sonoma County, two minutes from the town of Occidental, 25 minutes from the city of Santa Rosa, and an hour and a half from San Francisco. It's relatively easy for Sowing Circle's 11 members to bring in Bay Area-level salaries. Five are employed by OAEC in multi-skilled roles that include administration, grant application writing, gardening, maintenance and repair, and teaching workshops. The OAEC staff members began working for $10 an hour, with annual seniority raises, and salaries now range from $1,900 to $2,600 a month, depending on seniority. This is a low wage by Bay Area standards, but fine relative to the community's values. Sowing Circle's membership also includes a grade school teacher, a college professor, an environmental educator, and a home-based mom/political organizer. Another member, the president of a non-profit organization, works half-time at his home office and half-time in Berkeley, an hour and a half away.

2. Rural communities 30-45 minutes from a low-wage job market. Abundant Dawn is an hour from the small city of Roanoke, Virginia, and about 40 minutes from three other medium-sized towns, all with relatively few jobs and low wages. Their members' income-producing activities are typical of what rural community members with few nearby jobs must do. One works as a self-employed computer programmer (sometimes telecommuting and sometimes traveling elsewhere to jobs); two retirees own, repair and maintain their own local rental properties — and also bake bread for area restaurants; one offers a holistic health service in Roanoke and the three local towns — and also takes on other odd jobs; one formerly owned and operated a portable sawmill but now goes to college; and the four members of their income-sharing pod make and sell hemp hammocks, work part-time at a nearby CSA farm, and own and manage the fruit-distribution service for the CSA farm.

The situation is almost identical at Earthaven, which is 50 minutes from Asheville, and 20 and 30 minutes from two small towns, all of which also have few jobs and low wages. Some members are owners of an on-site forestry co-op that fells and mills trees and builds homes for other members. One member owns an herbal products business; another publishes *Permaculture Activist* magazine (both employ other community members part-time); another owns rental units in Asheville and an on-site general store. Two artists paint and sell landscape paintings; one woodworker makes wooden candle-lanterns and another makes custom stairways. Two work part-time administering and promoting workshops on sustainability for Culture's Edge, Earthaven's educational non-profit. Several are self-employed in full- or part-time service businesses: carpenters, permaculture teachers (one also does landscape design, another also teaches consensus), a massage therapist who commutes to Asheville, and a website designer/landscape designer. Two work as waitresses in a nearby town, one works three months a year as a publicist in a city in another state. Some work part-time or for a few hours a week for the community, coordinating its labor, doing repairs and maintenance, cooking for workshop participants, or managing the campground. A few live on the interest from investments; six are retired.

Lost Valley is within 15 minutes' drive from a few small towns and 30 minutes from the small city of Eugene, Oregon — all with relatively few jobs and low wages. Fifteen people (almost three-quarters of its members), work for the community's educational center business, either full time or part-time. One of the part-time employees also works as a massage therapist on-site, and others work part-time in Eugene or the nearby towns. Members who don't work for the educational center have full-time or part-time jobs off site as well — grant writer and consultant, part-time librarian, part-time park ranger, sales rep for a food distributor. Another member flies to a different city each weekend to represent products at trade shows. Another drives 12 hours to the San Francisco Bay Area for week-long trips eight times a year to work as an accounting consultant for clients there, but at Bay-Area wages.

Rural communities far from a job market.
Dancing Rabbit members have an even greater challenge, since they live so much farther from a job market — 45 minutes from a small town with low-paying jobs, and almost an hour and a half from the nearest city. Two members are self-employed in service businesses — a musician's booking agent and a freelance editor. Some have part-time or occasional work building homes for other members. Several have part-time jobs working for the Fellowship for Intentional Community at nearby Sandhill Farm, or in Sandhill's tempeh-making business, or for the Missouri chapter of a national organic certifying agency. Some work off-site for several weeks or months — a personal assistant who helps disabled people, a traveling sales representative, and carpenters who work construction in other cities. Several work a few hours weekly for the community doing accounting, answering correspondence, managing their intern program, or fund-raising for the community, and one works full-time eight months a year, growing the community's vegetables. Members of Skyhouse, the income-sharing sub-community, work a variety of telecommuting jobs, including computer programming, website design, and graphic arts.

As you can see, in rural communities away from thriving job markets, most people make do with various odd jobs, part-time jobs, one-person businesses with an uncertain income, or they telecommute. Few actually have "a job."

Starting a new business while also starting a community can be difficult to impossible; bringing a telecommuting job or an already-successful business to a rural community can work well. For example, the computer programmers at Abundant Dawn and Dancing Rabbit brought their professions with them and now telecommute. The income-sharing pod at Abundant Dawn was already making hammocks as subcontractors for Twin Oaks' hammock-making business before they began Abundant Dawn (they later launched their own independent hammock line). The owners of various businesses at Earthaven started them before joining the community.

The Risks of Community Businesses

Several founders of rural communities have told me it would have helped enormously, at the very start, if they'd had one or more viable community businesses to employ community members, and there's plenty of precedent from income-sharing rural communities formed in the late 1960s or early '70s. Twin Oaks in Virginia started its hammock business, and subsequently, a book-indexing service and tofu-making business — all still in operation today. Sandhill Farm in Missouri started an organic foods business — growing and processing sorghum syrup, honey, tempeh, garlic puree, horseradish, and mustard. The Farm in Tennessee started many businesses, including processing soy foods, manufacturing electronic equipment, video production services, and midwifery and midwife education. All these businesses continue today, although some are now owned as sole proprietorships by individual Farm members, or are owned by member collectives.

However, creating a community-owned business (or a non-profit educational center that pays wages to its employees) is not without its own risks. Start-up businesses fail at the rate of at least 95 percent, usually because they're undercapitalized or the founders didn't do adequate market research ahead of time. Start-up businesses require not only business experience and entrepreneurial skill to succeed, but often take 10- and 12-hour days for at least the first six months to a year. Even if you're a community of experienced, savvy entrepreneurs, where will you

PRIVATE ECONOMIES, INCOME-SHARING ECONOMIES

In a private or independent community economy, however members earn money — working at outside jobs, by owning their own businesses, through investments, or some other means — they keep their earnings and decide how they'll spend, invest, or save their own earnings. In other words, their finances are private and individual. They pay agreed-upon joining fees, site lease fees, and/or other assessments to the community for all community expenses, and the whole group decides how to spend or save their community assets. Most communities operate this way. In an income-sharing (communal) economy, however, members work for one or more community businesses and pool the profits in a common treasury, or work at jobs outside the community and pool their earnings from these jobs. The common treasury pays the mortgage payments, property taxes, insurance, maintenance, and other costs, and all members' basic needs for food, shelter, monthly stipends, and so on. All members decide how their common assets are spent. Relatively few communities do income-sharing, however members of Skyhouse subcommunity at Dancing Rabbit and the Tekiah pod at Abundant Dawn organize their economies this way. Meadowdance has a hybrid income-sharing economy. Everyone works for Meadowdance's community-owned businesses, and their basic expenses are paid from business profits. Members can also earn money they can use as they please by working at outside jobs or working extra hours for their community-owned businesses.

carve out the time and energy to set up a new community *and* a business, much less keep relationships intact with your partners and children? It's much worse if you try to do all this on raw land you're developing from scratch. New development either requires boatloads of money to hire professional crews, or long hard hours of your own sweat-equity labor, or both — usually over a period of several years. It's unlikely most community founders could pull this off *and* start a business. Bottom line — if you're planning a community-owned business, if at all possible, get it established and running well *before* moving to the land.

But there are several other ways to create on-site income for members besides the community becoming the employer itself. Several members could create a worker-owned co-op, for example, or could provide the community food, cooking, lumber, construction skill, laundry services, and so on for a fee. Or an individual or several members could start a business enterprise that employed some or all other community members.

A community-owned or member-owned business that employs other community members also has its own set of problems. On the one hand, community members would have on-site jobs, the entrepreneurs would have an ongoing source of close-at-hand workers, and, since it had an income source, the community would be more attractive to new members. On the other hand, just because some folks are fine fellow community members doesn't make them suited for a particular job role. What if the member was unsuited for the work, or made costly mistakes, or didn't show up for shifts, or came late and left early? What if the person was miserable, or even destructive, in the job? Imagine the amount of tension that could arise between that member and the business owners, whether the person was kept in the job (creating resentment in the owners and co-workers), or was let go (creating resentment in the person). Also, if some members owned the business and others didn't, a real or perceived power issue could arise between what could become the "owner class" and the "worker class." Or the needs of the business, driven by markets, cash flow, and other financial considerations, could slowly encroach on and even supplant the community's own visions and values for itself. Instead of being a servant to the community — providing income for members — the business could become its master. An antidote to this kind of "creeping takeover" would be to set up more than one member-owned business from the beginning, or a combination of community-owned, worker-owned, and individually or group-owned businesses, creating a more balanced "marketplace" of business activities and employment opportunities.

Another issue is whether a community business is really viable. A business might earn the community far less money per member than each person would make working outside, but as long as each member's expenses are low, their work-hours reasonable, the work itself satisfying, and their lives in community fulfilled and balanced, they're probably living better than their wealthier counterparts in the mainstream. As the saying goes: "Living below your means is a cheap way to be rich."

On the other hand, a community business could pay its overhead, satisfy its customers, fund all necessary community expenses, and seem firmly in the black, but at the cost of community members working inordinately long hours to pull it off. If members intersperse gardening, maintenance, cooking, and other community tasks with hours at the community business they might not really notice that by the end of the week they've worked 60 or even 70 hours at the business, and that their free time had diminished to nothing. Entrepreneurs and business consultants identify this situation immediately for what it is — a failing business that's actually in the red — but many communities can't see it.

This happens regularly at a rural income-sharing community I'll call Cranberry Valley. Its 20 members work at one or more community businesses — installing slate roofs, processing maple syrup for local stores, and operating a coffee house venue in town for local poets and musicians. But the hours are grueling and the community's newer members become exhausted and demoralized. (And in what I call "community macho," the long-time members remind them that it takes a lot of stamina to handle the intensity of community life.) Someone finally does the math and concludes that the coffee house loses so much money that everyone's actually working for $2.00 an hour, and their outrageously long hours are the result of trying to keep it afloat. Eventually, the newer members propose that Cranberry Valley cut its losses and close the coffee house so everyone can live normal lives again. The founders and old timers don't agree, saying that having a groovy coffee house was part of the community's vision from the beginning. Then there's a major exodus. The scene repeats itself regularly with new groups of members several months or years later.

Given these pros and cons of running a community business, here's how some communities manage it. And, although it's unlikely that any of the members in these community-owned, worker-owned, or individually-owned businesses will ever get rich, or even perhaps earn a normal wage by mainstream standards, they've found a way to live in a rural community and make a living there.

1. Income-sharing community-owned businesses. Meadowdance founders were convinced from the outset that a significant factor in a new community's success is whether people can afford to join it. They didn't want people to have

to eke out a living of odd-jobs and part-time jobs and still try to make land payments, so having community businesses was part of their community vision from the start. They chose two businesses, Vermont Software Testing Group and Wordsworth Typing and Editing, specifically because they weren't living in their permanent rural location yet and both businesses were portable, and because any members with basic knowledge of computers could be trained as effective software testers. As we've seen, because they didn't get their desired rural land, Meadowdance founders bought a large house in a town and launched their businesses from there.

For the first two-and-a-half years, these businesses made barely enough to pay overhead and marketing, house payments (mortgage, taxes, and insurance), food and household expenses, gasoline and maintenance of shared cars, and a tiny stipend for each member. Then the businesses began taking off, and the community could relax a bit. Even so, they consider these two businesses less than ideal in some ways, since both involve sitting at a computer for long hours. Now that they've purchased and moved to their new property, they'll found other community businesses, says cofounder Luc Reid, which most likely will be different in nature. Eventually they may phase out one or both of their computer-based businesses.

Meadowdance organized its income-sharing structure differently than other income-sharing communities. Income-sharing subcommunities, such as Skyhouse at Dancing Rabbit and Tekiah at Abundant Dawn, own their businesses through a 501(d) non-profit tax status and share one tax return, which gives them a definite tax savings. (See Chapter 16.) But to retain that tax status, members cannot work for outside businesses without sharing that income also, and any outside assets must either be put in trust or contributed to the common treasury. Meadowdance wanted to make it easy for anyone with enough motivation and energy to be able to earn additional income, and they didn't want to discourage anyone from joining who owned investments, real estate, or savings. So they don't own any assets through the 501(d) non-profit, but own their property as a Vermont Limited Liability Partnership, and each business as a Limited Liability Company. (See Chapter 15.) They file one tax form for the Limited Liability Partnership, and spread the tax burden among members equally. With this legal structure, as long as members meet their internal work requirements, they can work at outside jobs and do anything they want with outside earnings and other assets.

Lost Valley's Educational Center business is organized differently again. Fifteen members work full time or part time for the business, in administration and programs, consulting, accounting, promotion, gardening, or grounds maintenance and repair. The base pay is $6.50 an hour, with a seniority increase of 12.5 cents an hour more every year, plus 65 cents an hour additional if the employee has children. Full-time wages range from $845 to $1,040 a month (and full time is 30 hours weekly).

2. Member-owned community-service co-ops.
Eight Earthaven members decided to make a modest living on the land by addressing two of the community's challenges — the need to clear forest on arable bottom land so the community can grow enough food to feed itself, and the need for building materials and carpenters for community buildings and members' homes. They formed a worker-owned co-operative, Earthaven Forestry and Building Company (as a Limited

Liability Company), and taught themselves how to harvest trees sustainably, mill lumber, and build houses. It was a steep learning curve for many of them, as only two were carpenters, and they went into fairly deep debt with private loans from other members for a portable band saw, a dump truck, and other equipment. They are accomplishing their goals — clearing land, milling a surplus of lumber (and even finding a way to use smaller-than-normal dimensional lumber for innovative building methods), helping build community buildings and members' homes, and slowly paying off their debt. As of 2002, they were charging $16 to $25 an hour, depending on equipment used, whether the work involves heavy machinery or logging, and whether the work is on or off-site. They use part of this for overhead and debts, and split the rest, aiming for a $10 an hour wage. When they can't pay themselves that much, they pay what they can and credit the remainder to themselves for a future draw when the cash is available. Like OAEC and Lost Valley members, they're not getting rich, but they have found a way to make money in a rural community and simultaneously serve its long-term vision and goals.

3. Sole-proprietor businesses that serve the community.
Dancing Rabbit also wanted to find ways to meet members' needs and generate on-site incomes, so they formed the Cattail Food Co-op, which buys produce from several members with thriving vegetable gardens. The food co-op collects money from members and orders food items from a natural foods wholesaler that delivers monthly, but most of their funds go to the gardeners. In the April-October growing season, one member works full-time growing nearly all the community's vegetables for the co-op. As of 2002, he was making a very

modest living by ordinary standards, but one that works in Dancing Rabbit's low-expense environment. Three other part-time gardeners grow salad greens, herbs, and other edibles to sell to the co-op.

Keeping Member Assessments Affordable

There are probably as many ways to assess members for community expenses as there are communities. The total amounts vary widely, depending on the purchase price of the property (for example, it's considerably higher in California than in Missouri); whether it's developed, and to what degree; the amount of initial costs (down payment plus repairs, renovation, or development costs); the monthly land fee (loan principal and interest, taxes, and insurance); the number of members who will split these costs; and whether members will have equity in the property. Table 7 on the following pages illustrates some of these differences.

In each of the rural communities in the chart, the monthly land payments are affordable, given access to nearby jobs. In the years 1995 to 1999, when they were still paying interest-only payments on their three loans, SC/OAEC members paid $800 a month for the mortgage, taxes, insurance, utilities, repairs, maintenance, and further development, which was reasonable in this rural area near high-paying jobs. Now, after refinancing, and with 11 members, they each pay $815 monthly ($515 in land payments; $300 in taxes, insurance, repair, and maintenance). The community's operations expenses are not paid by member assessments, but by their $70,000 annual income from OAEC leasing their facilities. In rural areas with few available jobs, and where the property doesn't cost as much, the scale is lower. Earthaven members pay $15-$20 per month, and

Dancing Rabbit members pay $25 per month toward the land payment, and an annual assessment of two percent of each member's annual income, plus food costs and, if they rent a space from the community or Skyhouse subcommunity, a rental fee of $70 to $150 per month.

The monthly assessment for Abundant Dawn members for the land payment and other expenses ranges from $105 to $350 per month, depending on which pod (Tekiah or DaySpring Circle) the member is part of, his/her assets and monthly income, and other factors. In 2001, monthly assessments averaged $176 per member, and this fee will go down somewhat as more members join. If they rent community-owned housing, Abundant Dawn members pay from $50 to $150 monthly.

Lost Valley members pay a $250 monthly fee for utilities, taxes, insurance, maintenance, and loan payments, and $75 to $225 in rent for community-owned housing.

Food costs are usually figured separately. At Sowing Circle, Lost Valley, and Dancing Rabbit, where members share food expenses and eat together, food costs range from $100 to $150 per person per month. Abundant Dawn members pay for their own food, but are assessed $20 per month for bulk foods shared by the community. Meadowdance members pay nothing; their community businesses fund basic expenses and pay each member a small stipend. (See Table 7.)

Joining Fees

Joining fees vary widely, and some communities, such as Meadowdance and Dancing Rabbit, don't have them at all. The joining fee is $4,000 at Earthaven and $1,000 at Lost Valley. Abundant Dawn has no joining fee for individual members, but each pod pays a one-time

TABLE 7: INTERNAL COMMUNITY FINANCES

Community	Founders' Contribution Members' Joining Fee Site Lease Fee	Annual/Monthly Mortgage or Loan Payment
ABUNDANT DAWN	Founders paid $1,800 each plus a $300 nonrefundable security deposit. Each pod pays $5,000 to join Abundant Dawn. For Tekiah pod there's no joining fee. For DaySpring Circle pod, new members pay $3,000 to $4,000 to reimburse DaySpring Circle founders for the pod joining fee for Abundant Dawn, and for DaySpring Circle's infrastructure. No site lease fees.	$13,416 yearly; $1,118 monthly. Interest & principal to owner-financer.
DANCING RABBIT	No required founders' contributions. No new-member joining fee.	$20,750 yearly; $1,600 monthly. (CRP payments pay about half this.) Interest & (now) principal payment to private lenders. Members build homes on leased sites.
SOWING CIRCLE/OAEC	$20,000 founders'contributions. New members pay joining fee of $20,000+ which reflects capital improvements and increased property value.	(1995-2000) $37,500 yearly; $3,125 monthly. Interest-only payments on three mortgages.

Do Members Have Equity in the Community Property? Housing Arrangements	Annual or Monthly Member Assessment (excluding food)	Weekly Labor Requirement How Members Make a Living
PARTIAL EQUITY Undivided ownership of whole property; members lease sites. Members leaving after 3 years may be reimbursed 25% of their land payments, starting w/their 4th year, at community's discretion. Live in community-owned housing or owner-built homes.	9 members pay monthly land payment: amount varies per member (ranging between $105-$350 per member), depending on pod, member's assets & income, & other factors (average monthly fee in 2001 was $176). This Fee will decrease somewhat as more members join.	No labor requirement but labor averages 10-12 hrs. per week. Few jobs locally. DaySpring Circle members work in on-site member-owned businesses, off-site jobs, or telecommute. Tekiah members working in pod-owned hammock business and off site jobs.
NO EQUITY Property owned as Land Trust through 501(c)2 non-profit. Members lease sites for $25 monthly. Live in small owner-built cabins or rent community-owned cabins for $50-$150/month.	Annual assessment: 2% per member. 16 members (2002) hold 20 leases total. Monthly site lease for home, garden & business sites: $25 per 2500 sq. ft.	1.5 hrs labor/wk (75 hours yearly). Few jobs locally. Members work in member-owned on-site businesses, jobs off site, telecommute, or work for the community.
EQUITY Equal undivided interests in property. Live in community-owned cabins.	(1995-2000): 8 people. $37,440 yearly: $3,120 monthly. $800 per person/month for mortgage, operating expenses, development, & maintenance. (2001+): 11 people. $67,980 yearly; $5,665 monthly. $815 per person/month for mortgage, development, & maintenance. (Operations paid by OAEC annual lease fees.)	7 hrs week/average. Good job market locally. 5 members work for OAEC (approx., $1500/mo. take-home pay) or at off-site jobs.

Continued on page 162-163 (over)

Community	Founders' Contribution Members' Joining Fee Site Lease Fee	Annual/Monthly Mortgage or Loan Payment
EARTHAVEN	Founders paid $10,000 ea. for site lease. New members pay $4,000 joining fee & one-time site lease fee, which increases by $1,000 every year ($17,000 in 2002).	$50,400 yearly; $4,200 monthly. Interest & principal to EarthShares fund.
LOST VALLEY	No required founders fees. (One loaned money for acquisition and remodeling.) New members pay $1,000 joining fee.	Original property purchase loans are paid off; now pay $42,000 annually/ $3,500 monthly interest & principal to multiple lenders for further capital improvements.
MEADOWDANCE	No required founders' contributions; some gave loans; some didn't. No joining fee	Mortgage on house in town: $5,196 yearly; $433 monthly. Property Taxes: $4268 yearly; $356 monthly. Community businesses pay the mortgage.

$5,000 fee to be a part of Abundant Dawn. Tekiah, Abundant Dawn's income-sharing pod, has no joining fee for incoming members, and DaySpring Circle, its independent-income pod, requires $3,000 to $4,000 per incoming member to partially reimburse DaySpring Circle founders for their $5,000 pod-joining fee and expenses for their neighborhood infrastructure.

The joining fee for new Sowing Circle/ OAEC members is equivalent to the amount (adjusted for inflation) it would cost the community to reimburse a departing founder at the time the new person joins, even though no one is actually leaving. This amount is a combination of the $20,000 founder's contribution, plus the portion of the monthly loan payment that goes toward paying off the principal (but not interest, taxes, insurance, repair, maintenance), multiplied by the number of months (and years) the founder paid it at the time the new member joins. The joining fee is thus continually increasing; by 2002, it was close to $35,000. This may seem high, but consider that 11 members own a property that by 2002 was probably worth 2.8

Do Members Have Equity in the Community Property? Housing Arrangements	Annual or Monthly Member Assessment (excluding food)	Weekly Labor Requirement How Members Make a Living
EQUITY Undivided ownership of whole property. Members lease sites. Site lease fees $17,000 (in 2002). Leases may be sold to incoming members. Live in small owner-built cabins.	55 members. $120 yearly for operations; plus either $60 yearly facilities-use fee, or, for residents who use community kitchen, $130 yearly facilities-use fee.	1500 hours labor in the member's first 10 years (2 hour weekly minimum). Few jobs locally. Members telecommute, work for on-site forestry co-op, members' on-site businesses; or at off-site jobs.
NO EQUITY Property owned as 501(c)3 non-profit. Members rent community-owned housing.	22 members pay $20 monthly fee for shared infrastructure. Each pays monthly rental fee, from $75-$225 monthly, depending on size and amenities.	10 hours' labor weekly. Few jobs locally. 13 members work for educational center business; others work at off-site jobs.
NO EQUITY Community has option to financially assist departing members in setting up new living arrangements. Live in community-owned housing.	7 members. Community businesses pay all other expenses and give members a small stipend.	45 hour weekly (including work in community businesses). Members work for community businesses, though they may work at outside jobs if they choose.

million. If new members paid a joining fee that was a proportional share of the property value, with 11 members it would be almost $255,000.

When two new members joined the Sowing Circle community (as partners in relationships with founders), they were responsible for the full joining fee, which at the time was about $31,000. The community used this incoming revenue to remodel two of the cabins so they'd each be spacious enough for a couple. The new people each paid only about $20,000 of their joining fee in cash and are paying the balance in monthly payments (in addition to their $815 monthly mortgage payment, and food fees.) These payments will reimburse the community for cabin remodeling expenses beyond $20,000 per cabin. (See Table 7 above).

Housing Arrangements

These can vary widely as well. Some communities provide housing, others rent housing, and at still others, members must build their own homes. The monthly land fees at Sowing Circle/OAEC confers the use of a community-owned cabin. Lost Valley members pay from $75 to $225 for community-owned cabins or housing units, and Abundant Dawn members pay from $50 to $150 for community-owned space (although they can also build their own temporary or permanent housing, and/or bring in a temporary mobile home.) Dancing Rabbit members can rent community-owned (or subcommunity-owned) cabins for $70 to $150. Dancing Rabbit and Earthaven members lease their individual home sites, and must pay construction costs for building their own individual or shared homes. Meadowdance members share the house they own together.

Site Lease Fees and the Debt Load

Dancing Rabbit's founders wanted to keep expenses affordable, not only because of their values, but also because of the low incomes people would likely earn in a rural area as remote as theirs. So they set up their internal finances without a joining fee, and assess members two percent of their annual income every year.

They also set up a system of site leases with a minimum of about 2,500 square feet per person (an area corresponding to 50 by 50 feet, enough for a small cabin and a garden), and charge one cent per square foot per month, or approximately $25 a month per leased site. People can lease more than one site, depending on the size of their household and how much space they want, and can also lease business and gardening sites. They can also choose not to lease space, but rent community-owned housing instead. The founders set it up so that regardless of the number of members or any change in their debt load, this low monthly assessment remains the same.

For their first three years, from 1996 through 1998, they paid slightly over $1,000 a month

towards two of their private loans, and in 1999, at the end of their three-year grace period from their third loan, began paying about $2,750 a month. As of 2002, with 16 members leasing 20 home, garden, and business sites, this wasn't enough to make the payments, even with their annual income of approximately $12,000 a year from Conservation Resource Program payments. But this wasn't a problem, since they'd planned from the beginning to run on a deficit budget until they got enough members to lease enough sites, supplementing their site lease fees and CRP payments with money from their development/contingency fund. As soon as they lease 30 sites, they'll have enough monthly income, supplemented by the annual CRP payments, to pay their loans without dipping into any other sources. And with 40 sites, they'll have enough for maintenance, repair, capital improvements, and so on.

Earthaven's site lease arrangement is quite different. The founders raised the funds for their down payment and early development costs by paying one-time site lease fees of $10,000 for roughly quarter-acre residential and business sites. Some paid all cash, others paid half down with monthly payments, and some leased both business and residential sites. The next year, to pay off their owner-financers, they refinanced, creating the EarthShares fund with a series of small private loans from members, founders, and supporters.

They intended to pay off the EarthShares loans from additional one-time site lease fees as well as joining fees from incoming members over the years. The site lease fees had to meet the following criteria. (1) They had to be low enough to be affordable, considering that members would also pay a joining fee and construction costs for building their homes. (2) They had to represent a reasonable value, based on the increasing amount of community infrastructure. (3) They had to be high enough to generate enough annual income for Earthaven to meet its loan payments and maintenance projects, and generate enough total income to eventually pay off the EarthShares fund and build all the community's planned roads, bridges, and community buildings.

The founders met this challenge by planning a population of 150 adult members, their estimated carrying capacity of the land in terms of food self-reliance based on 55 to 66 quarter-acre sites. They set the joining fee at $1,000, raising it over the years to $4,000, and began gradually increasing the original site lease fee of $10,000. (As of 2002, the site lease fee was $17,000.)

They later added a compact site designation, roughly an eighth-acre for 60 percent of the full site fee, and are considering "common-wall" high-density sites of housing units in apartment-like buildings with shared yards for half of the full-site fee When all potential sites are leased and the community is full, maintenance and new development funds will come from members' monthly assessments, from annual fees from shorter-term leases for business sites, and from revenue-generating events and services for the public. (See Table 7.)

Labor Requirements

Another source of wealth in a community's internal economy is the labor it asks of each member on a weekly, monthly, or annual basis. Community labor tasks can range from construction, maintenance, and repair, to housekeeping of common areas, bookkeeping, various clerical tasks, and answering correspondence. If the community grows its own food and shares all or some common meals, labor tasks will also include gardening, shopping, cooking, and cleanup. If members work at one or more community businesses, that labor is included as well.

Communities need to create a budget for their labor needs, just they do for financial needs. This important step is easy to overlook unless you realize that your members' skills and energy are equivalent to money, and that each of you will be responsible for a portion of labor to help make the community viable. How much labor is required per person per week (or per month, per year, or for the first ten years) — and how you allocate it — depends on the number and kind of tasks you hope to accomplish (building a road, remodeling a building, creating a bookkeeping system or a website, and so on), how many hours you estimate each task will take, your number of members, and when you'd like to finish these tasks. If you don't create a labor budget, you'll be forever tempted to add new projects and ask the community to allocate labor credit for them, leaving you wondering why you have six half-done construction projects sitting around for years.

As with every other aspect of community economics, labor requirements vary widely, mostly depending on whether or not the group is developing raw land, how quickly the group wants to accomplish its goals, how much common space or common activities the group shares, and how many members are splitting the work. Groups that cook and eat together usually require a greater amount of community labor than those in which members have their own kitchens. Among the communities we've been examining, labor requirements vary from less than an hour a week to ten hours a week. Most communities include community meetings as part of their labor requirements. At Lost Valley, for example, four of the required ten hours weekly are for full-group or committee meetings.

As in most communities, Earthaven's founders spent an enormous amount of labor creating their financial and governance systems and their physical infrastructure, and wanted to find a way for incoming members to match that. So, in the late 1990s, they set up a system whereby all members owe at least 1,500 hours' labor in their first ten years of membership, which matches what most founders have already contributed. Although this averages out to about 3 hours a week, Earthaven members can arrange their 1500 hours any way they like over the ten years, as long as they work a minimum of 50 hours a year, or pay the equivalent in cash, measured at $7 an hour.

Abundant Dawn has a labor requirement but doesn't require a specific number of hours per week. They hold a labor review meeting every few months in which members let each other know what they've done since the previous labor review. Feedback in these meetings can include the observation that someone may be working considerably more hours than others, or asking someone to do more community work. Their amount of labor is related to the need; during one period it averaged about 10-12 hours per member per week.

Earthaven and Dancing Rabbit each set up internal currency systems (Dancing Rabbit "Hours" and Earthaven "Leaps") for exchanging goods and services with the community and with each other, and for keeping track of labor hours owed to the community. Both currencies are based on an hour's labor valued at $7.

Meadowdance members observed that they engage in many kinds of work that cannot be measured in durations of time, such as taking responsibility for a certain aspect of community life, or making sure other people are signed up for a particular job, so they made up a unit of work requirement called "Responsibility Points" or RPs. Even though some RPs are conferred for oversight or supervisory functions that don't necessarily take up time, RPs are nevertheless equivalent to about 15 minutes each. The community requires 180 RPs per member weekly (about 45 hours), which has averaged at about 16.5 hours working at community businesses and 28.5 hours working non-business community activities per week. Non-business activities include building maintenance, shopping, cooking, and cleaning, learning and recreational activities with the kids, computer repairs, and management activities such as dealing with taxes, insurance, paying bills, answering correspondence, and participating in whole-group meetings and committees (land search, work requirements, insurance, finance, and so on).

Sowing Circle/OAEC's labor system is also not based on required hours, but on requirements to accomplish different kinds of tasks in various time periods (although the hours average out to about 7-10 a week). For example, with ten currently active community members (at a community where they share all meals), each is required to cook once in two weeks and do dishes once a week, with an intern's help. Every member and intern must do a basic housekeeping-type task for the community listed on the "Chore Wheel," each of which takes three to six hours a month. Every two months they rotate the wheel and everyone gets a new chore. Every member participates in two-hour community meetings once a week, three-to-four-hour "deep check-in" meetings every other month, and half-day long-term planning sessions and half-day work parties every few months. In addition, each member is responsible for one of ten "work spheres" (for example, wildlands management, finances, development and planning, maintenance), with two or three other members assisting, so every member is involved in several work spheres. Each work sphere can take from a few hours to many per month, depending on a work sphere's requirements at the time, and how much energy the member responsible for it wants to devote to it. (See Table 7.)

Every community we've studied depends for much of its labor on interns — people who work for the community for several weeks to several months in exchange for room and board (and who sometimes pay a small amount for the experience). Interns are an invaluable source of community labor — and often a source of potential new members as well.

Building Equity

If a community as a whole owns all the property and no members hold title to their own lots or housing units, it's still possible for the members to build equity in the property — meaning they are reimbursed all or part of their founders contribution and/or land payments if they leave. Usually such reimbursements come from the funds of incoming members, often paid out in many installments over time. And even in those communities that aren't set up for anyone to build equity in the property, members may have equity in the home they've built, or in other improvements to their site, which they can usually sell to other members before leaving, depending on the community's agreements.

Sowing Circle/OAEC members have equity, but it's tied to how much they've paid in, not to property value. As described above, departing members would be reimbursed their founder's contribution and the total amount of principal they'd paid in monthly payments for all the months they'd lived there, adjusted for inflation

(about $35,000 by 2002). Funds for each reimbursement fee would come primarily from the joining fee of an incoming member, and would not be available unless a new member joined.

Earthaven members don't have equity in the strict sense of the term, since everyone owns all of the land (and its bylaws prevent it ever selling the land for speculative gain). Members can, however, sell their site leases back to the community at the same price they paid, depending on the community's financial health at the time, and the community can lease that site to an incoming member at the current lease fee. Departing members can also sell their houses, and any other site improvements, to incoming members.

Departing Abundant Dawn members who have lived there longer than three years have the possibility of partial equity in the property, depending on what the community decides at the time. If approved by the community at the time, departing members would be reimbursed 25 percent of their monthly land payments for every year they'd paid in after their first three years (minus certain adjustments), over the same number of years as they lived in the community after the three-year mark.

For example, if a household lived there five years and left, they'd be reimbursed 25 percent of the land payments they made in years four and five in payments over a two-year period. There's no profit on the 25 percent equity reimbursement, even though the property value will have increased, but the amount is adjusted for the cost of living. If the departing members had built a home, they could sell it to incoming members.

Departing members of Lost Valley and Dancing Rabbit aren't reimbursed any part of their assessments, but if they've built homes, they may sell them to incoming members. Departing Meadowdance members also receive no reimbursements, since they didn't pay into assessments for expenses (profit from businesses paid for this) or for building homes or housing units, as they intend that profits from the business will pay for members' homes also. However, depending on what the community decides at the time, departing Meadowdance members may be given financial assistance to help them get set up outside the community. If the departing members loaned the community money, loan-repayment priorities will be shifted in order to reimburse them sooner. (See Table 7.)

The combination of these assessments and fees, and issues of equity, helps determine not only how easily you can live in your community, but also how attractive you may be to potential new members.

Can People Afford to Join You?

In the late 1990s, Patricia Greene and John Charamella wanted to find the right community to join. As experienced communitarians, they assumed this would be reasonably easy financially, since they were debt-free and could sell their home for more than enough to pay a joining fee and build a modest house, and they could transplant their tile-laying business anywhere there were enough potential customers. They were seeking a community in which members had independent finances, in a rural area with no to low zoning and building codes. They assumed they'd pay from $10,000 to $15,000 in joining fees and site-lease fees or the right to build on a footprint of land, and about $40,000 to build a house with their own sweat equity. But after researching communities on the web, and by e-mailing and phoning communities and taking several extended trips to visit the most promising ones, they ended up wondering whether the average community seeker could afford to join any community.

At one end of the affordability scale they found a 25-year old community whose founders had long ago paid off and developed the land and weren't seeking reimbursement. Members lived in small, rustic cabins without water or electricity, and shared meals and took showers in a central community building. The community wanted to make living there affordable enough so members didn't have to work at outside jobs, so there was no joining fee, a nominal monthly fee for room and board, and an 18-hour weekly work requirement. To discourage new members from starting construction and then leaving behind a half-built building, the community was considering requiring a $10,000 bond from new members planning to build, to be returned to them when the house was built. And if members left, their home would belong to the community.

But mostly Patricia and John found communities at the other end of the affordability scale. One had a $80,000 joining fee, as well as monthly payments for overhead. Another community looked reasonable — at first. It was $5,000 to join, with a $250 per person monthly mortgage assessment. Because members shared meals and took showers in a central community building, Patricia and John figured it would cost about $25,000 to owner-build a small home without utilities. But when they added the $5,000 joining fee, a $25,000 home-building cost, and $250 for each of them monthly, after 10 years they would have paid $90,000, after 15 years, $120,000, after 20 years, $150,000 — all with no equity.

They liked a third community immensely. The joining fee was a modest $1,200-$2,400 sliding scale. The property was paid for, so there was no mortgage assessment. The monthly fees were $100 to $150 per person rent for one or two rooms and the use of all common facilities, and a $600 per person monthly assessment for food, health insurance, community utilities and maintenance. If they lived there without building, they'd pay $1,450 a month for both of them for three rooms, food and insurance. To build, they'd pay a one-time non-refundable infrastructure fee of $15,000, which went towards the community's maintenance and development of roads, water systems, and the off-grid power system. Added to this was approximately $40,000 to owner-build their house. The work requirement was 15 hours a week. But then they did the math. They figured what they'd pay over 10 and 15 years, and what they'd get, deducting what food and health insurance would have cost if they'd paid it on their own, and realized that the exceptionally high work requirement would prevent them from either building their home quickly, or from being able to work much outside and generate any savings. Coupled with the fact that they'd have no equity in the property, it just wasn't worth it.

Patricia and John's experiences illustrate how your community's internal finances can attract or repel the new members who could make your land payments more affordable. You'll need to create a balance between how affordable and attractive your community may be, and how much revenue and labor you'll need from each member to finish paying off your property pay-ments and building infrastructure. And part of this attractiveness is whether or not your community allows members to build any equity they could take with them if they left.

The Internal Community Finances chart illustrates the relative financial ease of joining some of the communities described in this book. Newcomers to Dancing Rabbit, Abundant Dawn, and Earthaven would need to bring their jobs or sole-proprietorship businesses with them or find a way to make a living in a rural county. Their highest expense would be the one-time cost of building a home, which they'd need to do with their own funds or private loans (or a bank loan if they had other property or assets as collateral). Building a home would most likely cost more at Earthaven, since members need to clear and grade their sites and set up off-grid power as well as build homes. If newcomers to Lost Valley didn't work for the conference center business they'd need to find a way to make a living in that rural setting as well.

In Chapters 15 and 16 we'll return to some of the most basic tools for growing a community — legal entities that help us buy, finance, develop, and own property in accordance with our values.

Chapter 15

Legal Entities for Owning Property

I HOPE IT'S ABUNDANTLY CLEAR by now that you should set up the legal entity for owning property *before* beginning the search. Choosing the right one for your community is a process of assessing available legal entities in terms of several different issues that will affect your community's functioning and well-being. You'll need to consider issues such as how you'll hold title to land, property rights, financing options, members' liability, tax consequences, and how attractive you'll be to new members. Not every legal entity will be ideal in every area, so you'll need to analyze them for the best balance of benefits in each of these areas.

Of course, you should seek the advice of a lawyer you trust about these matters. This book does not presume to offer legal advice, but rather to describe how some communities deal with these issues.

Checklist for Choosing a Legal Entity

Here's a checklist for the legal entities you're considering (based on a checklist created by Dave Henson, cofounder of Sowing Circle/ OAEC).

1. How will your community hold title to the land? Will this legal entity support it?

2. Will this legal entity (and the way you hold title to land) allow you to choose who will join you as a member?

3. Will this legal entity offer liability protection? For the group? For each of you as individuals?

4. Will it allow members to build equity in the community, and take all or part of it when they leave?

5. How would this legal entity influence banks or private lenders in deciding whether to refinance a mortgage or make a construction loan? For the community? For individual members?

6. Does this legal entity allow the community to assign its own criteria for decision making, in terms of how decisions are made and who can make them? (See below.)

7. Does it allow the community to determine the relationship between the amount of members' financial contributions and their ownership rights? Between their contributions and their decision-making rights?

8. How will your community collect contributions from members (joining fees, site-lease fees, periodic assessments)? And what will be its expenses (mortgage payments, property taxes, property insurance, maintenance,

capital improvements)? How will your legal entity treat this income and expenses for tax purposes?

9. Will your members share incomes? If so, will it be from profits of community-owned businesses, from earnings of outside jobs, or both? What kinds of member expenses will be paid by the community? How will your legal entity treat your shared income and expenses for tax purposes?

10. How easy will this legal entity be to set up or manage over time? How vulnerable is it to changes in the law, or to IRS or other governmental scrutiny? How much are annual filing fees?

11. How easy would it be to make changes in this legal entity's controlling documents, or to manage the legal and ownership implications of people joining or leaving?

12. Will this legal entity restrict your group from engaging in political activity?

While these questions may seem technical, their answers reflect your community's basic values. So the questions underlying all these other questions are: Does this legal entity inherently support your community's vision, mission, and values? Does it support your ownership, financing and decision-making structure?

Let's explore some of these questions.

How You'll Hold Title and Arrange Members' Use Rights

There are probably as many ways to organize land ownership and use rights and finance construction of homes in community as there are communities. You need to think about these issues now, before buying property, because your method of land ownership and internal financ-

ing both influences and is influenced by the legal entity you choose, and different legal entities resolve these issues differently. Let's look at some of the ways your community could do this.

Buying Raw Land

- Like Dancing Rabbit, you could buy property and lease individual homesites to members for quarterly or yearly lease fees. Or, like Earthaven, you could use 99-year renewable, transferable leases and receive substantial fees for homesites, almost like "buying" the sites.

- You could assign homesites to members without using leases at all, but assign them based on your members' equity contributions. Let's say you had 10 member households who each contributed $30,000 to buy a $300,000 property, and you designated a five-acre homesite for each. Or , if you got private financing or a bank loan to buy the property, you could assign yourselves the same homesites and each pay an equal portion of the mortgage.

- In any of the above scenarios, each of your member households could pay the construction costs for their own houses. Then you'd each own your homes but not the ground beneath them.

- The community could front the construction costs for each house, with members leasing or renting their houses from the community until they'd paid off the community's construction costs plus interest. Then you'd own the homes, but not the ground beneath them.

In all the above cases, if members left, they could sell their portion of equity in their houses to incoming members.

- As Meadowdance intends to do, the community could pay construction costs to build housing for members, with members working at community-owned businesses and receiving a small stipend. No member would own their own home, but all members own everything.

- Each member household could loan your community the money to build the homes, and trade the construction cost plus interest for as many years of free rent as it took to pay off each member household's loan. After the loan was paid off, you'd pay rent for the use of community-owned housing.

- You could subdivide the property, and individual member households could hold title to their own lots. If you had 10 member households and bought 50 acres, for example, you could split it into 10 five-acre lots, or into 10 three-acre lots and share ownership of the remaining 20 acres.

- In the same circumstances, you could create a cohousing community, with each member household owning title to its individual lot and housing unit, and everyone sharing ownership of all the rest of the property and all common facilities.

Buying developed land

- Like Sowing Circle/OAEC, you could each live in already-existing community housing, with your individual monthly land payments conferring that right.

- Like Lost Valley, you could each rent already-existing community housing, with money you received for working off-site or at a community business.

- Like Abundant Dawn, you could rent already-existing community housing or build your own temporary or permanent housing that you'd then own individually (but not the ground beneath it).

- Like Meadowdance (currently), you could all live in a house your community owns.

- Like Mariposa Grove, you could create a limited equity housing co-op and each own a share of the whole property, with a lease that allows you to live in "your" housing unit.

- You could arrange two or more of these methods in combination.

How you decide to arrange your ownership and use rights affects how attractive your community may be to potential members, how you can finance building your homes, and how much control you have over your membership process.

Attractiveness to Members

How you own land and apportion use rights will affect whether and how members may recover all or part of their equity if they leave the community, or if the community disbands. If you set things up so that it's relatively easy for members to recover equity from, say, site lease fees or construction costs, you'll attract members more easily. And thus, whichever legal entity you choose will make this particular choice of land ownership and use rights easier or more difficult to execute.

Affordability of Building New Housing

Your choices about ownership and use rights will also affect how affordable your members' housing might be if they have to build their own homes. For example, if your members held title to their own plots of ground or individual housing units, they could seek mortgages or construction loans, but if your whole community owns the land, your members could either pay cash to build their homes, or get private loans with other property or assets as collateral.

Control of Your Membership Process

Your choices about ownership and use rights will also affect how much control your community may have over who joins you in the future. If your members hold title to their own plots of ground or individual housing units, but to get members you offer these plots or housing units on the open market, you may have to sell to any interested buyer who can meet your terms. Thus, you have little control over who joins you as members. And even if someone leaving your community didn't intend their property for public sale, but to be sold only to incoming members who've gone through your member-screening process, the government may assume otherwise. The Federal Fair Housing Act was enacted to protect buyers from discrimination, so that sellers can't refuse to sell to a qualified home buyer on the basis of race, gender, age, religion, or national origin. If you decline to sell your community home to a qualified buyer who is not a community member, would a court say you are you breaking the law? Several real estate lawyers have told me that the penalties for breaking this Act, or even being accused of intending to break it, are so swift and devastating that they advise against testing it.

On the other hand, the buyers of property for sale in a community may be self-limiting, as many cohousing communities have found. Relatively few average home buyers are interested in buying homes in cohousing communities; usually, incoming members who buy the homes of departing cohousing members are interested in cohousing themselves, and it tends to work well for the community and the new residents. But not always — and when it doesn't work out, there's nothing the community can do about it.

As you can see, how your community holds title to land can cause a trade-off between affordable housing and control over membership. Again, you must think about this now so you can choose a legal entity that meets your needs in these areas.

Organizational Flexibility

The legal entity you choose will also impact your internal agreements about finances and rights and responsibilities. For example, if each member puts in differing financial contributions, do they have different rights and responsibilities in terms of paying taxes, responsibility for maintenance and repairs, liability for debts and damages, enjoyment of the land, choice of homesite, tax-write offs for tax-exempt expenses, and decision-making?

Whichever legal entity you choose will affect your freedom to determine these issues yourselves. A Limited Liability Company (LLC), for example, allows you to arrange these matters any way you like, as long as you spell it out in your operating agreements when you file with your state. State regulations for various kinds of corporations stipulate how you must organize these issues, although in some cases you can create internal community agreements that apportion these rights and responsibilities differently than your state's default requirements.

How You'll be Taxed

How you set up the internal finances of your community will affect the amount and kinds of income your community receives, which will affect how you'll be taxed, depending on your choice of legal entities. Since a community isn't usually a for-profit enterprise, what are sources of community "income" that could be taxed?

1. Fees collected from members for maintenance and repair of the community's land and buildings, income taxes and property taxes, and insurance.
2. Fees collected from members for mortgage payments or other loan payments.
3. Fees collected from members and saved for longer than a year, such as for maintenance and/or capital improvements, or savings for any possible future use.
4. Rental or lease fees for community buildings or land, from community members or non-community members (the IRS can tax these income sources differently).
5. Income from the sale of products, such as timber, firewood, or agricultural products, or the sale or lease of rights to products, such as water, mineral, or timber rights.
6. Interest from loans to members, such as when the community allows members to pay site leases or housing lease fees through monthly payments.

You may want to estimate your likely amounts of income from these sources ahead of time, and factor the taxation of that income into your choice of legal entity.

This chapter offers brief descriptions of Limited Liability Companies, homeowners' associations, condominium associations, housing cooperatives, and non-exempt non-profit corporations (which have no special IRS tax status), with advantages and disadvantages of each and examples of communities that use them.

Chapter 16 gives brief descriptions of non-profit 501(c)3 corporations (especially in conjunction with separate land-owning legal entities), 501(c)2 non-profits, land trusts, Community Land Trusts, and 501(d) non-profits, again with pros and cons and examples of communities that use them.

The information in this chapter and in Chapter 16 is simply an overview, and not meant as a replacement for your own further research — through additional reading (see Resources), talking with other community founders, and the advice of your group's attorney.

Having said that, let's start with a basic definition of a corporation.

Overview: Corporations and Non-profit Corporations

Corporations. A corporation is a legal structure that, like a person, can enter into contracts, buy and sell goods and services, borrow money, and pay taxes. It is considered an entity distinct from the people who own or operate it, so that any criminal charges, business claims, or lawsuits can be filed against the corporation but not against its owners, directors, officers, employees, or shareholders. They have "limited liability" and cannot be held personally liable for the corporation's debts. (It's "limited" rather than zero liability, because if the corporation is found to be operating solely so its owners can dodge taxes or break the law, the courts can prosecute them personally and/or attach their personal assets.)

Corporations are organized at the state, rather than the federal level, and are therefore regulated by the state. A corporation is created by filing articles of incorporation, paying the state's fees, and preparing bylaws and other required documents. A corporation can be formed for any lawful purpose, and most can issue shares of stock to people (shareholders) who invest money or property in the corporation or provide it with some kind of service. Shareholders receive money back on their investment when the corporation declares and pays dividends, or if any assets remain when the corporation is dissolved. One way of distinguishing types of corporations is by how they pay taxes; two of the most common taxation systems are C corporations and subchapter S corporations.

Non-profit corporations. Also called non-stock corporations, non-profits are a special kind of corporation organized to benefit the public or a certain group of people, rather than to make a profit. No income from a non-profit corporation may be distributed to its members, directors, or officers, although it can pay its employees reasonable wages or salaries, and sometimes its officers are paid employees.

Corporations intended to be non-profit must be so designated when they're created, and can only pursue activities permitted by the statutes for non-profit organizations. Like other corporations, non-profits can enter into contracts, have employees, pay taxes, and borrow money. While a non-profit corporation is accountable to creditors and any lawsuits, its founders, directors, officers, and employees are protected by limited liability.

Non-profit corporations don't issue shares of stock or pay dividends, and don't have shareholders. (Exceptions are certain hybrid corporations such as cooperative corporations used by certain kinds of co-ops, including housing co-ops.)

Like any other corporation, a non-profit corporation is created by filing the required documents with a particular state — the documents for a non-profit corporation will be slightly different from those for a for-profit corporation. Exemption from income tax is determined at the federal level.

Exempt non-profit corporations. The IRS offers approximately 20 different non-profit tax-exempt status types. Some of these the group can simply select each year, such as Section 528 for a home-

---

SOME BASIC TERMS

Limited liability. The protection offered by a corporation (for-profit or non-profit), which means the personal assets of the shareholders, founders, board members, officers, or employees are not vulnerable to most debts or lawsuits filed against the organization.

Double taxation. In a for-profit corporation such as a C corporation, any taxable income which is paid to its shareholders as dividends will be taxed twice: once at the corporate level, at a rate of at least 15 percent; and again when individual shareholders pay taxes on those dividends.

Pass-through tax status. A taxation method used by partnerships, limited liability companies, and subchapter S corporations, in which the legal entity pays no taxes directly. Any taxable income (or loss) is divided up and passed to its partners, members or owners, who pay taxes on the income (or deduct the loss) on their personal income tax returns. The purpose of pass-through taxation is to avoid the double taxation of most for-profit corporations. Pass-through taxation is a favorable tax method in circumstances in which a legal entity would pay dividends which would be taxed at both the corporate and individual level, and in cases in which the individual tax rate would be lower than the corporate tax rate.

owners association, while others, such as Section 501(c)3, must be petitioned from the IRS, and involve filling out many documents and awaiting the IRS's approval of this requested status.

Non-exempt non-profit corporations. When a group files with the state to form a non-profit corporation, but doesn't apply for or choose any tax-exempt status with the IRS, it could be called a non-exempt non-profit. A non-exempt non-profit pays taxes just as any other corporation.

Now let's examine five types of legal entities used by communities to own property.

Limited Liability Companies (LLCs)

The founders of Sowing Circle/OAEC set up two legal entities and a lease to support their intentions and goals. They own their property with a Limited Liability Company (LLC), which, like a corporation, offers its owners limited liability. They operate the OAEC with a non-profit 501(c)3 corporation, which leases the property from their LLC.

Advantages of LLCs

A limited liability company offers limited liability just as a corporation does, and pass through tax benefits, just as a partnership does. (It has far fewer requirements than a subchapter S corporation, as well; for example, there's no limitation on the number of owners.) As in corporations and partnerships, people put their money in the LLC and receive a percentage of ownership interest in return. A relatively new legal entity, the LLC was first introduced in 1977, and became more widely accepted after an IRS ruling in 1997. Now it's recognized in all 50 states, though its regulations differ somewhat from state to state.

Sowing Circle's LLC owns all the land, and individual members live in its cabins. Each member pays a monthly fee for community expenses, including the property's mortgage and other land-purchase loans. Because they own their land this way, they can control their membership process.

An LLC could also be used to own the original property that a community later subdivided into individually owned plots for members, which would allow those members to seek mortgages or other bank financing for building homes. If so, the community would no longer be able to control who joined them.

Each Sowing Circle member, through their monthly payments, is building equity in the community, most of which they can take with them if they leave, but only if a new member buys into the community, with the new member paying off the departing member. However, a community owning property with an LLC could certainly retain ownership of all the equity a departing member had paid into the community, or of any dwelling the departing member built. An LLC's members can decide such matters any way they like, as long as their policy is stated in the documents they file with the state, which is called an operating agreement.

Sowing Circle's founders included their most important agreements in the operating agreement — their vision, mission, and goals; how they will operate; how they will share ownership interests, profits, losses, rights, responsibilities, and liabilities; how they might sell any ownership interests back to the community; and what procedure they would use to disband the community and dispose of its assets. An LLC usually costs more than a partnership to set up, and unlike with partnerships, requires paying state filing fees.

As mentioned earlier, an LLC is considerably more flexible than other legal entities. For example, in an LLC the amount of ownership interest per member need not match the actual amounts of money contributed by each member, but can be apportioned any way the group decides. If six members each put in $20,000 and seven put in $5,000, all 13 members could receive equal ownership interest, equal decision-making rights, equal distribution of annual profits and losses, and equal shares of assets if the group ever disbanded and sold the property. Or, the 13 members could have ownership shares in proportion to their financial contributions, but their decision-making rights could still be equal. An LLC can also allow different kinds of decision-making rights for different kinds of members. For example, a community could have supporter/members who invest a certain designated amount of money but don't live at the property, and resident/members who do live there. Supporter/members could be involved in decisions that affect land value but not day-to-day decisions, which could be limited to resident/members only. If members do decide to apportion their rights differently than the amounts they each invest, or have several kinds of membership, they should state this clearly in their operating agreement so the IRS won't contest it later.

Like a corporation, an LLC must prepare and file organizational documents with the state, pay filing fees, and adopt operating rules that outline the basic legal requirements for operating under state law. Unlike a corporation, LLC s are not legally required to keep minutes, hold meetings, or make resolutions. An LLC passes its taxable income and tax-deductible expenses on to each member; however, an LLC can also choose to be taxed like a corporation to save tax costs in certain situations.

Disadvantages of LLCs

Pass-through taxation is only beneficial to individual members if they're in a 15 percent or

WHY NOT USE A PARTNERSHIP OR A SUBCHAPTER S CORPORATION?

A partnership offers pass-through tax status, and unlike an LLC, a community organized as a partnership can accumulate savings over the years without having to pass the tax liability for such "profit" onto its members. But a partnership offers no limited liability, and any partner can act on behalf of the whole partnership — including signing contracts and borrowing money for it-and such contracts or debts are binding on the partnership as a whole, even if no other partners agreed. Thus all partners are jointly and severally liable, which means each partner is liable for all the debts and liabilities of the partnership. A creditor or the plaintiff in a lawsuit can go after all of the members, or single out only the richest member, to collect the debts of or the court-mandated damages against the whole community.

Subchapter S corporations, created for small businesses, were more commonly used before LLCs came onto the scene. Most communities which would have previously chosen an S corporation (such as many cohousing communities) now use an LLC instead. An S corporation offers limited liability and pass-through tax status, but has more rules and regulations than an LLC, especially in terms of taxes, and is more complex to administer. It wouldn't work for a large community, as S corporations can have no more than 35 members.

"I'm not aware of any reason to form an S corporation over an LLC," says Sowing Circle/OAEC cofounder Dave Henson.

For more information about partnerships, limited partnerships, and other legal entities communities tend to choose less often, see the author's website <www.CreatingALifeTogether.org>.

lower tax bracket, (the same as corporate taxes). For any members with middle-class incomes, however, their tax rate would likely be 27.5 or 30 percent, almost twice the corporate rate. Also, the IRS will consider any savings the LLC accumulates by the end of the year to be "profit," and the tax liability for these funds must be distributed ("passed-through") to each member that year.

Homeowners Associations — Tax Advantages (and Disadvantages)

In Colorado's brilliant sunshine, a few miles east of Boulder where the Rockies meet the plains, is Nyland Cohousing. With 42 two-story townhomes, each painted a different brilliant color, Nyland is one of the largest cohousing communities in the United States. Members share a

COMMUNITY ASSOCIATIONS AND INTENTIONAL COMMUNITIES

Community Associations (also known as "common interest community associations" or "master planned communities") are generic terms for ways people can own shared property together. They include:

1. Homeowners associations, also called "planned communities" or "planned unit developments," or, by the IRS, "residential real estate management associations," generally own the common areas of the property.

2. Condominium associations own no property, but have a responsibility to manage and maintain all of the common elements; that is, all property outside the interior walls of the individual housing units.

3. Cooperatives, more commonly called housing co-ops, own the property, while residents own shares in the housing co-op and lease their individual units from it.

Community associations are regulated at the state level, and laws vary from state to state. What is called a homeowners association in one state may be called a planned community in another. Community associations are usually set up by developers of real estate

subdivisions and multifamily developments, and are used by the residents to own and manage their shared property together. Intentional communities can use these forms of property ownership as well.

Community associations are required to have a board of directors, regularly elected officers, and annual meetings, and, through an elected board of directors, make decisions about the operations of the association. Typically, either the board of directors manages and maintains the common property, or they hire a manager or management company to do it for them. In most real estate subdivisions or multifamily developments, the residents don't get involved in the day-to-day aspects of management. When intentional communities use a community association for property ownership, quite often all members are on the board and use that as the body for governing their community. Whether an intentional community chooses a homeowners association, condominium association, or housing co-op depends on the approvals and/or requirements of the state and/or the local planning department, what kinds of terms banks might offer, or how readily available financing might be in that state. Financing for housing co-ops is less available, and usually costs more than financing for either homeowners or condominium associations.

large wooden common house, a woodworking shop, a large organic garden, and acres of common land. As in most cohousing communities, people hold title to their own housing units and the ground beneath them. Nyland's 135 residents share ownership in the rest of the property as a homeowners association.

While laws for homeowners associations vary from state to state, in general they require that (1) the homeowners association owns the common areas such as pathways, parking areas, clubhouse facilities, and so on, and (2) all owners of housing units must be members of the association and pay regular assessments for the maintenance and management of its common areas. Intentional communities can also use homeowners associations, primarily because (1) they are recognized legal entities for owning shared property and getting bank financing for individually owned housing units, and (2) some states and municipalities require that a group intending to have individually owned housing units and shared common areas organize as a homeowners (or condominium) association before its development plan will be approved by the city or county.

Some cohousing communities, such as Sonora Cohousing in Tucson, Arizona, have arranged that residents are automatically members of the homeowners association's board of directors, and decide all community matters, not just those of property maintenance, in their regular community meetings. Others, such as Nyland Cohousing, set it up so that members elect a separate board of directors for their homeowners association, but all community members are still part of the whole group's decision-making body. Earthaven uses a homeowners association to own its entire property. Unlike in cohousing, members don't hold title to individual homesites, but lease them from

Earthaven's homeowners association with 99-year leases. All full, active members are members of Earthaven Association's board of directors, and, as such, decide all community-wide issues.

Creating a homeowners association requires forming a non-profit corporation. But rather than petitioning the IRS for a particular tax-exempt status (such as when seeking a 501(c)3 tax status), each year the community simply files under IRS Section 528, which means they can either pay taxes as a homeowners association and receive certain tax advantages, or pay as a regular for-profit corporation. (The IRS 528 tax status is different from the 501(c)3 non-profit tax status used by educational, charitable, or religious organizations to receive tax-deductible donations. And, unlike a 501(c)3, if a homeowners association disbands and sells its property, there's no IRS requirement that the assets be donated to another non-profit; the assets are disbursed to the property owners as in any other business.)

Financing advantages — sometimes. Banks and other lending institutions are familiar with homeowners associations and are willing to loan to them when they are used in the typical way, with each household holding title to their individual housing unit and sharing ownership of common elements with other residents. Thus, homeowners associations are advantageous to cohousing residents, who can seek mortgages for their individual housing units and recover their equity if they leave the community. But homeowners associations don't offer this advantage when a community uses it to own all their property in common, like Earthaven does. Since no Earthaven members hold individual title to their homesites, no one can use a homesite as collateral for a bank mortgage, and so homes must be built with existing assets or personal loans. (This is not a disadvantage of homeowners associations in general, but a result of Earthaven members not owning individual homesites.)

Membership control. However, when a community such as Earthaven uses a homeowners association to own all of its own land, and leases rather than sells its homesites, it is free to choose its members. (Again, this is not because of the homeowners association, but because homesites are leased to members rather than sold.) But in cohousing communities, individual housing units are sold on the open market (one of the requirements for bank financing), so the community as a whole has no actual control over who joins them. The Federal Fair Housing Act prohibits discrimination in the sale of real estate, and most cohousing communities I'm aware of have been advised by their lawyers to sell to whomever can meet the terms of sale. However, people buying in to new cohousing projects and through resales into existing cohousing communities tend to be self-selecting — only those with a fairly strong interest in the cohousing concept and cooperative decision making are willing to get involved in a lifestyle so unorthodox by mainstream standards.

Member equity. A member household leaving a cohousing community using a homeowners association simply sells their housing unit and recovers their equity. People leaving a community that uses a homeowners association like Earthaven does can recover their equity by selling their site leases back to the community (which resells them to incoming members) and sell their home and other site improvements to the incoming members.

Organizational control and flexibility.
Technically homeowners associations (and condominium associations) don't have as much flexibility in internal agreements about decision making or what degree decision making may be tied to the amount of each member's equity in the property. Like all organizations that create non-profit corporations with the state, homeowners and condominium associations must create bylaws which describe the organization's overall operations and how it makes decisions, and use the state-mandated boilerplate language for these bylaws, which stipulate one vote per housing unit. However, real estate lawyer Carolyn Goldschmidt has helped several Arizona cohousing communities overcome this limitation by adding a paragraph to the bylaws empowering the association's board of directors to create a policy manual that outlines their decision-making and other internal agreements. Then the policy manual, not the bylaws, becomes the community's flexible, easily changed document, which, if they like, can stipulate that they use consensus decision-making and other matters of community choice.

Tax advantages — and disadvantages. With a homeowners association, all income collected in any given year for acquiring property, construction, or managing or maintaining its physical infrastructure, is tax exempt. But using a homeowners association can also result in a tax liability, because the income and expense categories of intentional communities often don't fit the categories the IRS created for the mainstream housing developments that homeowners associations are typically used for. In order to get the special tax breaks of a homeowners association in any given year (rather than being required to pay taxes as a corporation), the community must meet the "60 percent test" — at least 60 percent of that year's gross income, known as "exempt function income," must come from members' dues, fees, or assessments for maintaining and managing that physical infrastructure. And it must meet the "90 percent test" — at least 90 percent of its expenses that year must be for the acquisition, construction, management, maintenance, or other operating costs of its physical infrastructure. But intentional communities aren't just about physical infrastructure. A community, unlike a suburban housing subdivision, might have other sources of income; for example, from a members' shared meal program, a childcare program, rental or lease income, income from the sale of firewood or building materials, interest on loans to members, or grants or donations earmarked for an education program or capital improvements.

And here's the first tax disadvantage: all of these sources of income are taxed at a flat 30 percent. And the second: if these sources total more than 40 percent of that year's income, it will reduce the community's non-exempt function income to less than the required 60 percent and the community won't be able to pay taxes as a homeowners association — with exempt function income — and must pay as a corporation.

And, if more than 10 percent of its expenses that year pay for similar activities that have nothing to with managing and maintaining physical infrastructure, such as implementing food or childcare programs, this reduces the community's expenses for physical infrastructure to less than the required 90 percent, and again, the community can't pay taxes as a homeowners association that year, but must pay as a corporation instead.

If the community spent all its members dues and assessments collected that year for physical operating expenses, paying taxes as a corporation wouldn't matter, as it would be a break-even situation. But if the community had capital expenses that couldn't be deducted that year, but which had to be depreciated over several years, or if it wanted to save money for future capital expenditures or maintenance that wouldn't be offset by expenses in the current year, it would not be a break-even situation, and the community would have to pay as a corporation.

Stuart Kingsbery, a CPA and tax lawyer, and Pam Ekrem Vogel, an accountant, examined various alternatives to this situation in *Cohousing* magazine (Winter, 1995). A community using a homeowners association could form a second, for-profit or non-profit corporation as a subsidiary, through which it conducted all community activities not involved with physical infrastructure — a food program, childcare program, educational grant program, and so on. (If the subsidiary corporation was for-profit it presumably would not pay taxes because it would break even, with any income being roughly equal to any expenses.)

If the community used the subsidiary to rent out space, the rental income would be taxable to the homeowners association, and should not total more than 40 percent of its income. In order to satisfy the IRS, the subsidiary corporation must have a separate board of directors, operate independently of the homeowners association, and not be considered an agent of that association.

However, there's no specific guidance from the IRS about whether creating a subsidiary corporation would really work for a community organized as a homeowners association, say Kingsbery and Vogel.

"Use caution," they warn, and first get the option of competent tax and legal counsel. Another alternative they consider is to create two different legal entities sequentially, starting with a homeowners association to collect and spend money almost solely on property acquisition, construction, management, and maintenance. Delay meal programs, child-care programs, grant-seeking programs, loans to members, and other projects or activities that don't involve infrastructure until later, when the initial building phase is done. Then dissolve and replace the homeowners association with a different property owning entity such as an LLC or non-exempt non-profit (making sure yearly expenses roughly match income), and which could operate any such social, member-loan, and educational programs without undue tax consequences. They advise tax and legal counsel for this idea as well.

Condominium Associations

Pioneer Valley Cohousing in western Massachusetts consists of 23 acres of woods and fields, an orchard and organic garden, and a concentric circle of attached and single family houses in red, blue, cream, yellow, green, and brown, plus a large common house, a workshop, and a home office building where several community members work. Pioneer Valley's 94 members own their property as a condominium association.

As mentioned earlier, in a condominium association residents generally own the air space inside their individual housing units and hold a fraction of ownership in the entire property, including all buildings and common areas. The condominium association manages and maintains the property, but owns nothing. The fractions of ownership are usually unequal, and are based on the square footage of the individual housing units.

Condominiums are more numerous in the East, and their laws vary from state to state

(although many states have adopted the Uniform Condominium Act). In Massachusetts, residents own not just the air space of their individual housing units, but the inside surfaces of the walls, ceilings, and floors. Still other states allow condominiums, called "air space condominiums," on plots of ground, such as that of Sharingwood Cohousing in Washington, in which people can individually own their own lots and houses, and a fraction of the entire property. (This form is most often used in rural areas where a drain field or leach field needs to be defined as part of the housing unit, although it can also be used in situations where the building footprint of a detached house is defined as the housing unit.)

Cohousing communities choose condominium associations for property ownership for the same reasons they choose homeowners associations: they can get bank financing for them, and some local zoning jurisdictions require either condominium or homeowners associations in order to approve the development.

Depending on state requirements and the group's preference, condominium associations are created by either forming a non-profit corporation or an unincorporated association, and as with a homeowners association, annually filing taxes under IRS Section 528. (Most real estate lawyers recommend that a group form a non-profit corporation rather than an unincorporated association, because the former offers liability protection.)

Advantages and Disadvantages of Condominium Associations

As with homeowners associations, banks are familiar with condominium associations and will loan to them. Cohousing residents can get bank loans for their individual housing units and can recover their equity if they leave. However, since individual homes are sold on the open market, the community as a whole has no control over who joins them. Again, as in cohousing communities that use homeowners associations, incoming members tend to be self-selecting.

Pioneer Valley chose a condominium association because they got better financing terms than they would have if they'd organized as a cooperative, the only other alternative for this kind of housing available in Massachusetts. Homeowners associations are not available in that state. Pioneer Valley residents elected a board of directors from among their members to carry out certain tasks. Most community decisions, however, are made by the membership as a whole at membership meetings.

Because condominium associations must maintain and manage the physical area, including the entire property (not just some commonly shared property), maintenance fees are usually proportionately higher than in homeowners associations.

Housing Co-ops — Separate Ownership and Use Rights

Members of a housing co-op (also called a cooperative or a co-op) are shareholders in a corporation that owns the property. Their shares confer many of the rights of ownership to a particular housing unit, and a proprietary lease confers the right to live in that unit. Housing co-ops are set up as either non-profit 501(c)4 mutual benefit corporations, non-profit 501(c)3 public benefit corporations, or, in some states, as cooperative corporations, a specialized legal entity created for cooperatives. Sometimes a cooperative's legal entity is a trust, and owners don't have shares, but have beneficial interests in the trust. Cooperatives are taxed according to their non-profit or cooperative corporation status.

If the housing units are of different sizes, or some are more desirable than others, members can either own specific shares for specific housing units (and these shares have different monetary values), or a higher number of shares for larger or more desirable units, depending on state law. Usually cooperatives are used for owning apartments in an apartment building, but land can also be owned this way. Miccosukee Land Co-op, for example, is a 279-acre intentional community near Tallahassee, Florida, founded as a cooperative in 1973. Miccosukkee's founders designated 100 homesites up to several acres in size, and share the rest of the property, including 90 acres of protected wetlands. One hundred shareholding families and individuals joined the community and built their homes on these homesites. Members don't have title to individual plots of land, and since getting a mortgage in a cooperative housing structure is difficult, Miccosukkee's members built their houses slowly over time, as cash flow permitted.

In a cooperative, shares can pass from one owner to another through sale or inheritance, but the right to live in the housing unit, conferred by a lease, must be approved by the whole group or its board of directors. Thus it is possible for someone to buy or inherit shares in a housing co-op but not be approved by the group to live there (which usually means they must sell their unit to a new shareholder approved by the co-op.)

Advantages and Disadvantages of Housing Co-ops

Like homeowners' and condominium associations, individual homeowners in a cooperative are eligible for bank financing, and can recover their equity when they leave. However, fewer banks loan to co-ops and loans are usually more expensive than they would be for other forms of

THREE LEGAL ENTITIES OF COHOUSING COMMUNITIES

From the late 1980s through the late 1990s, the first years of cohousing in North America, many cohousing communities created two legal entities: a subchapter S corporation for their land-purchase and development phase (or an LLC, once LLCs became widely used), and later, a homeowners or condominium association for common ownership of shared property. Some real estate lawyers, such as Carolyn Goldschmidt, who's worked with many cohousing communities in Arizona, recommend three legal entities, as follows:

Non-exempt non-profit corporation. First, the core group needs an initial legal entity that legitimizes it as a group. Carolyn recommends a non-exempt non-profit corporation, created by filing as a non-profit corporation with the state, but not applying for or choosing any tax-exempt status with the IRS. The non-exempt non-profit has a business name and bank account, and is used to collect any membership fees or dues and pay expenses (promotional costs, land search fees, lawyers fees, engineers' fees, and any other fees associated with the land search), and helps demonstrate to potential new members that the core group seriously plans to develop a multimillion-dollar project.

Limited Liability Company. This is usually created when the core group is about to buy their property, and is the vehicle through which they will buy the land, seek a construction loan, and develop the prop-

erty. An LLC may have corporations as well as people as members; usually the group's non-exempt non-profit is the LLC's first member, and the development or construction company they're partnering with is its second member. (See Chapter 14.)

Homeowners' (or condominium) association. This third entity is usually created after the group has bought the land. It is the vehicle through which the group will own its shared property once the land is subdivided (or not subdivided, if it's a condominium), and with which it will help get bank or lender financing for individual mortgages. Cohousing communities and any intentional communities intending to develop and subdivide their property as homeowners associations or create condominium associations are technically real estate developers. Some states as well as municipalities require developers to create a homeowners (or condominium) association for their future lot owners before they will approve the group's plat or site plan, and before any construction can begin.

Once the cohousing group has secured mortgages for their individual housing units, the community is built and people have moved in, and the last details of property development have been completed, the original non-exempt non-profit and the LLC are usually dissolved, leaving the homeowners (or condominium) association as the cohousing community's sole legal entity.

property ownership. (Pioneer Valley Cohousing considered organizing as a cooperative, for example, but the finance costs would have been so much higher that each housing unit would have cost $2,000 more than if they organized as a condominium.)

Because the right to live in a co-op must be approved by the whole membership, theoretically a community organized this way can choose its members, yet some real estate lawyers advise against this. While cooperatives have rejected potential members in the past, it's questionable whether a cooperative could reject members today without triggering any local discrimination laws, although housing co-ops are exempt from the Federal Fair Housing Act.

In a cooperative, ownership and decision-making rights are not always tied to the amount of equity contribution (although this varies from state to state), but are usually expressed as one vote (or one consensus decision-making right) per housing unit, regardless of the relative value of different units.

Limited Equity Housing Cooperatives

This is a special form of cooperative used to create affordable housing co-ops, senior housing co-ops, and student housing co-ops. In a limited equity housing co-op, the price of shares does not rise with escalating housing prices. Members make down payments and monthly mortgage payments to the bank; when they leave, they are reimbursed the amount of their down payment, plus an additional amount related to the cost-of-living increase, but no more. In some states, departing members do not recover any amount of the mortgage payments they made to the bank for the years they lived there. Their mortgage payments remain in the co-op as equity for the next incoming members who will live in those same housing units, and who will pick up the mortgage payments where the departing members left off. In other states, all assets can be recovered. Thus, owning a home in a limited equity housing co-op is not necessarily an investment in property, but a way to own a home without an undue financial burden, combining features of owning and, in some states, of renting.

Like owners, members must pay a down payment, which will be reimbursed when they sell, and they own their housing unit and have a say in the management of their shared property. Like renters (in some states), they have an unrecoverable monthly payment.

While the property for Mariposa Grove in Oakland, California was purchased and renovated by its founder, its members are considering reorganizing themselves as a limited equity housing co-op. To become a limited equity housing co-op, Mariposa Grove will incorporate either as a mutual benefit or a public benefit corporation (two kinds of legal entities offered in California).

Non-exempt Non-profit Corporations

Abundant Dawn in Virginia owns its property through a non-exempt non-profit corporation, which means it doesn't have a particular IRS tax designation such as 528 or 501(c)3. Rather, its founders indicated in the community's organizing documents that it was a non-profit or non-stock corporation (meaning it would not be organized to make a profit, and would have no stockholders and pay no dividends). Therefore, Abundant Dawn's tax rate is the same for as for any corporation: the first $50,000 of net income is taxed at 15 percent. Why would a community choose this form of corporation?

When Abundant Dawn cofounder Velma Kahn began researching legal entities, she considered homeowners associations, entities with pass-through tax status such as LLCs, various categories of tax-exempt and partially tax-exempt non-profits, and non-exempt non-profit corporations. She expected the community to receive income from various sources, primarily from members' fees, and compared how the community would fare at tax time under the various entities she was considering.

She rejected homeowners associations for several reasons, including the "60 percent" restriction on income sources and the rule that only income collected for maintenance and other expenses related to common property management is tax exempt. She also rejected entities with pass-through taxation such as LLCs and subchapter S corporations. While pass-through legal entities are taxed the same as directly-taxed corporations (in terms of the kinds of income and expenses that are considered tax exempt or tax deductible), Velma considered the pass-through tax status of an LLC or S corporation to be disadvantageous. For one thing, while members in low-income tax brackets would pay 15 percent on any passed-through income, members in middle-class tax brackets would likely pay 27.5 or 30 percent, almost twice the corporate rate. Velma also rejected pass-through taxation because she preferred that Abundant Dawn pay taxes at the community level, rather than the individual level, since it would mean less entanglement between the community's finances and its members' finances. If they were taxed at the community level, no members would ever need to wait to finish their tax returns until the community had figured its own taxes and determined each member's pass-through tax portions. And if there were a crisis in community finances, it wouldn't create a crisis in every member's personal finances. This left a simple nonexempt non-profit corporation as the most likely candidate.

Velma's next step was to consider which portions of the money coming into the community would be taxable income and which portions of its expenses would be tax-deductible. She knew most of the community's income would be from regular monthly payments from members, to be spent on property taxes and insurance, repairs and maintenance such as fixing the tractor, and buying food and seeds for the garden. If most of the money collected from members was spent on expenses that were by definition tax deductible (in that the monies were collected for the purpose of making these expenditures), then it really wouldn't matter whether their collected members' fees were treated as taxable income or not, as the tax burden would be negligible. But Velma saw two reasons why the community's tax burden might be unjust if the collected members' fees were treated as taxable income.

The first involves Abundant Dawn's potential savings. The community might want to save portions of their collected members' fees for several years, or simply carry over some funds from one year to the next. But if they did this, the amount collected from members' fees for this purpose would be considered taxable income, and any amount left unspent at the end of the year would be taxed.

The second reason involves buying their property, and to a lesser extent, buying other fixed assets. The portion of their mortgage payment applied to interest would be tax-deductible, but the portion applied to the principal would not be deductible. (When buying equipment such as a tractor, the payment could be deductible, but in some cases only through depreciation over a number of years.) As the mortgage would be paid down over the years, and increasing portions of the mortgage payment applied to principal, the community's tax burden could become substantial.

Fortunately, after researching tax law and case law, and receiving corroboration from a tax attorney, Velma learned that their member contributions for these expenses need not be treated as taxable income, for two reasons. First, Abundant Dawn members would be in the same position as stockholders, and their contributions would be akin to stockholder contributions to equity — a relationship which is well-substanti- ated in case law. Second, the community would act in the role of agent for the members, collecting money from several households for purposes

CAN YOUR GROUP BUY PROPERTY WITHOUT A LEGAL ENTITY?

If you buy property together with no legal structure, you have two choices: own it as tenants in common or as joint tenants. (The terms vary from state to state, as do the regulations for each.) If you don't choose, the state will automatically consider you Tenants in Common.

Tenancy in common. As tenants in common, each member of your group has an undivided interest in the property. Unless you agree otherwise on the deed, you will all have equal rights to the use of the property, and will all share equally in any liabilities or profits. Usually, this means sharing equally all mainte- nance costs and property taxes. However, as tenants in common, you can distribute ownership interests in the property however you wish. Your ownership interests could reflect the relative amounts of money each of you contributed, or you could choose equal ownership portions even if you'd each contributed different amounts. Taxes, maintenance expenses, profits, and the value of any improvements must be apportioned at the same percentages as everyone's shares of ownership.

As tenants in common any of you may sell, mort- gage, or give your ownership interest in the proper- ty to anyone you wish, and the new owner becomes the new tenant in common with the others. If anyone dies, their ownership share of the property passes to their heirs or assigns, not to the other people in your group.

Joint Tenancy. As joint tenants each of you has equal rights to the use of the property, and each of you also shares equally in liabilities and profits, and usually in maintenance costs, taxes, and work responsibilities. But if one of you contracts for improvements on the land, that person is solely responsible for paying the costs if the rest of you didn't consent to those improvements.

Joint tenants have the "right of survivorship," which means if one of you dies that person's share doesn't pass to their heirs, but passes automatically to the rest of you (free from any creditors' claims or debts the deceased person might have incurred).

Disadvantages of tenancy in common and joint tenancy. Both tenancy in common and joint tenancy are poor choices for communities because you could lose your property because of something one member does.

In a joint tenancy, for example, if one of you goes into debt, the creditor seeking collection could force the sale of the property to get the cash value of that person's share in the property. Also, any com- munity member could sell or give away their interest without the approval of the rest of you. This would cancel the joint tenancy, and property ownership would revert to tenancy in common.

And, as mentioned earlier, in a tenancy in com- mon any member can sell his or her ownership inter- ests to someone who isn't a community member. Worse, any disgruntled community member can force the sale of the property to get his or her money out.

which would not be taxable if the same expenses were paid by a single household (such as when a household pays property taxes or mortgage payments). The community would be collecting after-tax income from its members, and these members would have already paid income tax before paying their monthly community fees for shared expenses.

Velma knew they would pay taxes on other kinds of income, such as rental fees from members renting rooms or cabins belonging to the community, visitor fees, and subscription fees to the community's newsletter, and this was fine.

With these questions resolved, it was easy to choose a nonexempt non-profit corporation. Abundant Dawn members believed such a corporation would offer the lowest tax burden of any of the available legal entities, with no temptation to shift tax reporting to meet a particular legal entity's stringent requirements, such as those of a homeowners association. Moreover, they chose a corporation because regular corporate taxation is simple, straightforward, and easy to explain compared to the taxation of other legal entities they'd considered. "A non-exempt non-profit corporation was the cleanest," says Velma. "It didn't require any distortion of what the community is, or creating two sets of stories, one for the IRS, and one for real."

In Chapter 16 we'll look briefly at various kinds of tax-exempt non-profits.

~Chapter 16~

If You're Using a Tax-exempt Non-profit

IN THE EVERGREEN FORESTS of southern Oregon, Lost Valley Educational Center is organized as a non-profit 501(c)3 corporation. A 501(c)3 non-profit must offer a religious, charitable, educational, scientific, or literary benefit. (To the IRS, "religious" is not limited to recognized religions, but can include alternative forms of spirituality, which is why yoga ashram communities and meditation centers often use 501(c) non-profits.) Lost Valley can use a 501(c)3 because of its educational mission: to teach people about sustainable living. Sowing Circle/OAEC in California, Earthaven Ecovillage in North Carolina, and Dancing Rabbit in Missouri all use 501(c)3s to conduct research, offer documentation, and offer classes and workshops in sustainable living.

Again, neither I nor the publisher, nor any community members mentioned in this book presume to offer legal advice about tax-exempt non-profits. This information is intended to offer a variety of ideas for you and your community to consider.

Advantages of a 501(c)3 — Donations, Tax Breaks, Limited Liability

Tax-deductible donations. The primary reason for an organization to incorporate as a 501(c)3 is to receive foundation grants and tax-deductible donations. Donors can claim up to 50 percent of their adjusted gross income for such donations. People can leave money to a 501(c)3 in their wills, and upon their death their estate can receive an exemption from federal estate taxes. Also, having a 501(c)3 may make your community more desirable to donors and philanthropists for private loans with generous terms, as we saw with Sowing Circle/OAEC's refinancing.

Significant tax breaks. A 501(c)3 non-profit doesn't pay federal or state income taxes on income generated by any business activities related to its purpose. It does pay taxes on income generated by activities not related to its purpose, however. For example, Sowing Circle/OAEC pays no taxes on fees for its classes, workshops, and plant sales, but if for some reason it also repaired cars, it would pay taxes on all car-repair income, since that activity is not related to its purpose. In most cases, if a 501(c)3 owns land, it is often exempt from county property taxes. It does pay sales tax.

Other savings. As a non-profit, you are more likely to receive material donations and support from volunteers. You can get non-profit third class bulk postal rates for any bulk mailings, discounted space from some Internet service providers, lower advertising rates in some publications, and free radio and TV public service announcements.

Limited liability. As with all corporations, a 501c(3) non-profit confers limited liability on its directors, trustees, officers, employees, and members. However, courts hold non-profit board members and officers to a higher standard of conduct and accountability than those of for-profit corporations. Non-profits often buy liability insurance to protect their officers and board members.

On-site income for community members. If your 501(c)3 will be operating an educational or other kind of organization that requires full- or part-time staff, you can hire your own community members as employees, and pay their salaries from the non-profit's income (though these can't be exorbitant salaries). Rural communities often need community businesses in which people can earn money without commuting to jobs elsewhere, and depending on their purpose and scale, a 501(c)3's on-site activities can offer such jobs. This is how two-thirds the members of Lost Valley Educational Center and five of Sowing Circle's members make a living without leaving their land.

Disadvantages of a 501(c)3 — Onerous Requirements, Irrecoverable Assets

High set-up and maintenance costs. It can be costly to hire a lawyer to prepare incorporation forms and a tax accountant to prepare IRS applications. As mentioned in Chapter 8, you can save money by doing much of this yourself with the help of Nolo Press's book *How to Form a Non-*

profit Corporation and asking a lawyer and tax accountant to check your work. The total fees to incorporate in many states is less than $200, including the application fee for federal tax exemption, but annual registration fees may be high: in 2002 it was $800 per year in California, for example. (However, most states' annual fees for for-profit corporations are similar.)

Restricted access to bank financing. If you'll be seeking private loans from friends and supporters to buy your property or for projects that support your mission, having a 501(c)3 for lenders to loan to can be an advantage. But it can be a distinct disadvantage if you'll be seeking a bank loan, since most banks prefer not to loan to non-profits, preferring instead to loan to corporations or LLCs.

No equity in the property for members. Members of Lost Valley and Dancing Rabbit cannot build any equity in their property that they could take with them if they left the community, since these communities own their property as 501(c)3s (or 501(c)2s). Sowing Circle/OAEC members do build equity however, since their property itself is owned as an LLC and their 501(c)3 owns nothing but simply manages their educational center project.

Paper shuffling, number crunching. Like all corporations, a 501(c)3 requires ongoing record-keeping. This begins with the filing of the initial documents with the state, and continues with an annual report of activities and other mandatory forms. IRS requirements can also be intimidating. You must keep meticulous financial records with double-entry bookkeeping to prove that your 501(c)3 continues to deserve its tax-exempt status, prepare annual non-profit informational tax returns, and, if it has employees, deal with payroll tax withholding and reporting. Often the idealists who want to set up 501(c)3s are unfamiliar with these business procedures, but if they fail to do these things the IRS can freeze their bank account and bring all their non-profit activities to a halt. Most non-profits start out with a tax advisor or accountant to help them set up their books and create a system to prepare tax forms on time. Some non-profits get these services at no cost by arranging that a bookkeeper or accountant friend is on the board of directors.

Restricted politics. As a 501(c)3, a significant portion of your activities cannot be influencing legislation or endorsing or supporting candidates for public office. How much a "significant portion" is depends on the state.

Losing control of your non-profit. One critical point with 501(c)3s is that 51 percent of the people on its board of directors must be "disinterested." This doesn't mean uninterested (in the non-profit's activities); it means they must have no financial interest in your non-profit, and cannot materially benefit from its existence. If you own your land with a 501(c)3, at least 51 percent of your board members cannot live there, and if it operates your non-profit business, at least 51 percent cannot be its paid employees. Some non-profits initially organize themselves with a group of what's called "voting members" who elect their board of directors every three years. If you organize yourselves this way, 51 percent of your voting members must be disinterested.

While it's relatively easy to find supportive friends willing to become board members, you cannot predict or control what they might do in the future. Years down the road, as things and people change, you could find yourselves fighting desperately with your own board for control of the assets you yourselves donated. If the majority of your board members someday vote to radically change your mission, kick all of you off the property, or disband the community, you couldn't do a thing about it. (You couldn't' block such a decision in a consensus process, since state law requires that non-profit boards must use majority-rule voting. No matter what you might try to block, a 51 percent vote of your board members can change the course of your community's history forever.) "This is the biggest danger with a non-profit," warns Dave Henson.

At least one community has found a way to solve his, however, as we'll see below.

Irrecoverable assets. Once your community donates assets such as cash, securities, personal property, or land in a 501(c)3 non-profit, you can never get these assets out again. (This isn't true of loans. You can loan money to a non-profit, as two Dancing Rabbit founders did, and receive interest and recover part or all of the value of the loan if the community disbands or sells its assets to pay its debts.) If things don't work out and you disband, you cannot take back the value of the land and its capital improvements, but must either donate your property to another non-profit, or sell it and donate the proceeds of the sale to a non-profit.

For many communities this is not a disadvantage, since they choose a 501(c)3 primarily for this feature. When Dianne Brause and Kenneth Mahaffey bought the Lost Valley property, for example, they wanted to restore the land and protect it from ever being sold for speculative gain. They chose a 501(c)3, knowing that no community member could ever personally benefit from the sale of the property, which would act as a major disincentive for any future community members to disband the community and sell the land. Sometimes communities choose 501(c)3s for land ownership because the founders want to live out their ideals, intending to move to community and stay there. Nature's Spirit founders chose a 501(c)3 partly for this reason, and partly from a commitment to live a more spiritual way of life in a beautiful rural setting. Why would they want to leave?

However, one community's blessing is another's downfall. It's disastrous to start a project you can never recoup your life savings from if that's not explicitly what you intend at the beginning. What if things don't work out as you imagined? (Remember the 90 percent?) There's nothing more demoralizing than disillusioned communitarians grimly hanging on for decades because no one can afford to leave.

If you choose to own your property as a 501(c)3, be sure you understand all the implications. Be certain you're choosing it for the right reasons — not just because you think it's cool!

Land-Owning Entities and 501(c)3 Corporations — The Best of Both Worlds

"Think really hard before you use your 501(c)3 to *own* anything," advises Dave Henson. Sowing Circle community's non-profit OAEC owns nothing but its good reputation and some office supplies. Everything else — OAEC's office building, equipment, classrooms, dorms, dining facilities, and the grounds on which they host visitors and teach classes-is leased from the Sowing Circle LLC. The lease fee is $70,000 a year, and OAEC splits with Sowing Circle costs for repairing and maintaining the land and buildings it uses. The mission of Sowing Circle community founders is to live sustainably in

community and promote a more environmentally aware, ecologically sustainable way of life. They created OAEC as a 501(c)3 non-profit to help them carry out this mission by offering workshops and classes to promote the arts, social justice, environmental activism, and ecological sustainability. Sowing Circle founders also set up OAEC in order to provide income for community members, five of whom are salaried OAEC staff.

The OAEC non-profit makes money from a variety of sources, such as workshop and class fees, consulting fees, facility rentals, membership fees from supporting members, plant sales, foundation grants, and private donations (including volunteer labor and work exchange and donated in-kind services, such as printing).

The non-profit spends money on salaries for 20 full- and part-time employees (including off-site employees, and on-site residents who aren't community members), as well as associated expenses for Workers' Compensation; meals for work-exchange staff and course participants; wages for outside instructors; advertising and promotional costs; office supplies, postage, etc.; and when needed, materials or outside labor for repairing and maintaining leased grounds and buildings.

The Sowing Circle community's expenses, on the other hand, include mortgage payments, liability insurance, property taxes, food and other household expenses, and donations to OAEC for materials and any outside labor for maintenance and repairs. Because it's organized as an LLC, Sowing Circle's taxable income is divided up and passed to each member.

Sowing Circle receives income from members' monthly dues and OAEC's lease fees. In the beginning OAEC had agreed to pay $24,000 in lease fees, but the first year it could only pay half, and Sowing Circle wrote off the other half as a business loss. Several years later Sowing Circle hired a rural property appraiser and learned that, at market rates, their property could be worth up to $85,000 in annual lease fees (in year 2000 dollars). So Sowing Circle raised its annual lease fee to $70,000. The lease fee Sowing Circle charges OAEC cannot be any higher than the appraised market value of such a lease, or the IRS would consider it "self-dealing." To be safe, Sowing Circle charges OAEC $15,000 less than the appraised leasable value of their property.

In terms of decision making, all 11 Sowing Circle members make decisions about the relationship between their community and their educational non-profit. All OAEC staff members (including the non-community members), decide the non-profit's financial and other matters, and its board of directors make major policy decisions. Forty-nine percent of these directors are also Sowing Circle members. (To protect themselves, Sowing Circle's lease document has a clause which allows them to terminate OAEC's lease at any time for any reason. If a majority of OAEC's board tried for some reason to take the non-profit in a direction the community didn't want, the community could cancel the lease and OAEC would lose its teaching facilities.)

Sowing Circle community benefits from its business relationship with OAEC in several ways, including:

- Community founders can accomplish their educational mission without undue taxation or liability of their members or property. If OAEC were ever in financial or legal trouble, the community's land would be safe from any debts or lawsuits against the non-profit.

- Nearly half Sowing Circle's members, and six to ten other long-term residents and interns work for OAEC, and so don't have to leave the property to make a living.

- It earns $70,000 in annual lease fees.

- Most of its property and buildings are repaired and maintained by OAEC.

- Any grants or donations that come in to OAEC specifically earmarked for facilities improvement benefit the community's land and buildings (since they're the same), and result in capital improvements to the community.

- If Sowing Circle has taxable income left over at the end of the year it can donate it to OAEC for certain kinds of non-capitalizable maintenance and repair (that is, projects that don't improve the property long-term), and receive a tax break for the donation.

OAEC benefits from its business relationship with Sowing Circle community as well. For example:

- It has beautiful grounds and facilities for its educational activities.

- Its five Sowing Circle staff members are devoted to its mission, and live on-site.

- Its lease is relatively secure, because the same people, with the same intentions and vision, are the lessors and lessee. If for some reason OAEC couldn't fulfill its maintenance responsibilities, or couldn't pay its annual lease fee, there'd be a great deal of flexibility in solving the problem.

For information on setting up and maintaining a 501(c)3 non-profit, see Appendix 3.

How One Group Retained Control of its Board

"We never wanted to lose control of our own projects, or even fight with our board if things changed someday," one founder told me. She and her seven cofounders set up a 501(c)3 in such a way as to protect themselves from this kind of takeover.

They planned that 17 "voting members" (that is, a special group that elects their board of directors every three years), would elect eight people to their board. All eight founders became voting members. They needed nine more people to become the remaining voting members, so that at least 51% would be "disinterested." The founders asked nine of their closest friends to become voting members, explaining that their sole role would be to vote for the non-profit's board of directors every three years. The founders described their non-profit's mission and goals and gave their friends all of its documents. Then the eight founders nominated themselves as eight of the board members for the first three years. They asked these friends/voting members to approve or deny their slate of board member candidates (themselves), hoping, of course, that the friends would approve them. ("If any of you have a problem with our request to approve or deny the candidates," the founders asked them in advance, "then please don't agree to become voting members.") Since the friends knew and trusted the founders they voted to approve them as board members, as expected. The IRS looked very carefully at each of these nine voting members to make sure they didn't benefit materially from the non-profit, and they didn't. After the usual three-year period of close scrutiny, the IRS was satisfied. At this point, the founders asked their friends to disband the vot-ing membership aspect of the non-profit (which voting members can do), and increase the board to 11 members. The voting member-friends did this, and the founders asked three of them to join their board, which they did.

Now the community had all eight community members and three friends on the non-profit's board. Why did they want three non-members to join them? Whenever the board had to decide matters that benefited the community (such as adjusting the lease fee of the buildings it rents from the community), or raising salaries of community members who are also paid employees, they must remove themselves from the decision. They have three non-community board members so that for decisions like these, there will still be people left who can decide. (There are three so that if they disagree, one can break the tie. Of course, as friends of the community, they decide the way the community asks them to. If any of the non-community board members went against the community's wishes, the community would vote them off the board and replace them with someone more sympathetic.)

Title-holding Corporations — Collecting Income from "Passive" Sources

The primary mission of Dancing Rabbit in Missouri is to research, document, and educate people about sustainable living, and so they use a 501(c)3 non-profit to host workshops on sustainable living and carry out their other educational activities. However, another part of their mission is to preserve their land as a sustainable ecovillage and prevent it form ever being sold for speculative gain. So they formed a land trust, and own their property with a 501(c)2 title-holding non-profit, from which members lease small siteholdings.

A 501(c)3 non-profit can own property, but no more than 20 percent of its income may be from "passive" sources (rents, lease fees, and interest on loans or investments), or it can lose its tax-exempt status. So 501(c)2 non-profits were created in order to hold, control, and manage property and other assets for 501(c)3 non-profits, and they are often used as the land-owning entity in land trusts and community land trusts. A 501(c)2 cannot exist by itself, and must be paired with a 501(c)3. The 501(c)3 must exercise some control over its 501(c)2, such as having the same board members on each non-profit's board. Unlike a 501(c)3, a 501(c)2 cannot actively engage in any business activities, other than collecting rents, receiving interest, and so on. The 501(c)2 turns over all its income to its parent 501(c)3, and the two organizations file a consolidated tax return.

Private Land Trusts — Protecting the Land

A land trust is a legal mechanism to preserve the characteristics of a parcel of land, prevent it from ever being developed in an undesirable way, or protect it from being sold for speculative gain. Land trusts have been used to protect ecologically sensitive areas or the habitat of endangered species, preserve land as wilderness or farmland, and in urban areas, to protect affordable housing from the effects of escalating real estate values. A land trust either takes a property off the market forever or arranges that it can never be bought and sold at speculative market rates, or developed in a way that the donors of the land trust don't want. Intentional communities have placed their properties in land trusts for various reasons — to preserve its rural or agrarian character, to protect virgin stands of timber, to keep it as farmland, or simply to preserve it as an ecovillage for future generations.

Three parties are involved in a land trust.

1. The donor or donors are land owners who place the property in the trust for specific purposes. They can be the original land owners, or people who buy the land in order to place it in the trust.
2. The trustees or board of trustees administer the property and protect its mission. Selected for their alignment with the land trust's mission and goals, the trustees make sure the property is preserved in accordance with them. Over the years outgoing trustees are replaced by incoming ones, so the trust can continue in perpetuity.
3. The beneficiaries are the people and/or plants and animals who live on or otherwise benefit from the land. For a preserved wilderness the beneficiaries are its plants and animals and the humans who hike its trails; for an affordable housing project the beneficiaries are the people who live there.

The donors, trustees, and beneficiaries can all be the same people. Dancing Rabbit's founders purchased their property through their 501(c)2 land trust entity (making them functionally equivalent to donors of a land trust), are members of its board of trustees, and benefit from living on and enjoying the land.

A 501(c)3 and 501(c)2 non-profit are most often used for land trusts. The 501(c)2 holds actual title to the land and grants the beneficiaries long-term, renewable leases at reasonable fees.

Donors may deed their property to an existing land trust organization in their region, which serves as the trustees for that and other properties. Sometimes the donors have the right to live out their lives on the land, for example, if they donated their family farm to a land trust to be preserved as farmland. Other donors might donate their land as a wilderness area, in which case they wouldn't live there. The donor receives a one-time tax deduction for the appraised value of the property. In many circumstances, donors are required to pay $5,000 to $10,000 or more to the land trust's legal fund, so the organization can legally protect the property from any future threats to its mandated use.

Or people may create their own land trust and serve as its only trustees, in which case it's called a "private land trust." Private land trusts can be either revocable or irrevocable. If it's revocable, the donors can change their minds and develop or sell the property for another use. Once land is placed into a land trust it can be difficult to use as collateral for bank loans.

Land can also be preserved by creating a conservation easement, a legal restriction attached to its deed which limits all future use of the land to a specific purpose, such as to protect farmland, wetlands, a wilderness area, and so on. Sowing Circle created an "organic easement," possibly the first of its kind, to preserve its two locally-famous gardens as organically-managed in perpetuity.

Community Land Trusts — An Irrevocable Decision

A community land trust is designed to establish a stronger and broader board of trustees than those of a private land trust. While one-third of the trustees of a community land trust may live on the land (through lease agreements with the community land trust), two-thirds of the trustees must live elsewhere (be "disinterested"), receiving no direct benefit from the land. This ensures that any donors or beneficiaries who are also trustees cannot change their minds about the purpose or mission of the trust, or develop the land for some other purpose, or sell it. Having the majority of its trustees from the

wider community serves to guarantee the mission of the community land trust, because theoretically they are more objective, and are not in a position to be tempted by gaining financially from any change in the use of the land.

Community land trusts are irrevocable, which means the original owners of the land cannot remove it from the trust once they have donated it. As with private land trusts, once land is placed into a community land trust, it's not likely to be used as collateral for bank loans.

Private land trusts, and community land trusts especially, are options for founders wishing to ensure that the original purpose for their community and its land continues unchanged into future generations, unaltered by subsequent requirements for quick cash, loss of commitment, or personality conflicts among members.

For "Common Treasury" Communities — 501(d) Non-profit Corporations

Originally designed for the Shakers and other "Religious and Apostolic Associations" in the 1920s, 501(d) non-profits offer tax breaks for common-treasury religious communities that engage in business for the common benefit of their members. 501(d)s are also used by non-religious income-sharing communities, whose members work in one or more community businesses, and which provide members' basic material needs — food, shelter, monthly stipends, and so on. (Again, to the IRS, "religious" and "apostolic" does not necessarily mean a traditionally recognized religion; communities with alternative spiritual beliefs or secular beliefs have become 501(d)s.) The 501(d) tax status was originally created for groups that had taken a "vow of poverty," but Twin Oaks in Virginia successfully challenged this requirement, and the IRS no longer requires it.

Some communities, such as Twin Oaks and the Hutterite communities, use a 501(d) to own their land as well as their businesses. Other communities own their properties with one of the other legal entities, but a smaller group of members — a sub-community within the community — use a 501(d) to own their own income-sharing business. Abundant Dawn, for example, owns its land with a non-exempt non-profit, but Tekiah, a pod (sub-community) of Abundant Dawn, operates its shared hammock-making and market garden businesses with a 501(d). Dancing Rabbit owns its land with a 501(c)2 non-profit, and Skyhouse, a subcommunity, operates Skyhouse Consulting, a computer programming and website design business, as a 501(d). (The IRS was initially somewhat dubious about Skyhouse's petition to be taxed as a 501(d), because a high-tech telecommuting business with skilled, well-paid professionals was nothing like the hammock-makers or Hutterite farmers they were used to. But Skyhouse members demonstrated they were every bit as devoted to income-sharing, common-treasury principles as any other group, and the IRS granted the status.)

Advantages of 501(d) Non-profits

The main advantage of a 501(d) is income tax savings. The taxable income of a 501(d) is divided into equal parts and "passed through" to each member as if they were filing individual tax returns (as in an LLC or partnership). For example, if a group had 10 members and earned $100,000 one year, they'd each be assigned $10,000 as taxable income (even though they wouldn't actually receive it). Divided up like this, the rate of taxation is much lower than if it were one lump sum. A 501(d) can also choose not to pay self-employment taxes, which is often up to 15 percent of the annual income.

Depending on the amount of the community's annual income and how many members it has (and if it chooses not to pay self-employment tax), the amount assigned to each community member may not be enough to warrant being taxed, which happens most years with Skyhouse subcommunity at Dancing Rabbit. However, if a 501(d) community has a high income and few members, then the amount passed through to each member may be high enough to pay taxes on, which has also happened with Skyhouse. In this case, the community pays the taxes on behalf of the member.

If the community chooses not to pay self-employment tax they'll never get Social Security benefits and must set up some form of in-house retirement fund and take care of their members as they age. 501(d) groups can voluntarily pay self-employment tax to retain access to Social Security.

A 501(d) non-profit can engage in any kind of business, passive or active, religious or secular, since the IRS makes no distinction between related or unrelated income for a group with this tax status. A 501(d) can engage in any kind of political activity, such as lobbying, supporting candidates, or publicly advocating political causes. However, donations to a 501(d) community are not tax deductible, as donations to 501(c)3 non-profits are.

Communities organized as 501(d)s can choose their incoming members, and departing members may or may not receive equity when they leave, depending on the community's internal agreements.

Disadvantages of 501(d) Non-profits

To use the 501(d) tax status the community must be "income-sharing" in the sense that they share income not only from community businesses but also from any outside jobs, investments, or other forms of income. If, however, a substantial percentage of community income is derived from outside salaries or other sources, the IRS may rescind or deny the 501(d) status. (Unfortunately the IRS has not clearly defined what it means by "substantial," so this remains a gray area.) For this reason, Twin Oaks asks any members who have significant assets such as real estate, securities, or savings accounts to place these in a trust for the duration of their community membership.

Members of Meadowdance in Vermont are "income-sharing" in that they work at community-owned businesses, pool business income in a common pot, and provide their basic material needs from it. But, as mentioned earlier, they have a hybrid economy — each member is free to spend money from existing assets, and can earn extra money by working longer hours at community businesses, or working part-time outside the community. Meadowdance doesn't qualify for a 501(d) tax status nor does it want to be limited by the requirements of a 501(d), so they own their businesses as Limited Liability Companies.

The 501(d) non-profit is not applicable for most communities, but if your group plans to share income from community businesses and provide most of your members' material needs, it can offer an ideal way to save on the tax bite.

In Part Three we'll return to the essence of growing a healthy community — the "people skills."

Part Three:
Thriving in Community

— Enriching the Soil

Chapter 17

Communication, Process, and Dealing with Conflict: The Heart of Healthy Community

WHEN LARRY KAPLOWITZ and his wife Karin moved to Lost Valley in 1994, they arrived a few weeks after more than half the members had moved away for various personal reasons unrelated to the community. The remaining four members had desperately needed help for the community's conference center business and put out the call for new people. Larry and Karin were part of ten newcomers who joined in response. The rapid turnover was difficult for everyone.

"Here, suddenly, were ten of us; enthusiastic, full of our own hopes and ideas, hurts and defenses, and relatively short on the kind of experience it takes to make community living work," Larry recalls. "Lost Valley's community culture, delicately woven over the previous years, couldn't survive the onslaught. We began to sink in misunderstandings, resentment, and conflict."

"Within a year, conflict had practically paralyzed us. In our weekly business meetings, where we make decisions by consensus, almost every new idea or initiative, if not rejected outright, was resisted or undermined. Some people had become so uncomfortable with each other that they would go out of their way to avoid crossing paths. Resentments simmered but were rarely expressed directly, except in occasional outbursts of anger. At times the tension was so thick we felt like we were choking on it."

Eventually the people who were most at odds with each other left the community, and things improved a bit. But the experience had left people feeling hurt, discouraged, and cautious. For the next year, Lost Valley accepted no new members. People did their own thing and tried to stay out of each other's way.

"By the summer of '96 every one of us was frustrated, dissatisfied, and considering leaving," Larry says. "We agreed that if we were going to survive as a community we needed major change, which meant we would have to face our difficult issues directly."

Serendipitously, they learned about the Naka-Ima training. A Japanese phrase meaning "here now," Naka-Ima is an interpersonal healing method designed to help people reveal themselves honestly and connect with each other deeply. So the Lost Valley folks signed themselves up.

"By the end of the weekend training," Larry recalls, "the obstacles we all had in the way of being clear, compassionate, and honest with each other seemed to have dissolved, leaving a room full of radiant beings. We knew that the 'glow' would come and go, and that our obstacles, defenses, and wounds would continue to play havoc with us. But they no longer had the same power over us. As we integrated what we'd experienced over the next few weeks and months, we became increasingly honest with each other. We began taking the time to stop and address issues, conflicts, and hurts. We began making space for each other to express our feelings."

To save their community from continued stalemate and decline, Lost Valley members embraced what I call "good process" — communication skills and other techniques that help people feel connected and stay connected. Like great community property and a healthy internal economy, "good process" is another foundation for sustainable community. Learning good process skills nourishes the soil of healthy community. *Not* learning them is another set-up for structural conflict.

The "Rock Polisher" Effect

Most people drawn to intentional community are seeking a more harmonious and connected way of life than that of mainstream society. But we can't just wish it into existence. If we want to live better lives in community, we've got to do things differently there.

Most of us don't realize that our wider society is dysfunctional because it's just ourselves, doing what we habitually do, but multiplied and magnified by millions of people. When we see governments or corporations using manipulative, controlling, or punishing behaviors — through threats, terrorist attacks, or outright war — it frightens and disgusts us. But when we do the small-scale versions of these same ploys ourselves, we don't see it. We may revile "terrorists,"

but what about our own choice of words and tone of voice this morning with our partner or child? Those of us who think we do these behaviors the least are often the ones who do them the most. The more spiritual we imagine we are, the harder it is to see it.

This is why good process is so important to community. For life in community to be better than it was before, *we've* got to be better than we were before. In fact, we need good process skills *more* when we're involved in community, since the community process tends to trigger faster-than-normal spiritual and emotional growth. The "crucible of community" tends to magnify and reflect back to us our own most destructive or alienating attitudes and behaviors. We become magnifying mirrors for each other. The more intensely we dislike these attitudes and behaviors in other community members the more likely we have them in ourselves (or used to have them), although we may be unaware of it. The more we criticize other people for them, the more likely that we're unconsciously condemning ourselves for doing the same.

The close and frequent interactions with other community members about how we'll live and work together tends to evoke some of our worst and most destructive behaviors. And potentially, it can heal them. I call this the "rock polisher" effect. Rocks in a rock tumbler first abrade and then polish each other. In forming-community groups and communities our rough edges are often brought up and then worn smoother by frequent contact with everyone else's. But the rock-polisher effect can be so painful it ejects some people right out of the group, or the group becomes so fraught with conflict that it breaks up.

Through good community process we can make the rock-polisher effect more conscious.

Rather than suffer helplessly, we can use community as a powerful opportunity for personal growth. The process of sharing resources and making decisions cooperatively in community — and no longer being able to get away with our usual behaviors — is a wake-up call to the soul. Community offers us the chance to finally grow up.

Nourishing Sustainable Relationships

"At Lost Valley we learned that sustainable community must be based on sustainable relationships — relationships that give more than they take — that nourish, enliven, and inspire us," says Larry Kaplowitz. "Such relationships are a continual source of energy. They support us in becoming fully ourselves."

As you'd expect, the same kinds of communication and process skills that enhance love relationships do the same in community — sharing from the heart, listening to each other deeply, telling difficult truths without making each other wrong. This includes speaking to and perceiving others in ways that allow us to stay in beneficial relationships with them while discussing even the most sensitive subjects.

Here are some "good process skills" communities often use to create sustainable relationships:

Speaking more consciously. This involves speaking to one another in ways that tend to increase, rather than decrease, the level of harmony and well-being between people. When communication is "clean" enough, people feel confident they can talk to each other about anything, including disagreements or sensitive issues, and still feel good will and connection. These include using "I" rather than "you" messages, checking assumptions, describing feelings with real feeling words ("angry," "worried") instead of blame-words ("criticized," "manipulated"), and using neutral language to describe behaviors rather than characterizing people negatively.

The most effective communication skills I've found are those of Marshall Rosenberg's Nonviolent Communication process, which help people speak to each other in ways that tell the deepest truths while enhancing good will and deepening their connection. Many resources are available for learning these and other basic good communication skills (see Resources).

It takes time, energy, and willingness to change the ways we habitually talk with people, so that our conversations enhance, rather than diminish, our relationships. At first these methods may feel "unnatural." It helps to remember that all communication skills, including those we use now, are learned behaviors, and we can learn new ones.

Creating communication agreements. Conflict can arise because of the widely differing communication styles and behavioral norms that people

---

THE PROCESS TEAM

Some communities, such as Sharingwood Cohousing in Washington state, help maintain well-being in the community by establishing a team of consensus and process facilitators whose job it is to train meeting facilitators, introduce process methods (sharing circles, threshing meetings, the public/private scale, and so on), and keep an eye out for potential conflicts, and intervene when necessary. "Get your best facilitators and the people most interested in process," says Sharingwood process facilitator Rob Sandelin. "Encourage them and give them funds to get training in and bring good process techniques back to the group. The investment of time and money in good group process will more than pay for itself in community health and well being over the long run."

bring to community from different regions, sub-cultures, and socio-economic backgrounds. So some groups agree on and write down explicit communication and behavioral agreements. For example, is jumping in before someone has finished speaking considered a disrespectful interruption, or normal lively conversation? Is coming directly to the point considered respectful of each other's time, or brusque and preemptory? Are using swear words or explicitly sexual expressions of anger considered no big deal, or way out of line? Is inquiring about each other's romantic, sexual, financial, or health matters seen as friendly and intimacy-creating, or an invasion of privacy?

Check-ins: Check-ins can occur before decision-making meetings, or in separate meetings. Everyone around the circle tells what's going on in their lives at that time, their feelings about it, and perhaps their hopes and dreams about it. No one interrupts or responds — there's no sympathizing, criticizing, or offering advice. Usually there's a time limit, such as five or ten minutes per person.

Abundant Dawn allows 15 to 30 minutes of check-in time at the beginning of business meetings for members to let each other know what's going on that may affect how they communicate in the meeting, as well as any events that may affect community business itself. "If we just learned that someone's father died that week, for example," says member Joy Legendre, "then we'll all know why he hasn't been his normal self lately."

Sharing circles: Sharing circles are also sometimes called wisdom circles, the talking stick process, listening circles, heart shares, or the council process. These are sessions in which people share what's true for them and listen to each other deeply. Inspired by the Native American talking stick process, the purpose is not to solve problems or make decisions, but to explore issues and learn together, share personal stories and become closer to each other, or hear everyone's truth, pain, or joy about community issues.

People usually sit in a circle. Candles and ritual objects, including a small object such as a talking stick or a stone, are placed in the center. One person at a time picks up the talking stick or object and speaks from the heart. This means being honest and real, and allowing any emotions that might come up. It involves taking the risk to speak your truth without knowing how it will be received. Speaking from the heart often opens the door for others to do the same.

As in the check-in process, everyone listens respectfully, and no one comments (although in groups that follow Native American traditions, people often say "ho!" if the speaker's words have touched them deeply). When the speaker is finished, the talking stick or ritual object is returned to the center, and there is a short period of silence. The next person moved to speak does so, and then others, until everyone who wishes to speak has had a turn. Not every person needs to speak. In some sharing circles no one speaks twice; other groups encourage individuals to speak two or three times.

In another version of this process, when each speaker finishes, the ritual object is passed to the person on the left, who speaks next, and so on around the circle. Some groups go around at least three or four times, with each person taking one to three minutes each.

The Roots of Conflict: Emotionally-charged Needs

"Most of the time we no longer resist conflict, or ignore it, or try to tiptoe around it," says Larry Kaplowitz. "We've come to see it as an opportunity to identify our patterns, to uncover and heal our old wounds and distress. We're usually willing to stop what we're doing and address conflict, get to the root of it, and clear it.

"But we've accepted that it's not an instant process, nor a tidy one. Lifelong patterns don't give up the ghost without a fight. Sometimes we fall back on our denial and avoidance for days and weeks until it gets unbearable, but eventually someone always musters up enough courage or annoyance to shout 'Enough!'"

Community process consultant Laird Schaub defines conflict as at least two people having different viewpoints about something, with at least one of them having an emotional charge on the matter. Conflict also seems to be a

---

FIVE WAYS TO RESPOND TO CONFLICT

1. Ignore and suppress it. Rarely a conscious choice, but rather a lifelong avoidance pattern, this response erodes the quality of well-being in a group. Your members might not notice the buried resentments accumulating over time, but visitors certainly will. "Why does this group feel so heavy?" And like trying to squash beach balls by pushing them under the rug, ignored conflict always pops up somewhere.

2. Leave it. Leave the subject, leave the room, leave the group or the community. Another popular, mostly unconscious choice, this is usually a lose/lose situation, for the person and for the group.

3. Leap into it aggressively. Some people thrive on conflict, and enjoy how emotionally alive they feel when sparring with others. They may crave emotional intensity; or believe that aggressive criticism is equivalent to "being honest." They may unconsciously want to recreate a negative but familiar experience from early childhood. Some people may not experience their feelings consciously, so yelling at others gets them in touch with suppressed anger, and it feels great to let it out. Other people can only feel connected with someone once they've had a fight — as if they're testing someone's solidity or strength before they can trust them. By leaping into conflict people may meet their own needs for aliveness, authenticity, healing, connection, or trust, but their strategy of fighting with people to meet these needs can drive others right out of the room and right out of the group.

4. Change how you feel about it. In this response to conflict, emotional upsets are considered opportunities for personal growth and spiritual development. You don't address issues that upset you, but rather go deeply into any anger, fear, or sadness as a result of the problem in order to release these feelings and enter a state of tranquility. This can empower individual members, and certainly prevents angry confrontations in the group, but it doesn't necessarily empower the whole community or help create sustainable relationships. Gary may continue blasting his loud music at 3:00 am and annoy the hell out of everyone else, no matter that you've become enlightened because of it.

5. Use the conflict to strengthen the community. Lastly, you can use conflict to generate more understanding and connection, and make changes in behavior to improve how everyone gets along — in other words, use it as part of "good process." Handled well, dealing with conflict can make a community stronger, more connected, and lighthearted in the long run.

multi-layered process. On the surface it may seem to be about differences in ideologies, priorities, and values, especially about such controversial community issues as children, food, labor requirements, and pets. But below that layer, it seems to be about fear, guilt, or resentment, and below that, deep longings from early childhood for certain basic human needs — for acceptance, approval, control, love, and so on.

Psychologists recognize that besides physical needs for food, water, warmth, and so on, certain emotional needs must be met for infants and children to develop into emotionally healthy adults — including nurturing, affection, love, acceptance, empathy, connection, being valued, and being respected, to name a few. When an infant or child doesn't experience nurturing and affection in adequate amounts, for example, these needs can become highly charged because they're associated with the pain of loss, which creates the unconscious fear that the person will never get enough nurturing or affection. Hence, buried pain from long-ago unmet emotional needs can trigger conflict in community 20, 30, and 40 years later.

Having deeply-buried emotionally charged needs is not the problem. The problem is believing that at some level that community will somehow meet these needs. The secret, silent *demand* that community or other community members must provide what seems to be missing adds a cutting edge to conflict. This is why arguments about what on the surface seem like ideologies, priorities, or values, can be so intense. I may assume that community means valuing inclusion (because I desperately needed acceptance as a child and didn't get it); *you* may assume community means freedom for each of us to do our own thing (because you desperately needed autonomy as a child and didn't get it). So we end up having fierce fights about what "community" means.

What can we do about it? We can develop good communication and process skills, learn to accept and welcome feedback and do course-correction when necessary, find ways to heal our individual issues, and deal constructively with conflict when it arises.

High Woundedness, High Willingness

"We've learned that it's the little things — the minor hurts, the small resentments, the petty judgments about each other — that subtly yet pervasively undermine and limit the degree of well-being in our relationships," says Larry Kaplowitz. "Even a small degree of mistrust can prevent us from really being open with each other. Uncleared, this can quickly spiral downward into disconnection, avoidance, more resentment, and conflict."

Clearing these issues often involves offering feedback, by which I mean telling someone about something they did or said and how it affected you negatively.

COHOUSING AND CONFLICT

Cohousing founders tend to excel at the logistics of forming a community — acquiring land and financing, and dealing with development — but tend to stumble over interpersonal communication, often becoming embroiled in intractable conflict once they move into their beautifully constructed buildings. Founders of non-cohousing communities, however, often stumble over business and financial hurdles but seem to instinctively value good process and communication skills. (Founders of more recently built cohousing communities, however, seem more aware that the human connection is as important as the construction loan.) We certainly need both sets of skills! Let's hope members of cohousing and non-cohousing communities will learn from one another, and we'll all benefit.

Many people attracted to community have so many highly charged unmet needs that they are easily triggered into hurt, anger, and defensiveness. They give feedback in brusque, unskilled ways and resist any feedback that others try to offer them. They have what I call "high woundedness." Yet others attracted to community, equally wounded, are also willing to do what it takes to heal themselves and learn good process skills. Such people have what I see as "high willingness and high woundedness." Even though dealing with critical feedback is difficult, they often learn good communication skills well enough to give feedback compassionately, and develop enough self-esteem to hear and thoughtfully consider any negative feedback offered by others. They often become community's best facilitators, counselors, and mediators.

Before dealing with the art of giving and receiving feedback, however, let's examine some common kinds, as well as some common sources, of community conflict.

Seven Kinds of Community Conflict We Wish We'd Left Behind

Here are how certain habitual "old paradigm," "dominator culture" behaviors and attitudes are often expressed when transplanted to intentional community. We can begin to dismantle these behaviors in ourselves by first realizing that if we want to live more sustainably and harmoniously in community than we did in mainstream culture we've got to change ourselves too!

1. Founder's Syndrome (I). Unconsciously assigning parent and authority figure roles to founders and acting out adolescent rebellion and self-identity issues by resenting, undermining, and/or challenging the community founders' wisdom or experience, and/or the validity or relevance of the community's values, vision, or purpose.

2. Founder's Syndrome (II). Founders' clinging to an unconscious self-image as parents or authority figures; assuming a wiser, superior, or more privileged status than other members; and resenting, undermining, or challenging any efforts to question the founders' authority or otherwise offer the community innovation, new perspectives, or change.

3. Visionary Abuse. When dynamic, energetic, visionary founders, burning with a spiritual, environmental, or social-justice mission, work grueling hours in primitive, cramped, uncomfortable, or health-risking conditions, and happily expect all members, interns, and apprentices to do the same. Related to eco-macho, sustainabler than thou, campground macho ("We all lived in tents for three years with no heat, electricity, or running water, and you should too"), and community macho ("Community is not for wimps: *we* can take it, can you?").

4. Violating community agreements. The resentment and erosion of community trust that occur when a few people don't follow the community's agreements and policies consistently, while others follow and uphold them.

5. Letting people get away with violating community agreements. The further resentment, erosion of trust, and breakdown of community well-being that results when a member isn't called on disregarding agreements and so continues disregarding them. By default the person becomes a kind of community aristocrat with the privilege of living outside the normal rules. Often perpetuated by interpersonal power imbalances.

6. Interpersonal (as compared to "structural") power imbalances. Conflict, resentment, and the breakdown of trust in community when some members have more power than others because of behaviors that others are reluctant to or afraid to deal with. These can include:

- *Intimidation power:* Habitually emanating anger, suppressed rage, "panic-anger," and burning intensity; speaking sharply or harshly, bossing people around, criticizing people frequently, and sometimes name-calling and shouting people down. The person with intimidation power wields power over other members because it's difficult to muster the courage or energy to disagree with their opinions or ask them to change their demeanor. People may have tried many times to ask for change and have given up, or the person is now less aggressive as a result of past feedback and others are too worn down to ask for further change, or the person also offers such beneficial qualities that others resign themselves to having a mixed blessing and let it go.

- *Undermining power:* "Bad-mouthing," discrediting, and undermining another person's behavior and/or character to other community members; assuming the worst about the targeted person's motives and then criticizing those motives to others ("He's just trying to rip us off," "She's just trying to control everyone"); not distinguishing between one's own fears about the person and objective reality; not talking about these concerns with the targeted person or setting up a third-party mediation. The undermining person wields power over others in the community because s/he operates behind

people's backs, and others are reluctant to voice concerns about this behavior for fear they'll be targeted next.

- *Hypersensitive power:* Reacting to even mildly worded feedback or requests for change as though it were an intolerable personal attack; becoming visibly upset when others disagree with one's views or beliefs; responding with such defensiveness and self-justification so that people give up: "You can't tell Reginald *anything.*" This wields power over other community members because no one has the energy or patience to deal with this person's high level of fear and drama. People with hypersensitive power, like those with intimidating or undermining power, maintain their power over others because they rarely receive feedback.

7. Assuming the worst about other people's motives. Resenting and criticizing someone not only for what they may have done, but also for the assumed "worst-case scenario" motives for their actions (He's trying to cheat us," "She just wants to bully everyone," "He's always trying to show off") and using these assumptions as proof of the person's malfeasance or character flaws without (1) realizing these are assumptions, not facts, and (2) not asking the person if the assumptions are true.

Twenty-four Common Sources of Community Conflict

"Structural Conflict" Set-ups

1. Vision and values differences. Arguments over how money should be spent, or how time and labor should be allocated, based on differing values or visions about the community. (See Chapter 4.)

2. "Structural" power imbalances. Resentment and blame arising from real or perceived power differences in terms of how decisions are made and who makes them, or who has more influence than others in the group, either because of persuasive influence, expertise, or seniority in the community. (See "Interpersonal power imbalances," above.)

3. Exhausting, divisive, or unproductive meetings. Resentment and anger from too-frequent, overlong, or dragging meetings that accomplish little and go nowhere, or meetings characterized by resentment or hostility. (See Chapter 6.)

4. Lack of crucial information. Arguments about whose fault it is that we're suddenly stopped in our tracks, or must raise unexpected funds because we didn't adequately research something earlier; for example, not knowing that our local zoning regulations don't permit our planned population density or clustered housing, or not knowing composting toilets are illegal in our county.

5. Remembering verbal agreements differently. Eruptions of resentment, blame, or hostility because some community members appear to be dishonest or trying to cheat others, because we all remember our financial or other agreements differently. We can't just look up the agreements because we didn't write them down. (See Chapter 7.)

6. No communication or behavioral agreements. Misunderstandings and resentments because group members have widely divergent communication styles or behavioral norms. What are our norms for how people talk to each another, or express disagreement and strong emotion?

7. No processes for accountability. Resentment, blame, and flying accusations because some of us didn't do what we said we'd do, and certain projects can't move forward because some earlier tasks are unfinished, causing us to lose money or miss important opportunities.

8. No membership criteria or new-member screening process. Resentment and mistrust arising because new people enter who don't share our values and vision, don't align with our community culture, or can't meet our financial and labor requirements. (See Chapter 18.)

9. Being swamped with too many new members at once. Disorientation, overwhelm, depression, loss, or panic because the "container" of our shared history, values, and culture is threatened or damaged by the sudden influx of more people than we can assimilate easily. (Forming community groups and communities do better to add new members slowly.)

10. High turnover. Disorientation, overwhelm, depression, and associated emotions because too high a percentage of members are continually coming and going for the community to establish a sense of itself. The center does not hold; there's no "there" there.

Differences in Work and Planning Styles

11. Processors vs. Doers. Conflict between group members who want to process emotions or clear up points of meeting procedure, and those who want to focus on facts, strategies, and "real" things, but who sometimes override other people's feelings or ignore agreed-upon procedures.

12. Planners vs. Doers. Tension between those who want to gather facts and data and make long-term plans before taking action, and those who want to leap in and get started.

13. Spiritual vs. physical manifesters. Annoyance and impatience between those who want to use visualization, affirmation, or prayer as the primary means to manifest community, but may not feel comfortable with budgets, mortgages, shovels, or power tools, and those who want to use strategic plans, cash flow projections, and work parties as the primarily means to manifest community, but are leery of "invisible stuff."

14. Differences in information processing. Disrespecting, dismissing or devaluing people who may process information differently (visually rather than aurally, in wholes rather than step by step), or at a different pace than we do.

15. Differences in communication style. Socioliguistic differences based on region, ethnicity, subculture, socio-economic background, gender, or whether a member has lived in communities for decades or just arrived from the mainstream.

Fairness Issues

16. Work imbalances, or perceived imbalances. Resentment toward those who work less often or less rigorously on community projects than we do, or than they've previously agreed to.

17. Financial issues. Arguments over who's expected to pay for what, and if and when money can be reimbursed. Resentment and tension over the relationship between financial contribution and the amount of influence in decision-making.

18. Time-crunch issues. Disagreements about the amount of time spent in meetings and on community tasks versus. time with one's family or household. Conflict over the best times to schedule meetings or community projects so they're convenient for everyone. Arguments over how consistently community members should contribute to the group and whether it's OK to take periodic breaks.

19. Gender imbalance and power-over issues. Power imbalances and resentments if there are considerably more members of one gender than another, or one gender dominating some areas, or one gender consistently teasing, behaving suggestively towards, or dominating the other.

Neighbor Issues

20. Behavioral norms. Conflict over what's considered acceptable behavior in community; for example, to what degree people might intervene in or restrain potentially unacceptable, unsafe, or destructive behavior of other people, their children, or their animals. Can community members request changes in parents' child-raising style, or request that others restrain, train, or fence their animals? What are standards of acceptable behavior outside the community, where someone's behavior might reflect on the community?

21. Boundary issues. Tension about what community members do on their homesites, in their adjacent homes, or shared common spaces, that can be seen or heard by others, including what noises may too loud or disruptive to others during certain hours or what physical objects might be an eyesore to others. What behaviors — such as disciplining children, having loud arguments, butchering livestock, drinking, taking drugs, nudity, displays of affection, or sexual expression

— are fine for some to overhear or view are fine and which are "over the line." To what degree can fellow community members borrow each other's personal items without asking? What degree of playful, affectionate, or sensual physical touch is welcome to some and unwelcome to others?

22. Care and maintenance issues. Conflict about standards for taking care of and maintaining jointly owned equipment or tools, and who's responsible.

23. Cleanliness and order issues. Tension over standards for cleanliness in common rooms, and cleanliness of jointly used items and how they're stored, particularly in kitchens and bathrooms, and who's responsible.

24. Lifestyle issues. Conflict arising from items some members may own or activities they may enjoy privately — smoking, liquor, drugs, guns, pesticides, and meat eating — which may be no big deal for some but disturbing to others. Conflict over the degree to which relationships between families, couples, or households may be the business of other members, such as parents' discipline or lack of discipline with children, open marriages, polyfidelitous relationships, or gay or bisexual relationships. To what degree is how people treat each other in their love relationships the business of other community members?

Every one of these conflicts can be reduced or prevented by well-crafted agreements and procedures, good training in group process, or both.

The Fine Art of Offering Feedback

Offering feedback is *not* an attempt to assess or guess or criticize the person's intentions or motives. If you do that, it'll probably trigger defensiveness and escalate the problem. And although you can also request that the person do things differently in the future, this can also make things worse, if wanting the person to change is the only reason you're giving the feedback.

"Get in touch with your motives for offering feedback," advises process consultant Paul DeLapa. "If your intention is to offer information about how the person's actions or behavior affected you, there's a good chance the person can hear and accept it. But if your motive is to change them, it probably won't work."

Don't try to convince or coerce them. "People don't resist change itself as much as they resist 'being changed'," says Paul. So offering feedback can support someone's own willingness to change something if the feedback is offered in a way that doesn't register as a demand or as an implication that they're somehow bad or wrong.

How you say it has everything to do with how feedback will be received. It requires all the best communication skills we can muster — using neutral language, describing what the person actually did rather than assessing his or her character or motives, and using real feeling words rather than blame-words. Again, the best process I know of for offering feedback constructively comes from the Nonviolent Communication process.

Receiving Feedback — Listening for Kernels of Truth

Even if you learn to offer feedback skillfully, much of the critical feedback you may hear about yourself could be delivered in a graceless manner. Even people committed to good process can still speak awkwardly or harshly when they're trying to deliver a difficult message. You could get feedback that implies or outright states that you're wrong, bad, or defective in some way.

You can hear guesses and presumptions about your motives stated as facts. You can be told you "always" do such-and-such or "never" do such-and-such. You can be armchair-psychoanalyzed as to what childhood factors cause your malfeasance. This can be so painful it completely obscures the important information the person is trying to give you.

Hearing critical feedback can hurt. Not only because of any harshness in the delivery, but also because of the possibility that, to whatever extent, it may be true. It helps to keep some principles in mind:

1. Just because feedback is delivered in a critical, exaggerated, or hostile manner doesn't mean it doesn't contain a kernel of truth — or maybe a lot of truth.

2. On the other hand, it could be a projection of the person's own issues onto you, with nothing to do with your own actions or behaviors.

3. And even when delivered skillfully, feedback might still be exaggerated, or partially or wholly invalid.

Hearing critical feedback requires at least two skills: the ability to respond to the person in a way that doesn't make things worse — for you, for them, and for the whole community; and listening for the kernel of truth in what they say and finding ways to check it out objectively.

Suppose Jason says: "I'm annoyed and frustrated by the mess in the kitchen after you've used it. I've been cleaning up after you and I'm getting tired of it. I wish you'd clean up after you're done."

Constructive responses could include (depending on how accurate you think Jason's observation may be): "Thanks for telling me," or "Thanks, I'll consider that," or "Thanks, I'll do something about it," or just "Thanks."

But what if he'd said: "You're a slob who leaves a mess every time you use the kitchen! We always have to clean up after you!" With a message like this, it can take a great deal of patience and tolerance not to retaliate in kind. If you do, you, Jason, and the whole community will probably feel worse. If you respond more neutrally as suggested above, you'll have helped the community's well-being by not adding to the burden of ill will Jason has just dumped into it.

How do you know when feedback is true? Introspection, self-observation, and any manner of self-awareness techniques, including asking for inner guidance, can help you assess its degree of truth. Even better, you can ask other community members directly. I recommend doing this in relatively straightforward way, for example: "Excuse me, Sally, do I sometimes leave a mess in the kitchen?"

Sally could say, "You sure do. I've been meaning to tell you about it. Would you please take more time to clean up after you're done?"

Or she could say, "Hmmm, let me see. Well, maybe once or twice, but not all the time."

Asking various people and getting a consistent response one way or the other is one way to gauge the accuracy of someone's feedback. Asking questions in a straightforward way gives you a better chance of getting neutral, accurate information.

But suppose you felt so hurt or angry by how Jason criticized you that you exaggerated and "horriblized" what he said when you tried to verify it: "Jason says I'm a horrible slob who always leaves a mess in the kitchen and everywhere I go. He says everyone always has to clean up after me! Is that true?"

This defeats your chances of getting accurate feedback, because Sally would probably say something like: "Of *course* not! You don't leave messes everywhere!" And you'll have missed the kernel of truth that you do, in fact, *sometimes* leave a messy kitchen.

We can help create sustainable relationships by giving feedback as skillfully as we can, without expecting or demanding that other people are any good at it. We can sift through any graceless or harsh criticism for whatever helpful truths about ourselves we can glean. This is a lot to ask. Yet it's the rock polisher in action, and it's one of the best ways we can use community to grow and heal ourselves and strengthen our relationships there.

HEALING OUR INDIVIDUAL ISSUES

If several people say give us the same feedback, maybe we should do something about it. But what? How can we get along better with each other, and help our lives become happier, lighter, and more enjoyable?

"Emotional Freedom Technique (EFT)" is a relatively new method for releasing hurts and wounds from the past that may be influencing perceptions and attitudes in the present. I've tried various therapies over the years, but never found anything so effective, painless, cheap, and fast. It can take only three or four sessions, for example, to make a noticeable difference. EFT doesn't require re-experiencing or even understanding old upsets, or using visualization or affirmations. It's essentially a mechanical technique involving certain acupuncture points, but without the needles, and one can do it at home, without a therapist. It seems to work by healing issues at the core — for me it's like pressing the "erase" button on a tape recorder, unbelievable though that sounds. I recommend this healing tool for any community members seeking an exceptionally fast and simple way to peel away the negative layers that can get in the way of sustainable relationships. (See Resources.)

Threshing Meetings

"The amount of time and energy conflict can suck out of a community can endanger its viability," says Dave Henson of Sowing Circle/OAEC. He's right — and it's everyone's business to resolve small conflicts before they become community-wide conflagrations.

Most communities profiled in this book have regular meetings to unearth small conflicts before they escalate to larger ones. Threshing meetings are like safety valves that periodically let off pressure, and can include giving appreciative as well as critical feedback, venting frustration or anger, asking people for specific changes in behavior, or simply exploring controversial issues.

Using processes like threshing meetings to handle conflicts early, when they're small, often prevents them from mushrooming into major conflagrations later on. It's also much easier for a group to resolve large conflicts once they've learned to handle smaller ones.

Abundant Dawn members set aside an hour and a half twice monthly for what they call "personal/interpersonal time." People describe what's going on in their lives, says Joy Legendre, as well as delve into any conflicts. "Just knowing that space is there for us to bring these issues up helps defuse the little tensions and problems. It's easier to let them go and not get bothered by them, just knowing that we can always discuss them at the meeting."

But they're not called "threshing" meetings for nothing. "Public feedback sessions can be risky," cautions process consultant Paul DeLapa, "because it risks undermining trust between people instead of building trust." Many people aren't willing to offer feedback one-on-one, and will criticize people behind their backs rather than speak to them directly. In public feedback sessions such as threshing meetings these are usually the people who suddenly feel free to unleash the floodgates of pent-up frustration and resentment. For the person receiving the feedback it can feel as thought they're being ganged up on. If everyone in a group plans to give one member feedback, Paul recommends that the person sets up some boundaries, such as what kind of feedback they'd be willing to hear, and how they'd prefer it be delivered. Establishing some boundaries first empowers the person and helps them feel less vulnerable.

But in some circumstances feedback offered in a group setting can be easier to take than one-on-one. If Vaughan gives Sally critical feedback, and other group members say they've never had that experience themselves, it could offer Sally a wider perspective and lessen the sting. And if Vaughan were to offer feedback in a harsh way, other, more skilled communicators could intervene, and remind him to alter his language.

The public/private scale exercise, first suggested for the visioning process can help people in a threshing meeting (or any meeting) break the ice in discussing an issue that they're reluctant to talk about publicly. Let's say it's believed that someone repeatedly breaks community agreements or has seriously breached behavioral norms, or some members cannot meet their financial obligations to the community, or it's rumored that someone may be harming a child — and no one wants to bring it up. Using the public/private scale and framing the issue as a series of questions makes public the range of members' opinions about the issue, which can help induce people to speak up and address the matter directly. (See Exercises, Chapter 5.)

Creating Specific Conflict Resolution Agreements

Some groups create a set of agreements about how community members will handle conflict when it comes up. Here are the agreements Sowing Circle made, excerpted from their "Conflict Resolution Policy."

Sowing Circle Community: Conflict Resolution Policy

When confronted with conflict of any kind, the community agrees to adhere to the conflict resolution principles and steps outlined below:

I. **Problem-Solving Ground Rules.** All members agree to attempt to solve problems by first dealing directly with the person or persons with whom he/she is experiencing problems. Implicit in this agreement is a commitment to honest, direct problem-solving. All members will agree to the following ground rules when involved in conflict resolution efforts:

1. A commitment to mutual respect.
2. A commitment to solve the problem.
3. No put-downs.
4. No intimidation, implied or direct.
5. No physical contact.
6. No interrupting.
7. Agreement to use the conflict resolution protocol, below.

II. **Conflict Resolution Protocols.** Community members in conflict will:

- Make a good faith effort to resolve the problem between/among themselves. If this does not work, the members in conflict will:

- Ask a mutually agreed-upon member to help mediate and solve the problem with those having the conflict. If this does not work, the members in conflict will:

- Formally request assistance from the community in solving the problem.
- If the community is unable to assist in resolving the conflict, and all avenues of conflict resolution have been exhausted, then the community may choose to engage in outside mediation to solve the problem.

III. Third Party Confidentiality. We recognize the importance of the conflict resolution protocol outlined above, and agree to abide by it in principle and practice. As non-involved parties, we will encourage conflicting parties to deal directly with one another. However, we also recognize the need, at times, to discuss, seek advice, or seek comfort from others while in the midst of conflict. Such a situation requires confidentiality. As "third parties" who are approached for solace, advice, etc., we agree to provide these things in the spirit of helping to improve the situation.

We do not wish to contribute to rumors, gossip, "bad-mouthing," or the perpetuation of problems. If a person who is experiencing a conflict with one or more people on the property approaches a neutral "third party" it is understood that the person is responsible for keeping the health and well being of the community in mind. That is, while maintaining confidentiality, the third party should remind the conflicted person of the conflict resolution protocol, if necessary. In addition, by virtue of being privy to the conflict at hand, the third party is also responsible for monitoring the situation. If the feelings, issues, etc., are leading to greater conflict or to a weakening of the community, then the third party should take steps toward facilitating resolution, even if this means exposing the fact (not details) of the problem at hand to others in the community.

IV. Confidentiality with Regard to Internal Community Conflict. In the spirit of protecting the privacy and rights of members of the community, we are committed to maintaining confidentiality regarding individual and community issues of a sensitive nature when speaking with people outside the community.

Helping Each Other Stay Accountable to the Group

One of the most common sources of conflict in community occurs when people don't do what they say they'll do. As in business, this often causes repercussions "downstream," since some people count on others to finish certain preliminary steps before they can take the next steps. But by putting a few simple processes in place, community members can help each other stay accountable to one another in relatively painless, guilt-free ways.

One is to make agreements about tasks in meetings, and keep track of these tasks from meeting to meeting. This involves assigning tasks to specific people and defining what they're being asked to accomplish and by what time. It also involves having a task review at the beginning of every meeting — the people or committees who agreed to take on these tasks report whether they have been done, and if not, when they will be.

It also helps to create a wall chart of assigned tasks with expected completion dates and the person or committee responsible for each. Assign someone the task of keeping the chart current and taping it on the wall at meetings.

Community activist Geoph Kozeny suggests creating a buddy system, where everyone is assigned another group member to call and courteously inquire, "Did you call the county yet?" or "Have you found out about the health permit?" This is not about guilt-tripping; it's about helpful inquiry and mutual encouragement. These methods rely on the principle that it's more difficult to forget or ignore responsibilities if they're publicly visible. Social pressure can often accomplish what good intentions cannot.

If not completing tasks becomes an ongoing problem with one or more people in the group, you can add additional processes. For example, when anyone accomplishes a task, thank and acknowledge the person at the next meeting. When someone doesn't accomplish a task, the group as a whole asks the person to try again. After awhile, the simple desire not to let others down usually becomes an internalized motivator for more responsible behavior.

If someone still frequently fails to do what they say they'll do, you can use a graduated series of consequences. (See below for a more detailed explanation of a graduated series of consequences.) First, several people could talk with the person, for example,. describing the repercussions to the group of failing to follow through. If that doesn't resolve it, the matter could be taken up by a committee convened for this purpose. Last, it could become a matter for the whole group.

Why is this such a common source of community conflict? I think it's about developing the habit early in life of procrastinating or agreeing to take on more than is possible, and not having enough motivation to change. When we live alone or live with our families, it's relatively easy to change our minds about whether or not, or when, we'll do something we said we'd do, or just plain let it go. But in a forming community group or community, this can have widespread negative impacts on other people, and we'll certainly hear about it. It can take time, energy, and commitment to shift from "live-alone" or "single-family" mode to consistently considering how our actions will affect others.

GETTING OUTSIDE HELP

Sometimes conflict gets so entrenched and seemingly irresolvable that communities call in process gurus, consensus facilitators, or other communication consultants to help sort out the problem. These consultants are skilled in process and conflict-resolution methods, and, since they're often community veterans themselves, their community experience gives them a context for the unique challenges that arise when people attempt to live more closely and interdependently. (See Resources for suggested community process consultants.)

When people repeatedly don't do what they promise and others continue to hold them accountable, it usually results in the person either changing their habits or eventually leaving the group.

A Graduated Series of Consequences

It's especially painful for community groups when someone consistently violates agreements or behavioral norms, or refuses to make changes repeatedly requested by other community members regarding behavior or communication style. One remedy is to agree on and implement negative consequences for such offenses. In order to protect a community, it's possible to design a graduated series of fair, compassionate consequences, from mild to increasingly serious, that treat people with respect while inducing them to make necessary changes.

Many communities have no consequences for such breaches, partly because most of us feel uncomfortable considering such matters, and partly because having negative consequences seems no different than the fines and jail sentences of mainstream society. It's difficult for community members to propose or implement coercive methods of governance when what they really want is a finer, kinder, more conscious society than the one they grew up with. For the same reasons, the communities that do have consequences are often reluctant to enforce them.

Still other communities have consequences, but the consequences are too severe for the offense, so people are loathe to employ them. For example, one large income-sharing community has just one consequence for members who get too far in the "labor hole" (failing to do their share of labor) or the "money hole" (borrowing too much against future stipends) — eviction from the community. But this requires polling the members for 100 percent agreement to take this action. While many people in this community have gotten into the labor hole or money hole over the years, this consequence is rarely proposed. And when it is, usually enough friends of the member in question vote against it so he or she doesn't have to leave. Everyone loses here. The community continues to financially carry members who contribute less and take more, and the offending member continues to get away with irresponsible behavior and has little motivation to change.

Occasionally, community members need a series of consequences to finally understand that they must make changes. When all else fails, coercion can give a person a needed kick in the pants. Community Alternatives Society in Vancouver, Canada, had no real "rules" until they were forced to create agreements about behavior, and more importantly, institute a graduated series of consequences if anyone breached them. This community's series of consequences treats members with respect, yet has "teeth." Here's what they do if someone seriously violates behavioral norms or repeatedly breaks community agreements:

1. One person talks with the member in question about the problem and asks him or her to make changes.

2. If this doesn't work, four people meet about the problem — the first two and a trusted friend of each, again, requesting that the person make changes.

3. If this doesn't solve it, the person meets with the Accountability Committee to resolve the problem.

4. If this still doesn't solve it, the Accountability Committee creates a five-month contract with the member that outlines how he or she will make the necessary changes, and meets with the member monthly for updates. The purpose of the contract and meetings is *not* to punish or humiliate the member, but to encourage and support their making the changes.

5. If even this doesn't work, the whole community meets specifically to decide what action to take, which may include asking the person to live somewhere else for a while, and possibly also revoking his or her membership. The member can participate in this meeting, but has no blocking power.

6. If most members want to take this action but one or more people block it, the committee meets with the member in question and the those blocking the proposal to seek resolution together.

The number of consequences a group has, and how far it goes (a whole-group meeting? expulsion?) will depend on the size of the group and how deeply connected people feel — often a function of how long they've been together.

Isn't it drastic to put a member back on a provisional membership status, or ask them to live elsewhere for a while, or worse, to ask them to permanently leave the community once you're all living on the land? Yes, it is drastic. And sometimes, when the violation is severe enough or the conflict too wrenching, it's the only way to protect your forming community group or community from breaking up altogether.

After they took the first Naka-Ima workshop, Lost Valley members noticed two divergent trends developing in their community. Most members wanted to move in the direction of more cooperative and shared resources, but felt frustrated because other members wanted more independent lives. At that time, as a relatively small consensus-based group of ten members, it seemed that without something changing nobody would be able to get what they really wanted — especially since using consensus requires a common purpose.

"To those of us who held the cooperative vision," Larry recalls, "it seemed necessary to break with precedent and ask the others to leave, freeing the energy to move forward. We didn't feel we had enough of a foundation to tolerate that kind of diversity. This was the first in a series of courageous and risky choices that we believed we must take to restore our integrity as a community."

The people did leave, and Larry reports that the community became more harmonious because of it.

Asking someone to leave your group or community is probably the most disruptive and painful way to deal with apparently irresolvable conflict. It is far easier to address the likelihood of such conflict ahead of time by carefully choosing the people who join you. We'll address this controversial topic in Chapter 18.

IDEALISM AND DISILLUSIONMENT

Community founders and newcomers often assume that they won't need conflict resolution methods, ways to help each other stay accountable to the group, or consequences for violations agreements — since none of these issues will ever come up in their community. They assume they won't be living in the "old paradigm," so why have remedies for it? But a few months or a few years into the process they see that heir community does not at all resemble the harmonious and deeply connected "new paradigm" family they envisioned, and disillusionment sets in.

Usually they blame the community itself ("We're so screwed up!") or particular members ("If only Ollie would leave!"), rather than realizing they had unrealistic expectations to begin with, and they are having a typical (some say, inevitable) community experience.

Community life is more functional and satisfying than life in mainstream culture — but often not as functional and satisfying as we'd hoped!

Community is like crossing a bridge between win-lose culture and the more harmonious and sustainable culture we aspire to and would like to leave to our children. Community members are traversing the bridge, passing from one realm to the other, helping generate that future as we keep learning better how to interact and communicate with each other in cooperative, win/win ways, resolve conflicts successfully, and so on.

Utilizing the processes described in this chapter isn't evidence of our community's failure. These processes are like training wheels; they're small, helpful, devices to help us travel more easily from we've been to where we're going — toward communities that are socially, ecologically, and spiritually sustainable.

⇜ Chapter 18 ⇝

Selecting People to Join You

IN THE MOUNTAINS AND HIGH DESERT valleys of southwestern Colorado, six professional women in their forties through sixties planned a small community I'll call Pueblo Encantada. After awhile it became clear that a seventh person who'd recently joined the group, whom I'll call Regina, couldn't afford the $20,000 land-purchase contribution. Everyone assumed she'd no longer be involved, but Regina, deeply moved by the vision of a rural community in a beautiful setting, was convinced it was her destiny. "I *know* I should be there," she said. "It's calling to me spiritually." So the other members, moved by the desire not to exclude anyone for financial reasons, and unwilling to go against anyone's strong spiritual conviction, took Regina into the community, bought an 11-acre property, and placed her name on the deed with everyone else's.

Most of the women lived and worked in town and visited the land on weekends, planning to move there as soon as they could afford it or after they retired. But a few, including Regina, lived on the land full time.

After about six months, tension arose over land use. Regina had acquired a horse, and insisted on certain requirements for pasturage and access to water, although this limited the other members' use and enjoyment of the land. As a consensus-based group, no one could force the issue unless everyone agreed, and Regina didn't. (And because they were new to consensus, no one realized there had been no real agreement in the first place since they'd never decided as a group to allow Regina to use that amount of land.) The conflict grew steadily worse. The other women resented Regina for behavior that seemed unfair and demanding, especially since they had literally gifted her with community membership out of their own pockets. Over the next several months feedback sessions didn't work, threshing meetings didn't work, outside mediation didn't work. Finally, the others offered to split the 11 acres, with Regina retaining an acre and a half, although not the portion she wanted. She could reimburse the others in monthly installments, with no down payment. The community would continue, minus Regina, on the remaining nine and a half acres. But she refused. By now an intolerable situation, the only recourse the women had was to sue Regina to force the sale of the property and get their money out. This they did. In less than a year and a half, Pueblo Encantada had become Pueblo Nada.

If this weren't bad enough, because Regina was on the deed as co-owner, the court disbursed to her one-seventh the proceeds of the sale, in spite of the fact that she'd paid not a dime. But this wasn't the worst part. The worst part was that every one of the six women had felt uneasy about Regina when they'd met as a core group. Her energy, her communication style, and her near-insistence that she belonged on the land, had raised red flags for everyone. But no one had said a word, not wanting to appear unkind, or worse, "selfish." Wanting to be generous, unwilling to heed telltale signs, and ashamed of their feelings of aversion, no one voiced her private misgivings. Being "nice" cost them their dream.

Select for Emotional Maturity — the "Narrow Door"

Pueblo Encantada's story is not at all unique; I've heard many variations of this tale in the years I've been watching forming communities.

Accepting someone into to your core group or already-established community who isn't aligned with your vision and values, or who triggers strong reservations, doesn't work. It can potentially lead to spending hours of meeting time on conflicts that leave everyone drained and exhausted, or worse, to lawsuits and community break-up. And, because people project so much idealism onto community, we tend to make the same kinds of mistakes choosing community mates as we do choosing lovers: leaping before we look, projecting idealized archetypes onto ordinary folks, refusing to pay attention to telltale signs.

The antidote is to put in place a well-designed process for accepting and integrating new members and screening out those who don't resonate with your group. Since community living involves getting along well with others, you'll

want to select people whose lives demonstrate they can do this. Ideally, you'll select for emotional maturity and self-esteem. *Not* having a membership selection process can be a heartbreaking source of structural conflict later on.

"If your community front door is difficult to enter, healthy people will strive to get in," says Irwin Wolfe Zucker, a psychiatric social worker and former member of Findhorn and other communities. "If it's wide open, you'll tend to attract unhealthy people, well-versed in resentful silences, subterfuge, manipulation, and guilt trips." Once these people become members of the group, he warns, everyone's energy may later be tied up in getting them out again.

A membership screening process usually means a period of time visiting the core group or community as an observer, answering questions, being interviewed by the group, and acceptance through the consensus process. In forming-groups, this can include paying membership dues and/or fees towards land purchase. In already-established communities, this usually means a more rigorous set of questions, a longer visiting period, a six-month-to-a-year provisional membership, and possibly higher membership fees.

An important part of the screening process is how accurately the group describes itself publicly. Done well, your promotional materials (brochure or other handouts, inquiry response letter, website, classified ad in *Communities* magazine, listing in the *Communities Directory*), will draw those people aligned with your values and vision, and who are able and willing to meet your time, energy and financial requirements.

Your promotional materials can help you draw the kinds of people you're seeking and deter anyone else. You can be explicit about this if you wish. One community's brochure reads:

We're looking for people who feel confident and good about themselves, who have achieved a degree of emotional maturity, and who can get along with others in a group situation.

We're interested in people who don't feel that they've been harmed or taken advantage of by others, or who don't get the feedback that they're moody, or touchy. We're seeking people who enjoy the company of others, and are willing to ask for what they want and need.

It makes sense to have a formal member-screening process once you're living together in community, but is it reasonable to ask someone to go through all this simply to attend meetings of your core group? It doesn't make sense for visitors who will simply observe and offer comments. But it does if they will become decision-making members who'll help influence the future of your community.

Another reason to screen new core group members involves keeping the ones you've got.

WHO DOES WELL IN COMMUNITY? Interview questions/quiz?

1. Someone who doesn't "need" it. People who are fulfilled and doing well in their lives are more likely to thrive in and contribute to community.

2. Someone with a healthy sense of self. People with emotional maturity and self-esteem, who know what they want and know their strengths and weaknesses, and who are seeking personal growth for themselves, tend to do well in community.

3. Someone who is open to and able to hear other points of view. The aggressive, competent business executive or entrepreneur who instinctively knows best and makes decisions quickly tends to feel frustrated and impatient in community until he or she becomes comfortable with cooperative decision-making. Then such a person can thrive in community and contribute a great deal.

4. Someone with a sense of connection to people and an interest in the well-being of others. Obviously a socially confident person who likes people will enjoy community, but people who are shy or natural loners can have difficulty at first. They can be insensitive to other people's needs and have no idea

what's expected of them. But with enough "high willingness," such people can use community as a learning opportunity and become fully contributing members.

5. Someone willing to abide by group agreements. Some people fiercely guard their autonomy, find the idea of interdependence with others unsettling, and tend to bristle when asked to do follow rules or perform a task. Again, with enough "high willingness," such people can move from "I" consciousness to "we" consciousness without losing their sense of self. It feels good to be interdependent with others; however, for some people it takes a certain amount of self-confidence and trust even to try it.

6. Someone willing to speak up. People who are willing to take the initiative, say so when they disagree with others, and ask for what they want, tend to do well.

7. Someone willing to be quiet and listen. People who always know what's best, or who are dynamic, assertive, and full of ideas, may need to tone down that energy somewhat in group meetings in order to give others the space to speak.

Once you're living in community, it's not easy for someone who's fed up with a newcomer's behavior to leave. But until a core group's level of commitment has increased, for example, after buying land, if someone joins you who annoys or disrupts the group, anyone in the core group could become annoyed enough to walk away and never return.

But is it Community?

Many people don't think it's "community" unless the group is inclusive and open and anyone can join. Doesn't community mean offering a more accepting, inclusive culture than mainstream society?

Most experienced communitarians would reply that not having criteria for new members — admissions standards, if you will — is simply an invitation for emotionally dysfunctional people to arrive. Without realizing it, they seek out communities in order to heal childhood hurts and wounds. They look to community to provide the loving family they never had. (One community founder told me that their community sign out front might as well have read: "Emotional Hospital — Welcome.")

When I bring this up in workshops, many people shift uncomfortably in their seats — it goes against the grain to consider excluding people. I can always spot the experienced community members though; they're the ones rolling their eyes with "you can say *that* again" looks. They've usually learned this through bitter experience; there's no reason you should learn it the hard way too.

"An intentional community is a scarce and valuable commodity in our culture," observes communitarian Harvey Baker of Dunmire Hollow in Tennessee, "existing only because its founders have invested a lot of time and human resources. It'd be a shame to let in someone in who could destroy what has taken so many people so many years to create."

But what about the rock polisher effect? Aren't everyone's rough edges worn smoother by contact with everyone else's? Veteran communitarians often point out that most people naturally mature in community because of the (hopefully) constructive feedback they'll receive and the natural tendency to learn from the (hopefully) good communication skills modeled by more experienced members. Many groups know people who were difficult to be around when they first arrived, but were so motivated to learn that they became model community members.

But the rock polisher effect appears to hinge on the willingness of the potential new member to learn and grow and change. I've seen forming communities — even those with otherwise fine process skills — break apart in conflict and sometimes lawsuits because even just one member didn't have enough self-esteem to function well in a group. The person's "stuff came up" — as everyone's does in community — but theirs was too destructive for the group to absorb. When a person is wounded and having a difficult time, he or she can certainly benefit from living in community, and, ideally, can heal and grow because of the support and feedback offered there. But a certain level of woundedness — without "high willingness" — appears to be too deep for many new communities to handle. I believe one deeply wounded person can affect a group far more than ten healthy people — potentially derailing the community's agenda and draining its energy.

Passive Victims, Outraged Victims

Consider the person who has had the misfortune of being abused as a child and hasn't had much healing before approaching your group. Such a person usually feels needy at some level, and tends to interpret other people's inability or refusal to meet his or her needs as simply more abuse.

Sometimes the person seems timid, passive, or insecure, which people sometimes characterize as having "victim" energy. Others, equally hurting, have the opposite traits, appearing edgy and intense, or erupting into anger rather easily. In both cases, it appears that on an unconscious level, the person expects to be victimized, and is "ready for it" in advance. Such a person tends to either seek out abusive situations or provoke normally mild-tempered people to anger. They can perceive angry or abusive behaviors where they don't exist, and conclude, "See, I knew you'd abuse me."

The problem is not that the person was once victimized, which obviously wasn't their fault. The problem is the ongoing interpretation of other people's actions as victimizing them still.

Here's how this often plays out in community. Let's say Darleen arrives at your door, or begins attending meetings of your core group. She's in difficult life circumstances; you feel compassion and want to help, so you do. You feel good about this, and all is well for awhile. But soon tension builds between Darleen and other members. At sharing circles she retreats. Attempts to offer her feedback are rebuffed. Requests for minor changes in her behavior are seen as attacks. Any "good process" attention the community gives her is seen as persecution. At first Darleen thought you were allies, but look: just like everyone else, you're out to victimize her too.

For some reason "Darleen" often shows up in communities as a single mother on welfare with several small children and two dogs which the children are very attached to. The mother has environmental illness, one of the children has special needs, the dogs have fleas and the mange. (The potential drama and cost to the community escalates if the father of Darleen's children is trying to take them away from her, or wants to move in and abuse her further.) Darleen is exhausted and desperate, and of course you want to help her. By all means feed the family, give them shelter for a few nights and a little money, if you like. Encourage Darleen to get help with county social services. Just know what you'll be taking on if you let her join you.

Lost Valley once rescued a single mother in circumstances like these, and she ended up resenting and blaming the community no matter how they tried to help. "We didn't have what it took for her to continue accepting our charity," Dianne Brause recalls wryly.

Or let's say Mike arrives at your door. Angry with the corrupt powers that plunder the Earth, he's certain of his convictions and passionate about social change. He knows community — your community — is part of the answer. He joins and you welcome his zeal. All is well for awhile.

Soon tension builds between Mike and a few others. The feedback he gets is wrong; requests for change are power-plays; sharing circles are for wimps. Any "process" attention the community gives Mike is coercion. At first your community seemed like righteous allies in the struggle, but look: you're just corrupt power-mongers like everyone else.

Darleen is operating out of fear, Mike out of rage. Both are victims.

What kind of communities can people in these circumstances join, besides therapeutic communities, or service communities organized to offer support to people in need? A large, old, well-established community can sometimes take on difficult or wounded people without much damage to itself. A mature oak tree, after all, can handle being hit by a truck. But don't take on this challenge if your group is small, or brand new. You're just a seedling, not an oak tree, and still too vulnerable.

Membership Screening and the Law

As mentioned earlier, if you have housing units or lots for sale on the open market, you can't pick and choose your members, but must sell to anyone who meets your terms. If, based on your membership criteria, you choose some buyers and reject others, courts could interpret this as discrimination. Cohousing communities face this issue, but, as mentioned earlier, usually find that only those people who want more community in their lives are interested anyway, so their membership selection process becomes self-selecting.

But sometimes a cohousing core group sees a red flag and does something about it. This was the case with a forming cohousing group in the Northwest, which I'll call Redwood Commons, and a member of their group whom I'll call "Cal." Cal spoke in a monotone and had little facial expression, what psychologists call "flat affect." Everyone noticed his unusual, somewhat mechanical demeanor. Some felt compassion and were kind; others were unnerved. When it was time for Redwood Commons to put money down on a property and move forward, some didn't want Cal in the group. "What if he 'snaps' someday and harms one of our children?" they asked. Others were heartsick about it. They wanted to be kind to Cal, who was obviously hurting and would benefit from community living, but they didn't want to risk it. So a few members took Cal aside, and rather awkwardly, asked him to leave the group, which he did. They

didn't point out that he had every legal right to buy in. To this day many Redwood Commons members feel ashamed of the way they asked Cal to leave; it was obviously a painful experience for him. Could they have done it more kindly, they ask? Should they have discouraged his meeting attendance earlier in the process? And were they just dead wrong? Cal could have been a fine community member. Frequent contact with neighbors, particularly children, could have brought needed warmth into his life.

Yet even though this issue is painful to contemplate, I think these core group members did the right thing by following their instincts and taking the action they thought best for the community. Unlike Pueblo Encantada members, Redwood Commons people didn't let shame about their feelings of unease stop them from speaking up.

Dealing Well with Saying "No"

Whether a group has homes or lots for sale on the open market, or owns its property and can thus choose its members, is it worth it to ask someone to leave, given how badly they may feel? Consider this: someone who is not accepted for membership in a group or community feels disappointed, gets over it, and moves on. But someone who is accepted as a community member, moves to the community and lives there for awhile, and is later asked to leave, may be deeply scarred. It is far easier on everyone concerned to take this painful step at the beginning.

I'd much rather see a new community get established, sink roots, and grow strong and healthy for a few years before taking in a wounded person who might be disruptive but could benefit from community, than see them try this when they're first starting out and risk everything in the process. You're propagating from seeds here. You need all the protection you can get.

This can be so difficult that people don't deal with it at all, especially if they were raised to believe that it's not "nice" to say "No." Like Pueblo Encantada members, people can feel ashamed of their feelings that something's "not right," and judge themselves for being "judgmental" or worse, for being "discriminating."

"Judgmental" means to criticize someone as unworthy, whereas what you're doing is assessing whether this person resonates with your visions and values, is aligned with your behavioral norms, and can meet your financial and labor requirements. And to "discriminate" means to recognize the differences between various choices; to differentiate, to discern. And discern you must, since you could be living near and sharing property with this person for the rest of your life.

How Can You Tell?

Since most of us are wounded to some degree and are in various stages of recovery, how can we tell in advance who might be wounded severely enough to drain and exhaust the group? Most people with serious emotional difficulties don't give off signals like Regina and Cal, but seem just like anyone else at first.

SCREENING NEW MEMBERS

Communities organize their membership screening process in various ways.

At Earthaven, for example, people learn about the community's vision, values, membership requirements, and other information through its website and information packet (which includes magazine article reprints and a video). Interested people can take a tour, attend the community's Council meetings, and arrange weekend visits.

The first stage of membership is to become a "supporting member," which is an opportunity for the person and the community to get to know each other in a relaxed way without too much being asked of anyone. A supporting member can visit anytime, can live in the community if accommodations are available, can attend Council meetings but not participate in discussions, and receives the community's newsletter and emailed copies of Council minutes. Supporting members pay a small monthly membership fee and sign an agreement saying that they understand the community's vision and values.

When people decide to join the community they become "provisional members" for at least six months first (although it can be longer), which allows them and the community to get to know each other far better, with a fair amount of commitment on either side. Provisional members can participate in community meetings (although they cannot block proposals) and they're encouraged to live in the community. They pay the community's $4,000 joining fee and sign a contract agreeing to pay a site lease fee at the time of full membership. They are required to attend at least two committee meetings a month, work 48 hours per quarter on community tasks, and get to know as many community members as possible.

Supporting members apply for provisional membership by filling out a questionnaire about themselves and their community aspirations (which is shared with the whole group), as well as telling aspects of their life story at a whole group meeting convened for this purpose. If no one objects in to the person's provisional membership status in the three-week period following

This is what two founders, whom I'll call Celeste and Brad, asked after their upper Midwest community, which I'll call Faraway Lake, broke up in conflict and heartbreak.

Celeste and Brad are two of the most likable, capable, and spiritually grounded people I know, so when they began planning a new community I was sure it would be a success. They wrote a beautiful description of their vision for Faraway Lake and attracted five other cofounders, each of whom seemed equally grounded and capable. The group met for months at each other's homes to make plans.

After looking at over 50 properties the group found an ideal site by a lake, with everything they'd been looking for. While they had enough money for a down payment, they didn't have enough to buy the land outright, so began a search for a mortgage. In the meantime they rented a cabin near their intended property and camped in the yard or slept dormitory-style in the attic. In order to make a living in their rural setting they started a small, cooperatively owned manufacturing business, for which Brad and Celeste and two others invested savings and borrowed start-up funds from friends. They rented and renovated a nearby factory space and set to work. Over the next few months the group toiled

the storytelling evening, he or she becomes a provisional member. (If the community doesn't ultimately accept the person as a full member, the fee is returned. But if the person decides not to join the community, the community keeps one-third the fee as a deterrent to anyone's joining too casually.)

In six months, if the person has met the labor and other requirements, he or she can apply for full membership. Community members are polled for their comments and whether they support the person's becoming a full member. The questions include: "Have you been able to get to know this person? If not, why not?" and "How do you think this person could best contribute to the community?" and "Do have any concerns about this person as a member? If so, have you met with the person to discuss them?" If a member does have a concern, he or she must meet with the provisional member to attempt to resolve the concern. If issues cannot be resolved, or if the community as a whole has concerns about the provisional member, the person may be asked to continue in that membership status for awhile, and apply for full membership again later. If no one has any objections, the person is proposed for full membership at a Council meeting for consensual agreement. Then everyone celebrates.

Meadowdance has a similar process with successive levels of membership, but with more checkpoints; at the first-month, fourth month, seventh month, and 13th month, when the person becomes a full member. At each membership stage the person can participate in meetings, but cannot block a proposal. Meadowdance's process must necessarily be more regulated than joining a village like Earthaven, since Meadowdance members join a household, share a kitchen, and work for the community businesses.

Most of the "successful ten percent" have similar multi-step membership processes.

long hours at the new business, but still managed to take time out to enjoy stories around the campfire, go hiking and sailing, and meditate by the lake at sunrise.

Unfortunately their new business had a series of unexpected setbacks. The financial uncertainty, along with the fact that they lived in crowded conditions, strained their good will, and soon they began bickering. This didn't alarm Brad or Celeste, who'd lived in community before and were old hands at group process. But in one member, whom I'll call David, rage was growing. In sharing circles or feedback sessions, he seemed to be listening and understanding, but was secretly becoming even more angry, resentful, and entrenched in his position. He took a particular dislike to Celeste, who had asked him to change certain attitudes and behaviors toward people outside the community with whom they were doing business. As conflict escalated over the next few months and Celeste, Brad, and others attempted to give David feedback, the more he singled out Celeste as the cause of the problem. As their conflict grew worse, it got framed as a power struggle between the two of them. Celeste wanted David to become more conscious of and alter certain behaviors; he wanted her to stop trying to "dominate everyone." As experienced communitarians, Brad and Celeste believed that since they all lived under one roof and were financially interdependent, David's or any other member's behavior was everyone's business, but for David, it was an outrageous invasion of privacy. The group split into factions. Distrust and tension mounted.

Just when it seemed as though things couldn't get any worse, the business failed, still deeply in debt. Exhausted and demoralized, the group felt it had no choice but to call it quits. Everyone moved away. After fourteen months Faraway Lake was no more. David, who'd put no money into the cooperatively owned business, refused to make payments towards reimbursing its loan. Living on their own again, dejected, and feeling strangely ashamed of the failure of their community dream, Brad and Celeste worked for the next three years to replace their savings.

"How could we have known how David would react to living in community?" Celeste later asked. "No one could have guessed by meeting him. During the months of planning he was one of the most engaging and delightful people you'd ever hope to meet. How could we have *known?*"

Questions, References, "Long Engagements"

"Look for good history of love and work," advises Irwin Wolfe Zucker. According to psychological studies, past behavior is the best predictor of future behavior, so he recommends asking questions, through questionnaires and interviews. Let's say you're seeking people who are financially stable, emotionally secure, and, ideally, have some experience living cooperatively. The more intimate the community you're planning — in terms of physical proximity, the amount of shared resources, and the amount of financial interdependence — the more direct your questions might be.

For example, besides the usual questions about the person's community aspirations, you might ask:

- How have you supported yourself financially?
- Can you describe some of your long-term relationships?
- What was your experience in high school or college?

- How much schooling did you complete?
- If you chose to leave school, why was that?
- Have you pursued alternative educational or career paths such as internships, apprenticeships, or on-the-job training? Where, and for how long? Did you complete them?
- Have you lived in shared or cooperative living situations before, such as college dorms or student housing co-ops, shared group households, or other intentional communities?
- Do you have a significant love and/or family relationship now? How long have you been together? Do you plan to live together in community?
- If you're a single parent, what is your current relationship with your children's other parent? Are you on good terms and share parenting or are you estranged? Does the other parent want custody of the children?
- Will you be able to meet our labor and financial requirements? How?

While these are certainly personal questions, keep in mind that you're considering this person for a truly personal relationship, involving aspects of both marriage and a business partnership. You're expecting him or her to be responsible and trustworthy as a close neighbor and someone who may be a friend to your children, as well as someone with whom you'll own property and make important financial decisions.

By the way, not having the money to pay a share of land-purchase costs or membership fees but wanting to join anyway is sometimes a predictor of trouble later on, as was the case with Regina and David. But not always. Some of the most active and contributing members of Earthaven, for example, are young people who joined without funds, and are paying off membership and site-lease fees through a labor exchange with the community.

You could also ask for three or four references — from former partners, current and former employers, landlords, housemates, and/or traveling companions. What if new people just give names of friends who'll only say good things, you ask? Consider that even the way people respond to the request for references tells you something. If they are happy to provide references and do so immediately, it's a good sign. I once called references for people interested in visiting a small forming community. (References were asked for before, rather than after a proposed visit, so that if the references didn't check out, the visitors wouldn't have wasted their time or travel expenses.) I learned that you can get a pretty good sense of how others may feel about someone by about the third or fourth reference call. And it certainly would have benefited Faraway Lake if Brad and Celeste had sought references or a background check on David. They later learned he had been fleeing court-ordered judgments for punitive damages and reimbursement of funds owed former business partners in two different past businesses, and had been attempting to go underground, "hiding" in various intentional communities.

But wait a minute — is past behavior *always* the best predictor of future behavior? What about people who change and grow? People definitely can mature and become more stable, compassionate, and responsible over the years and we must allow for that possibility. I suggest asking people about this directly: "What were you like in your twenties? Have you changed in any significant ways since then?" We need to seek a balance between considering people's past behavior (and for some, perhaps during only the past five or ten years), and their current state. Questions and interviews, references, and a long getting-to-know-you period where we can experience the new person on a day-to-day basis all help with this process.

But, wait another minute — what about the people who started the core group or the community? If they screened themselves for all the same membership criteria would they have gotten in? Do they even meet their own requirements?

People often do tend to seek higher standards in new members than they exemplify in themselves. It seems to be human nature to aim high, perhaps like the father for whom no boyfriend is good enough for his little girl — even though old dad doesn't meet his own standards. My advice is for founders of core groups and communities to seek a balance between new-member requirements that are so idealistic that few could pass them (and certainly not themselves!) and so lax that the requirements don't accomplish their intended purpose — attracting capable, like-minded people who will help the community achieve its goals.

Besides getting information about the person, membership requirements usually also involve a "getting to know you" period, and various kinds of fees. Time and money requirements also help separate serious community seekers from the merely curious.

I'm a firm believer in "long engagements:" extended guest visits or provisional memberships of six months to a year or more, so the group and the prospective member can continue to get to know each other. Most long-lived communities have discovered that this length of time is important. Sometimes it takes a year to find out what someone is really like, or more importantly, what they're like under stress, and whether it seems they'll be able to live happily with your community agreements.

Finally, it's important to have a process to integrate new members into your group or community. Besides sharing your decision log and making sure the new person knows your agreements and financial and labor requirements, you'll want to share as much community history and "community culture" as you can with this person, and invite him or her to participate in as many work parties, shared meals, and celebrations as you can. Most of this will naturally occur over the period of provisional membership (and in forming-community groups, during the "visiting observer" period). Sometimes communities take it a step further; for example, having a series of orientation sessions and/or assigning the newcomer a sponsor who's available to orient the new person and answer any questions.

The most critical part of any orientation however, should be making sure that the new person is familiar with your decision-making process. If you use consensus, you'll want the person to fully understand its philosophy and practice, and especially the blocking privilege. Some groups require that new people complete a weekend consensus workshop before becoming a full member with decision-making rights, which seems like an excellent idea to me.

The suggestions in this book for planting the seeds for your ecovillage or intentional community and helping it grow and thrive are by no means all you need to know; nor is this the end of your learning. It is, of course, the beginning.

You and your friends in community are pioneers in the finest sense. Your choice to live cooperatively with others, share resources, and evolve a more harmonious and sustainable way to live, has the potential to benefit others in far greater proportion than your numbers. Through slow, small increments, as people hear about your community and visit you — and hear about and visit other ecovillages and intentional communities across North America — they'll be influenced by a vision for human settlement that's potentially so inviting it ultimately makes a positive difference in our culture.

Creating community may be one of the most meaningful ways you can spend your time. I wish you every good fortune on the journey.

≈ Appendix 1 ≈

Sample Community Vision Documents

Lost Valley Educational Center , Oregon

A community can alter its vision documents to reflect changed circumstances and insights.

Vision (1996):
- To be a vital resource for the creation of sustainable culture for the Pacific Northwest.

Mission (1996):
- To support people in creating sustainable lifestyles by providing learning opportunities to develop skills and awarenesses that promote cooperative, harmonious, sustainable and joyous ways of living in relationship with each other and the Earth.

Goals (1996):
- To offer and develop high-quality learning opportunities to develop skills and awarenesses for sustainable living.
- To provide a nourishing, supportive, and responsive environment that facilitates participants in achieving their goals and deriving full value form their learning experiences.

- To provide financial and operational resources to support and enhance the activities of the educational center.

Vision Statement (1999):
The mission of Lost Valley Educational Center is to create and foster mutually beneficial relations between humans and all parts of the web of existence. We believe that these relationships provide a means to well-being as well as survival.

In fulfilling this mission, our purpose is to create and maintain an intentional community and an educational center dedicated to three goals which guide us in all activities:
- To educate broadly in areas such as ecology, sustainable agriculture, human-made environments, personal and spiritual growth, and community development.
- To live an ethic in which we are open to spiritual diversity, demonstrate right livelihood and sustainable economics, support individuals in their personal growth and healing, and steward the land to sustain and heal the Earth for generations to come.
- To participate in the global community, network with others, and facilitate the

evolution of cooperative societies and socially responsible relationships at every level.

We dedicate ourselves to learning and teaching this way of life.

Earthaven Ecovillage, North Carolina

The following is excerpted from Earthaven's "New Vision" document:

We are the members and pioneers of a planned permaculture ecovillage, actively engaged in building sacred community, supporting personal empowerment, and catalyzing cultural transformation.

We share a vision of a community with a vital, diversified spirituality, healthy social relations, sustainable ecological systems, and a low maintenance/high satisfaction lifestyle.

Earthaven's "ReMembership Covenant" outlines the following purpose and goals:

Purpose:

To be an evolving village-scale community dedicated to caring for people and the Earth by learning, practicing and demonstrating the skills for creating holistic sustainable culture, in recognition and celebration of the Oneness of all life.

Goals:

1. Make conscious our connection to Spirit and Earth and our interdependence with the web of all life.
2. Facilitate our transition toward a life of elegant simplicity.
3. Nurture an increasingly abundant world by enhancing living systems, while reducing consumption of resources.
4. Foster the lifelong learning and growth of every community member, recognizing each individual is both teacher and learner.
5. Preserve our landholding through proper stewardship, designated wilderness areas and ecologically sound use of our resources.
6. Create a learning center that serves as a living demonstration of this holistic vision.
7. Envision a positive, restorative future and develop the skills needed to create and sustain it.
8. Promote personal and planetary healing on all levels.
9. Serve and reach out to the local and global community, encouraging spiritual and cultural diversity and other forms of creative expression while providing a sense of inclusion, integration and celebration through responsible community activities.
10. Encourage the growth of our village until we have at least 66 site holders.
11. Encourage the establishment of member-owned and managed, ecologically sound businesses.
12. Actively support the intentional communities, permaculture and land reform movements as we are able.

Abundant Dawn, Virginia

Following is Abundant Dawn's vision statement:

- We are creating a loving and sustainable culture. We live close to one another, cooperate, and share resources, so that we may live more lightly and joyously on the earth.

- As we seek to realize ourselves through service, and work towards ecological and social responsibility, we respect the diversity of our members' life choices.

- Whether in times of peace or conflict, we meet each other face to face, with openness and caring. We are each individually committed to reaching through our hurts and fears to find and share our deepest truths.
- We honor the spark of the divine in all beings.

The following is excerpted from Abundant Dawn's vision documents:

Abundant Dawn intends to be a large community (possibly 40-60) made up of four or five smaller subgroups, which we call pods. Pods are small enough for all the members to sit in a room together and make a decision. Decisions regarding such important matters as membership, children, housing, and level of economic cooperation are decided at the pod level, with input from the wider community when appropriate.

This structure gives us some advantages of a large community (diverse population, sharing a large property, tractor and community center) as well as some advantages of small communities (intimate living groups, direct input into life-affecting decisions, face-to-face meetings).

Each pod has a few acres designated for its use and control. Within the guidelines of our vision statement, land plan, ecological guidelines, and other broad agreements, pods are encouraged to develop their own ways of living together. We intentionally include a spectrum of economic models from full income sharing to independent household incomes.

Major decisions, such as our overall land plan, are made by a consensus of the full members of Abundant Dawn. This may shift to consensus by pod representatives as we grow larger.

⫷Appendix 2⫸

Sample Community Agreements

Decision Log, Buffalo Creek Community

The following excerpt in the Decision Log of Buffalo Creek Community (not their real name) illustrates the kinds of agreements a forming community makes in their early stages, before beginning the land search. Buffalo Creek's vision was to live in a spiritually focused community of deeply connected friends in a rural setting. While they took detailed minutes of their meetings, this document records only their decisions, by date. They used this document as a "group memory" when considering new issues, and to orient visitors and new members to the group.

Sept 15: We named the community "Buffalo Creek." Our emphasis is on personal connection with each other, with community living as a subset of that.

Oct 21: Five criteria determine an active member of the community: (1) Being in alignment with the Buffalo Creek Community Mission Statement and Agreements; (2) Payment of $150 (or $75 for waiting list); (3) Participation in at least one action group and general meetings; (4) Missing no more than two consecutive general or action meetings; and (5) financial prequalification to buy a lot and build a house.

Active members are entitled to a reserved housing unit, participation in decision-making, and access to our community lending library.

At least one-third of all households will be reserved for families with children under 16.

All meetings are open and anyone may attend. Non-active members may be asked to only observe at meetings. They would not participate in consensus or other decision-making processes.

If a vote is called for, each household is entitled to one decision-making right, which may be split if members of that household chose to decide differently from each other.

Number of households to target for: 24.

Dec 16: We will pay for an option or down payment on land only after we have 24 active households.

Jan 19: A household can sell its place (3rd, 16th etc.) on the membership list. As a place is vacated, all households that follow move up one place on the list.

Mar 16: The Waiting List is limited to 50 percent of active members. For example, there maybe 12 members on the waiting list when there are 24 active households.

Apr 20: For any decision to be binding on the entire community, two-thirds of all households must agree to the decision.

A decision made by consensus will be considered to meet the requirements of the two-thirds rule.

May 18: The Coordinating Team is given the authority to approve, by consensus decision making, expenditures of up to $500. If their decision is not unanimous, or if the expenditure exceeds $500, it should be proposed to the whole group for approval.

Jun 15: We established a Site Fund. Each active community household is required, beginning August 1, to deposit $250 quarterly to the Community Treasury to be held for necessary expenses for obtaining the community building site, including but not limited to professional, legal, or other help. Further, this "forced savings" will be held in a safe interest-bearing account.

The primary decisions of our next meeting will involve creating an "exit clause" for any active members who wish to leave the Buffalo Creek group, as well as a "default clause," for any active members who do not meet the quarterly payments.

"Ode" of Respects & Responsibilities: Community Alternatives Society

Community Alternatives Society members, who live in their own apartment building in downtown Vancouver as well as a farm in the countryside, called this agreement an "ode," rather than a "code" of behavior, because it sounded more poetic and less bureaucratic. I suggest using this as a stimulus for your thinking when you consider the issues of any behavioral agreements your group makes.

Seven Areas of Respect

1. Respect personal boundaries, touch others appropriately, and refrain from violence. (Physical Respect)
2. Respect other people's feelings and emotions, and take responsibility for my own. (Emotional Respect)
3. Be honest, use respectful forms of communication with others, hear what others are saying to me. (Verbal Respect)
4. Respect my own and others' right to privacy, solitude, quiet, and security in their personal space, and negotiate the use of communal space. (Territorial Respect)
5. Care for individual, communal, and community property. (Material Respect)
6. Respect the diversity of people's age, sex, racial origin, sexual orientation, spiritual practices, and physical and mental capabilities. (Respect for Diversity)
7. Respect the community structure and consensus decision-making process. (Community Respect)

Seven Areas of Responsibility

1. Be conscientious in my attendance of community meetings.
2. Take responsibility for communicating my ideas and feelings.
3. Contribute time and energy to the community in the form of work parties and chores, and negotiate the duration and terms of any reduction in community participation that I may require.
4. Serve as a contributing member of a committee and the planning team during my rotation.

5. Be open and conscientious regarding my financial responsibilities.

6. Inform the community about guests staying for extended periods of time and any changes in my personal situation which affect the community and/or my ability to contribute to it.

7. Promptly inform the appropriate people about any violence or serious violations of the "R&Rs" that I witness.

Steps Toward Conflict Resolution

1. *Direct One-to-One Communication* between the involved parties. (If an individual feels unsafe, go directly to #2, below. If any individual witnesses or experiences a flagrant violation, go directly to #3, below.)

2. *Hear and Clear Session(s).* Each person involved in the conflict invites a trusted community member to the session as their advocate and the four individuals work toward the resolution.

3. *Consultation with the "R&R" Accountability Committee.* Advocacy/resolution groups may consult the committee for assistance when avenues #1 and #2 have not proven successful. If the involved parties are not willing to resolve the conflict, they will be requested by the committee to engage in a contract of self-empowerment with the community.

4. *Self-empowerment Contract.* The party(s) in question will be given one month to submit in writing and present to the community, a plan of action that outlines how that person will make the necessary changes in his or her life. The community will expect monthly updates and this contract will have a duration of five months. At the end of this period there will be a marked improvement in the situation or the community will proceed to #5, below.

5. *Community Action Meeting.* In the case of a serious flagrant violation the community may go to this step directly. In a situation where all other attempts at resolution have failed, and where the party(s) in question has not honored his or her Self-Empowerment Contract with the community, and is therefore exhibiting a lack of commitment to the community, a Community Action Meeting shall be called. The involved party may attend this meeting but may not be involved in the decision making. If the rest of the community reaches consensus, the involved party shall be evicted (6a) and may also have his or her membership in CAS revoked.

6. *Lack of Consensus.* If consensus is not reached at the Community Action Meeting, the planning team will meet with the person(s) who blocked the proposed action and the person(s) who violated the Self-Empowerment Contract to seek a solution.

Pet Policy, Abundant Dawn

Abundant Dawn's Pet Policy, although unfinished, demonstrates the kind of broad and deep thinking community members must undertake when dealing with especially controversial subjects, such as pets. I suggest you use it as a starting point when considering the issues of your own pet policy. (Yes, you'll need one.)

Special terms: "pod," a subcommunity or neighborhood within the larger community; "wild side," the steeper, more forested side of their property; "mild side," the more gentle slopes and pastures they intend to develop.

This document covers our agreements regarding dogs, cats, and house pets. It does not cover our agreements regarding pasture animals, such as cows, whether or not they are pets.

Pets in General: We agree to clearly state to visitors/potential members our concern about having pets on this land because of wildlife, noise pollution, quality of life standards, etc. We agree to write up our experiences with and discussions about pets so new members understand the "why" of our policies.

We will have no pets on the wild side, except, as it is beyond our control, free-ranging cats.

Dogs: Every pod will have 1.5 dog chips (one chip represents the right to have one dog). Chips are loanable, holdable, sellable, negotiable among pods. Chips cannot, however, be transferred permanently, but at maximum for the life of the animal in question. The dog chips (and thus the dog limits) are applicable to both indoor and outdoor dogs.

There will be a membership process for all dogs.

We will have no dogs running free on the property. Dogs may be walked on leash on mild side of land. We will have no dogs on the wild side.

The community will fund a fenced dog park (perhaps 0.5 to 0.75 acre) within which dogs may run and play, with the amount of human supervision to be determined in future deliberation. There will be a regular fee for dog owners (applicable to owners of both indoor and outdoor dogs) to pay back the expense of building the park, fund upkeep of the dog park and fence, and pay other dog-related expenses. Dog owners will be responsible for the labor of building the dog park and maintenance.

Whole pods will not be fenced. There can be a fenced yard, run or pen for dog(s) within the pod.

Dog owners will be responsible for the care and control of their dogs.

Dogs who are heavy barkers, or aggressive to people, cannot live here.

Dog owners must deal with dog shit, especially keep it off paths.

Dogs must have rabies vaccinations.

Dogs must be spayed/neutered.

Noise, odor, flea and other nuisance issues will be addressed by the dog owner to the community's satisfaction. Dog owners will prevent fleas by method of their choice. If it is not sufficient, owner will be open to feedback and to changing their method to a more effective one.

Cats: *Definitions.* "Free-ranging" cat means an unconfined outdoor cat (which may also have access to indoor space). "Confined cat" means a cat which is confined in a building and/or a yard with an effective cat fence.

Every pod will have one cat chip (one chip represents the right to have one cat). Chips are loanable, holdable, sellable, negotiable among pods. Chips cannot, however, be transferred permanently, but at maximum for the life of the animal in question. The cat chips (and thus the cat limits) are applicable to free-ranging cats only. There is no community-level limit on confined cats, except insofar as there are problems with noise, odor, fleas, etc.

There will be a membership process for all free-ranging cats.

Free-ranging cats must have a bell to minimize the effect on wildlife.

All cats must be spayed/neutered. A variance can be applied for related to an confined cat.

Noise, odor, flea and other nuisance issues will be addressed by the cat owner to the community's satisfaction. Cat owners will prevent fleas by method of their choice. If it is not sufficient, owner will be open to feedback and to changing their method to a more effective one.

Cats must have rabies vaccinations.

Owners of free-ranging cats will work out cat-fighting issues in acceptable ways, possibly taking turns confining their cats.

Future issues: Abundant Dawn is still in the process of agreeing on standards for pet care.

Issues still to be decided: What is the minimum amount of space in which dog or cats of various sizes might be confined? Under what circumstances might the community intervene in terms of suspected mistreatment or abuse?

The community has not yet written a policy regarding pets other than dogs and cats.

≈ Appendix 3 ≈

Setting Up and Maintaining a 501(c)3 Non-profit

Creating a 501(c)3 non-profit and keeping it going can be time-consuming, and may not be worth it unless (1) your organization generates a surplus of taxable income each year, (2) you want to attract tax-deductible donations, and/or (3) you want to apply for public or private grant monies.

Filing

First, file your Articles of Incorporation with the state, noting your intentions to be a non-profit corporation, and then create your bylaws and other necessary documents.

Preliminary Ruling, Final Ruling

You must request either a preliminary or a final ruling as a 501(c)3. As you'll see below, a final ruling is more desirable.

In order to apply for a final ruling, the IRS asks for (1) your budget for the current tax year, and (2) budgets for either three prior tax years or your proposed budgets for the next two years. This means you'll need to make a good guess as to your expected expenses for the next two years, or that you've operated for two or three years already, through another kind of legal entity (and

are switching to a 501(c)3), or that you've operated as the project of another non-profit (and thus can give evidence of your budgets and other financial data for two or three years). In order to seek a final ruling, OAEC submitted their budget for the then-current tax year, plus for two past years (during which they'd operated as a project of the non-profit Tides Foundation), and an estimated budget for the following year. "It definitely helps to show the IRS any previous years' budget activity to get a final ruling," says OAEC's Dave Henson. "If your group has no history of non-profit activity, you'll need to estimate two years' future budgets, and the IRS will likely take longer to give final approval."

The other option is to seek a preliminary ruling. Whether you seek a preliminary or final ruling, the IRS will grant you a temporary 501(c)3 status and monitor your activities for three to five years. If you've applied for a preliminary ruling, after three to five years you may apply for a final ruling, basing the required budget and other data on your first years of operation. If, after examining your organization's posters, flyers, brochures, and letters, the IRS considers most of your activities in that period to be related to your purpose, they'll grant you a final 501(c)3 ruling and will stop scrutinizing you so closely. If the IRS determines that most of your activities are *not* related to your purpose, and thus not really non-profit activities, they can delay your organization's final 501(c)3 status and continue close examination of your activities until you can show that you're actually doing what you said you would.

If this happens, and the IRS doesn't grant a final ruling after three to five years, it affects your organization retroactively, since everything you were doing was based on the assumption that you'd receive that final 501(c)3 status. This means anyone who gave you a tax-deductible donation during that period must now pay taxes on it, because donations to your organization during that time are no longer tax-deductible. Thus, it's hard to get grants until you have a final ruling.

For this reason, experienced non-profit activists strongly suggest you make your mission statement as broad and general as possible when you first apply for non-profit status. If sometime later you decide to do different activities than you originally envisioned, the wording of your mission statement can be interpreted to include the new activities and you don't endanger your non-profit status.

However, you may want to apply for a final ruling right away, if you have a history of activity and can give four years of information on your budget and activities (the previous two years, and estimates for the current year and the following year). OAEC applied for a final ruling in their initial IRS application. For two years they'd been a project of the non-profit Tides Foundation, so they could estimate their future budgets reasonably well, and they had a history of activity. They got their final ruling much sooner than they could have if they had requested their preliminary ruling first, making it easier to seek grants in their first few years.

Related and Unrelated Business Activity

Probably ninety percent of all 501(c)3 non-profits receive no other income aside from grants and donations. But some engage in business activities, such as running a conference center, for example, which generates an income. If a 501(c)3 were set up to run a conference center for a particular kind of educational activity, which was so stated in its Articles of Incorporation, the IRS would consider all income from the conference center as related to the 501(c)3 non-profit's purpose.

As noted earlier, any income from activities not related to the 501(c)3's purpose (called "unrelated" activities), is taxable. No more than 50 percent of a 501(c)3 non-profit's income can be unrelated; most must be derived from activities related to your purpose, as stated in your Articles of Incorporation. If the IRS discovers that more than 50 percent of your income-producing activities seem unrelated to your purpose, they can rescind your 501(c)3 status. Also, to maintain your 501(c)3 status, no more than 20 percent of your income can be from "passive" sources such as rents, lease fees, and interest on loans or investments.

"Disinterested" Board Members

As mentioned earlier, at least 51 percent of your board members must be "disinterested." If you use a voting membership to elect your board, 51 percent of the voting members must also be disinterested. The IRS will watch this closely for the first three years of your non-profit's existence.

The "Public Support Test"

Every year you must pass the "public support test" by demonstrating to the IRS that at least one-third of your financial support comes from the public, through the sale of goods and services, membership fees, and/or donations.

Other Tax Exemptions

You must apply separately for tax-exempt status at your state, country, and/or city level.

≈Resources≈

My website, DianaLeafeChristian.org, offers many more resources for topics covered in these chapters, including consultants experienced in working with communities and forming community groups. The site also features a schedule for my upcoming public talks and workshops about forming new communities, my upcoming public talks and workshops about forming new communities, how to schedule a workshop for your group or arrange a consultation, by phone or in person, and how to subscribe to my free online ecovillage newsletter. What follows is a list of some of the best resources from my website. What follows is a list of some of the best resources from my website.

Books and Magazines

Communities Directory 2007. Fellowship for Intentional Community (2007). Information on over 900 communities in North America — where they are, what they're doing, how to contact them, maps, comparison charts, articles about community living. *store.ic.org/directory*

Fellowship for Intentional Community. Articles from experienced communitarians on various aspects of community living, covering the wide range of communities in North America from ecovillages to cohousing. *communities.ic.org*

Ecovillages: New Frontiers for Sustainability. Jonathan Dawson. Green Books/ Chelsea Green (2006). The best book I know of about ecovillages. Jonathan Dawson is president of Global Ecovillage Network (GEN), co-director of GEN-Europe, and a member of Findhorn Foundation, an ecovillage in Scotland.

Ecovillage at Ithaca: Pioneering a Sustainable Culture. Liz Walker. New Society Publishers (2005). An excellent first-person account of how one group founded their community. *www.newsociety.com*

Cohousing: A Contemporary Approach to Housing Ourselves, Kathryn McCamant, Charles Durrett, and Ellen Hertzman, Ten Speed Press, Second Edition (2003). The book that introduced cohousing to North America. *store.ic.org/catalog*

The Cohousing Handbook, Revised Edition. Chris ScottHanson & Kelly ScottHanson, New Society Publishers (2005). Practical advice and step-by-step processes for forming a core group and developing and building cohousing communities. Much of it, especially the first half, is useful for founders of non-cohousing communities as well. *store.ic.org/catalog*

Finding Community: How to Join an Ecovillage or Intentional Community. Diana Leafe Christian. New Society Publishers (2007). The benefits of living in an intentional community, the different kinds of communities to choose from, and how to research them thoroughly, visit enjoyably (getting the most out of your visit), evaluate what you've seen intelligently, and join your chosen community gracefully. Diana is the author of this book. *www.newsociety.com*

Introduction to Consensus, Bea Briggs, Self-published (2000). This is the book I recommend most to forming community groups because of its clear, straightforward format. *store.ic.org/catalog*

On Conflict and Consensus: A Handbook on Formal Consensus Decision-making, C.T. Butler and Amy Rothstein, Food Not Bombs Publishing (1991). A political activist and consensus trainer, C.T. Butler developed the Formal Consensus process as a more structured method than other consensus processes and the "principled objection" test for blocks to a proposal — the block must be based in the vision or values of the group.
You can download the whole book for free from the website or order a copy mailorder. *www.consensus.net*

Nonviolent Communication: A Language of Life, Marshall Rosenberg, PuddleDancer Press (2003). Nonviolent communication (NVC) is one of the most powerful, and effective tools to create a sense of connection between people, turn conflict into an experience of mutual understanding, and reduce the frequency and intensity of future conflict situations. *www.cnvc.org*

"Emotional Freedom Technique (EFT)" is the fastest, cheapest, most effective and painless self therapy I've seen yet, and is ideal for helping individual community members transform attitudes and behaviors that can disempower the individual and the group. *www.emofree.com*

Getting Real: 10 Truth Skills You Need to Live an Authentic Life, Susan Campbell, New World Library (2001). One of the best guides I know of to the communication approach which, like nonviolent communication, works well in the "rock polisher" of community — telling the truth and being transparent.

The Mediator's Handbook, Jennifer E. Beer and Eileen Stief New Society Publishers, Revised and Expanded 3rd Edition (1997). Overview of conflict and mediation, a step-by-step mediation process, skills and approaches for the three main mediation tasks — supporting the people, controlling the process, and solving the problem. *www.newsociety.com*

Nolo Press. Practical, plain-language information and advice to help people in the United States set up their own legal entities and solve their own legal problems with confidence, and whenever possible, with minimal need for a lawyer. Books, CDs, legal forms, corporation kits, downloadable data, and legal information online. See especially Nolo Press books: *Form your Own Limited Liability Company*; *Incorporate Your Business*; *A 50-State Legal Guide to Forming a Corporation*; *How to Form a Non-profit Corporation*; and *How to Write a Business Plan*. www.nolo.com

Self-Counsel Press. Similar to Nolo Press, but for a Canadian readership. *www.self-counsel.com*

Introduction to Permaculture. Bill Mollison and Reny Mia Slay. Tagiri Publishing, 2003. Permaculture basics: how to feed and house yourself in any climate the least use of land; energy; and repetitive labor.

Permaculture Activist. Quarterly publication serving the permaculture movement in North America with useful, practical information about permaculture projects "on the ground." *www.permacultureactivist.net*

Organizations and Associations

Fellowship for Intentional Community (FIC). Membership organization serves intentional communities and community seekers in North America with information and networking. Publishes *Communities* magazine, *Visions of Utopia* video, the *Communities Directory*, and more. *www.fic.org*

Northwest Intentional Communities Association (NICA). Network of intentional communities in the Pacific Northwest that provides information and mutual support, and hosts regional gatherings. *www.ic.org/nica*

Global Ecovillage Network (GEN). Supports and encourages the evolution of sustainable settlements worldwide with information and networking. *www.gen.ecovillage.org* Also GEN Europe and Africa *www.gen-europe.org* and GEN Oceania and Asia *www.genoa.ecovillage.org*

Ecovillage Network of the Americas. The GEN organization for South, Central, and North America. *www.ena.ecovillage.org*

The Cohousing Association of the United States Promotes and encourages cohousing communities in North America through networking and information. Quarterly e-mail newsletter; biannual mailed newsletter. Much of their information can be adapted to fit non-cohousing communities. *www.cohousing.org*

Canadian Cohousing Network. Promotes cohousing communities in Canada through public education and networking. *www.cohousing.ca*

Federation of Egalitarian Communities (FEC). Support network for North American intentional communities that value income-sharing, non-violence, participatory decision making, and ecological practices. *www.thefec.org*

Community Associations Institute. Provides information and advice to community associations (homeowners associations, condominium associations, and housing cooperatives) through books and booklets, courses, and certification programs. *www.caionline.org*

National Association of Housing Cooperatives. Offers technical assistance and training to founders and board members of housing co-ops. *www.coophousing.org*

Institute for Community Economics. The organization that developed community land trusts in 1967. Offers information and assistance for creating community land trusts through consultation, books, and a revolving loan fund. *www.iceclt.org*

E.F. Schumacher Society. Information, book publishing, workshops, and consulting on local economic self-reliance, through community land trusts, microlending, local currencies, and community supported agriculture farms. *www.schumachersociety.org*

Websites

Author's website. Many more resources for topics covered in this book, the author's upcoming public talks and workshops about forming new communities, and how to schedule a workshop, arrange a consultation, or subscribe to the author's free online ecovillage newsletter. *www.DianaLeafeChristian.org*

Community Bookshelf. Mail-order books on intentional community living, ecovillages, cohousing, consensus decision-making, effective meetings, conflict resolution, and sustainable living. *www.store.ic.org*

Videos, Workshops, and Other Resources

Visions of Utopia: Experiments in Sustainable Culture [video; 90 min.], Geoph Kozeny, Fellowship for Intentional Community (2002). Profiles seven diverse communities, explores the "glue" that holds communities together, offers candid assessments from community members of what works and what doesn't work. *www.store.ic.org*

Starting a Successful Ecovillage or Intentional Community. Workshops with *Creating a Life Together* author Diana Leafe Christian. *www.DianaLeafeChristian.org*

Starting and Sustaining Intentional Communities. Three-day courses with Dave Henson and Adam Wolpert at Sowing Circle/OAEC. *www.oaec.org*

Workshops at Earthaven Ecovillage. Workshops and community internships in permaculture design, natural building, water catchment, constructed wetlands, and forming new intentional communities or ecovillages. E-mail culturesedge@earthaven.org *www.earthaven.org*

Living Routes — Ecovillage Educational Consortium. Organization hosts live-in educational experiences at ecovillages in Europe, India, and the US for college credit. *www.livingroutes.org*

Lost Valley Educational Center. Workshops and community apprenticeship programs in permaculture design, natural building, and organic gardening. *www.lostvalley.org*

Occidental Arts and Ecology Center. Workshops and community apprenticeships in permaculture design, natural building, and forming land-based intentional communities. *www.oaec.org*

Sirius Community Educational Programs. Workshops and community apprenticeships in permaculture design, natural building, and organic gardening. *www.siriuscommunity.org*

Communities Profiled in this Book

Abundant Dawn
www.abundantdawn.org

Dancing Rabbit Ecovillage
www.dancingrabbit.org

Earthaven Ecovillage
www.earthaven.org

Lost Valley Educational Center
www.lostvalley.org

Mariposa Grove
www.mariposagrove.org

Meadowdance
www.meadowdance.org

Sowing Circle OAEC
www.oaec.org

⋙Index⋘

About the Author

Since 1993 Diana Leafe Christian has been editor of *Communities* magazine, a quarterly publication about intentional communities in North America. She has been interviewed by NPR and the BBC about intentional communities and contributed a chapter on forming new communities to *Creating Harmony* (Gaia Trust, 1999). Her articles on ecovillages, financial and legal aspects of communities, children in community, and communication and group process issues in community have appeared in publications ranging from *Mother Earth News* to *Communities* magazine, the *Communities Directory*, and Canada's *This Magazine*.

Diana leads workshops for forming-community groups and educational centers nationwide and at communities conferences, on the practical steps to create ecovillages and intentional communities, including the land-purchase, zoning, and legal stages of these projects.

She lives at Earthaven Ecovillage in North Carolina, one of the "successful 10 percent" communities she began researching for this book.

Website: www.CreatingALifeTogether.org

If you have enjoyed *Creating a Life Together* you might also enjoy other

BOOKS TO BUILD A NEW SOCIETY

New Society Publishers' mission is to publish books that contribute in fundamental ways to building an ecologically sustainable and just society, and to do so with the least possible impact on the environment, in a manner that models this vision.

Our books provide positive solutions for people who want to make a difference.
We specialize in:

• **Sustainable Living** • **Ecological Design and Planning** •
• **Natural Building & Appropriate Technology** • **Environment and Justice** •
• **New Forestry** • **Conscientious Commerce** • **Resistance and Community** •
• **Nonviolence** • **Progressive Leadership** • **Educational and Parenting Resources** •

For a full list of NSP's titles, please call 1-800-567-6772 or check out our web site at:
www.newsociety.com

New Society Publishers

ENVIRONMENTAL BENEFITS STATEMENT

New Society Publishers has chosen to produce this book
on New Leaf EcoBook 100, recycled paper made with 100% post
consumer waste, processed chlorine free, and old growth free.

For every 5,000 books printed, New Society saves the following resources:[1]

45	Trees
4,076	Pounds of Solid Waste
4,485	Gallons of Water
4,836	Kilowatt Hours of Electricity
7,410	Pounds of Greenhouse Gases
32	Pounds of HAPs, VOCs, and AOX Combined
11	Cubic Yards of Landfill Space

[1] Environmental benefits are calculated based on research done by the Environmental Defense Fund and other members of the Paper Task Force who study the environmental impacts of the paper industry.

For more information on this environmental benefits statement, or to inquire about environmentally friendly papers, please contact New Leaf Paper – info@newleafpaper.com – 888•989•5323.

NEW SOCIETY PUBLISHERS